CAMBRIDGE TEXTS IN THE
HISTORY OF PHILOSOPHY

FRIEDRICH SCHLEIERMACHER
Lectures on Philosophical Ethics

CAMBRIDGE TEXTS IN THE HISTORY OF PHILOSOPHY

Series editors
KARL AMERIKS
Professor of Philosophy at the University of Notre Dame
DESMOND M. CLARKE
Professor of Philosophy at University College Cork

The main objective of Cambridge Texts in the History of Philosophy is to expand the range, variety and quality of texts in the history of philosophy which are available in English. The series includes texts by familiar names (such as Descartes and Kant) and also by less well-known authors. Wherever possible, texts are published in complete and unabridged form, and translations are specially commissioned for the series. Each volume contains a critical introduction together with a guide to further reading and any necessary glossaries and textual apparatus. The volumes are designed for student use at undergraduate and postgraduate level and will be of interest not only to students of philosophy, but also to a wider audience of readers in the history of science, the history of theology and the history of ideas.

For a list of titles published in the series, please see end of book.

FRIEDRICH SCHLEIERMACHER

Lectures on Philosophical Ethics

EDITED BY

ROBERT B. LOUDEN
University of Southern Maine

TRANSLATED BY

LOUISE ADEY HUISH

CAMBRIDGE
UNIVERSITY PRESS

PUBLISHED BY THE PRESS SYNDICATE OF THE UNIVERSITY OF CAMBRIDGE
The Pitt Building, Trumpington Street, Cambridge, United Kingdom

CAMBRIDGE UNIVERSITY PRESS
The Edinburgh Building, Cambridge CB2 2RU, UK
40 West 20th Street, New York, NY 10011-4211, USA
477 Williamstown Road, Port Melbourne, VIC 3207, Australia
Ruiz de Alarcón 13, 28014 Madrid, Spain
Dock House, The Waterfront, Cape Town 8001, South Africa

http://www.cambridge.org

First published 2002

Printed in the United Kingdom at the University Press, Cambridge

Typeface Ehrhardt 11/13   *System* LATEX 2ε   [TB]

A catalogue record for this book is available from the British Library

Library of Congress Cataloguing in Publication data

ISBN 0 521 80982 7 hardback
ISBN 0 521 00767 4 paperback

Contents

v

Introduction

Friedrich Daniel Ernst Schleiermacher (1768–1834) – father of modern liberal theology, founder of modern hermeneutics, translator of Plato into German, co-founder (with Wilhelm von Humboldt) of the University of Berlin, and early advocate of civil rights for both women and Jews – was clearly a man of many talents and interests. But over the years a number of German scholars have argued that it is in fact Schleiermacher's philosophical work in ethics that constitutes his most outstanding achievement. For instance, August Twesten, Schleiermacher's student and later successor at the University of Berlin, claimed in 1869 that Schleiermacher's ethics was "in truth the key to understanding all of his scientific works." And Otto Braun, in the Foreword to his 1910 German edition of Schleiermacher's works, summarized his criterion of selection by stating that "ethics is the crux of Schleiermacher's philosophy; all of the writings belonging to ethics therefore form the foundation of the edition." Hans-Joachim Birkner, founding editor of the more recent (and still incomplete) *Kritische Gesamtausgabe* (critical edition) of Schleiermacher and German editor of the ethics lectures translated below, begins his discussion of Schleiermacher's ethics by proclaiming that "without a doubt, Schleiermacher's philosophical ethics represents his most important achievement, and in the history of ethics constitutes a completely original project." Finally, Gunter Scholtz, in a more recent study, argues that Schleiermacher's ethics, in comparison with all other areas of his work, "has a far greater

I would like to thank the Board of Trustees of the University of Maine System for awarding me a 2001–2 Trustee Professorship, which greatly facilitated my research on Schleiermacher's ethics. Thanks also to Karl Ameriks, Peter W. Foley, Patrick Frierson, and Daryl Morazzini for their comments on an earlier version of this Introduction.

significance: it tackles the more important problems, has a much wider perspective, and can lay claim to greater originality."[1]

However, in the Anglo-American world Schleiermacher's philosophical ethics has long remained a well-kept secret. How did his ethics develop and take shape? What does his mature ethical theory look like? And can the above claims be justified?

Steps along the way: Schleiermacher's ethics before 1812

Schleiermacher's writings before 1812 (the year in which parts of the following lectures were first delivered at the University of Berlin) cover a wide range of topics and genres, and include some of his most famous publications – e.g. *On Religion: Speeches to its Cultured Despisers* (1799) and the *Monologues* (1800). Many of them were never published or even completed during his own lifetime. But, overall, ethical themes and concerns dominate these early writings as well. As one recent critic notes, "if we view them with hindsight and in light of where Schleiermacher's numerous interests eventually led him, it is fair to say that moral philosophy, broadly understood, occupied the young Schleiermacher far more than religion or theology."[2]

The pre-1812 writings of Schleiermacher's that are most relevant to the development of his mature ethical theory are the following:

"Notes on Aristotle: Nicomachean Ethics *8–9" (1788)*

This is, as far as we know, Schleiermacher's first philosophical work – written when he was twenty years old and still a student at the University of Halle, studying under the Wolffian philosopher Johann August Eberhard (1739–1809). Originally intended as a contribution to a complete translation of and commentary on Aristotle's *Nicomachean Ethics*,

---

[1] August Twesten, "Zur Errinerung an Friedrich Daniel Ernst Schleiermacher" (lecture, Berlin, 1869), p. 10. As cited by Hans-Joachim Birkner, *Schleiermachers Christliche Sittenlehre im Zusammenhang seines philosophisch-theologischen Systems* (Berlin: Alfred Töpelmann, 1964), p. 36 n. 28. Friedrich Daniel Ernst Schleiermacher, *Werke. Auswahl in vier Bänden*, edited by Otto Braun and Johannes Bauer (Leipzig: Felix Meiner, 1910–13; reprint ed. Aalen: Scientia, 1967), I, xxxiii. Birkner, *Schleiermachers Christliche Sittenlehre*, p. 37. Gunter Scholtz, *Ethik und Hermeneutik: Schleiermachers Grundlegung der Geisteswissenschaften* (Frankfurt: Suhrkamp, 1995), p. 7.

[2] Brent W. Sockness, "Was Schleiermacher a Virtue Ethicist? *Tugend* and *Bildung* in the Early Ethical Writings," *Zeitschrift für Neuere Theologiegeschichte* 8 (2001): 10. (I am indebted to Sockness's analysis on a number of points in the following survey of Schleiermacher's early ethics.)

the project was abandoned in 1791 when another scholar published a new German translation of the same text. Perhaps the essay's most telling feature occurs in the opening sentence, when the author asks "How then are we to reconcile" duty (*Pflicht*) and feeling (*Empfindung*)?[3] – a question that gains prominence in many later writings, as Schleiermacher begins to interweave the Kantian philosophy he was raised on with the new Romanticism which he himself helped to create. On a more general note, this early comment on Aristotle (particularly when combined with his later and more ambitious Plato translation project) serves as an important reminder that a very important source of Schleiermacher's ethical theory is ancient Greek philosophy. One of Schleiermacher's main goals as an ethical theorist is to integrate what he regards as the one-sided approaches of ancient and modern ethics – to bring together the teleological doctrines of good and virtue on the one hand with a deontological doctrine of duty on the other. As he notes in his Introduction to the *Brouillon zur Ethik* (*1805/06*): "With the ancients, the highest good and virtue; with the moderns, virtue and duty. These [latter] two are in opposition: if virtue is given, duty stops; as long as one must inculcate duty, virtue is not yet there" (*WA* II, 84; see also 256, 555). However, unlike certain late twentieth-century virtue ethicists whose passion for Aristotle (and/or dislike of modernity) was so strong that it led them to try to "do ethics without ... the notion 'morally ought,'"[4] Schleiermacher proposes a more pluralistic program: one that incorporates the strengths of both the ancient and modern traditions of ethical thought.

The most significant representative of modern ethical thought (particularly for a young German intellectual writing at the end of the eighteenth century) is of course Immanuel Kant – by far the deepest and most pervasive influence on Schleiermacher's earliest writings. While

---

[3] Schleiermacher, *Kritische Gesamtausgabe*, edited by Hans-Joachim Birkner with Gerhard Ebeling, Hermann Fischer, Heinz Kimmerle, and Kurt-Victor Selge (Berlin: Walter de Gruyter, 1984–), I.1, 3. Future references to Schleiermacher's writings are cited in the body of the text by division, volume, and page number in this edition (hereafter abbreviated as *KGA*). Most recent English translations of Schleiermacher's ethics writings contain the *KGA* pagination. References to Schleiermacher's *Grundlinien einer Kritik der bisherigen Sittenlehre* (1803), *Brouillon zur Ethik* (*1805/06*), and *Ethik* (*1812/13*) (not yet reprinted in *KGA*) are cited in the body of the text according to volume and page number in Braun and Bauer, eds., *Werke. Auswahl in vier Bänden* (hereafter abbreviated as *WA*).

[4] Elizabeth Anscombe, "Modern Moral Philosophy," *Philosophy* 33 (1958): 1–19; reprinted in *Virtue Ethics*, edited by Roger Crisp and Michael Slote (New York: Oxford University Press, 1997), pp. 34, 33. For a critique, see my "On Some Vices of Virtue Ethics," *American Philosophical Quarterly* 21 (1984): 227–336; also reprinted in *Virtue Ethics*.

many of Schleiermacher's pronouncements concerning Kant's ethics are extremely critical, the impact of the sage of Königsberg on his ethical theory was both lasting and profound. As he notes in an often-quoted letter to his friend Karl von Brinkmann in 1790: "All this must strike you as rather anti-Kantian; nevertheless I can sincerely assure you that with each day my faith in this philosophy increases" (2 February 1790, *KGA* V.1, 191).

On the Highest Good

This second text was written in early 1789, also during Schleiermacher's student days at the University of Halle. It is primarily a response to certain issues raised in the Dialectic of Kant's *Critique of Practical Reason* (namely, the doctrine of the highest good, and the related postulates of God and immortality), which had been published the preceding year. At bottom, Schleiermacher seems here to be trying to out-Kant Kant, pleading for a more rarified concept of the highest good that is completely detached from all-too-human empirical concerns for happiness. To include happiness along with virtue within one's concept of the highest good, as Kant does (while warning readers that they "are two specifically quite *different elements* of the highest good"[5] that cannot be reduced to one notion – *contra* eudaimonisms both ancient and modern), is, Schleiermacher claims, "to present to us a prostitute . . . who only knows how to flaunt charms of a sordid and . . . revolting variety" (*KGA* I.1, 96). Also of note in this essay is Schleiermacher's scornful dismissal of Kant's moral arguments for God and immortality as "postulates" or necessary presuppositions for the connection between virtue and happiness, a critique which foreshadows Schleiermacher's later battle in *On Religion* to put a stop to reductionist Enlightenment efforts to make religion merely "a saving support of morality" (*KGA* I.2, 202).

The mere fact that Schleiermacher chooses to criticize Kant's concepts of the highest good and the postulates rather than other concepts that are more central to his ethics (such as duty or the categorical imperative) may be taken as yet another sign of the strong influence of ancient Greek ethics on the development of Schleiermacher's own ethical theory. At this

---

[5] Immanuel Kant, *Kants gesammelte Schriften*, edited by the German Academy of Sciences (Berlin: Walter de Gruyter, 1902–), 5: 112. Future references to Kant's writings are cited in the body of the text according to volume and page number in this edition. (References to Kant's *Critique of Pure Reason* are cited in the body of the text according to the traditional A/B pagination.)

point, however, it is clearly Plato rather than Aristotle who emerges as Schleiermacher's hero in the history of moral philosophy. Plato "saw the moral law as independent of the idea of happiness, as lying in reason"; and he also (unlike Kant) understood that the highest good "is possible and definable only through reason" (*KGA* I.1, 109). Aristotle, on the other hand, is criticized for viewing ethics as "nothing but the doctrine of happiness," and thus for constructing a "vacuous" and "hideous" system. Aristotle "simply did not know that reason could be practical of itself" (*KGA* I.1, 109–10).

However, despite Schleiermacher's professed Platonist (not to mention Kantian) endorsement of the fundamental tenet that moral action needs to be based on reason rather than feeling, he also shows signs of wavering here. "Ours is not a will that can be determined by the moral law directly, this can only happen indirectly by means of subjective motivating grounds" (*KGA* I.1, 100). For Kant, on the other hand, "what is essential to any moral worth of actions is *that the moral law determine the will immediately*" (5: 71).

The above quarrels with Kant notwithstanding, Schleiermacher remains committed throughout his ethical writings to the fundamental Kantian claim that we have a duty to promote the highest good; to make the material world around us agree "as far as possible" with our idea of a truly "moral world" – i.e. a world in conformity with moral principles chosen by free and rational beings (A 808/B 836; see also 5: 113). In *On the Highest Good*, this duty is summarized as the promotion of "the totality of what is possible through rational laws" (*KGA* I.1, 92); in Schleiermacher's mature ethics it translates into the goal of a "steady dissemination [of reason] across the whole earth, the total field of the cultural task" (*WA* II, 284; see also 92).

On Freedom

Schleiermacher's next substantial early work in ethics is *On Freedom*, described by Günter Meckenstock as "the most comprehensive, ambitious, and no doubt also the most difficult work in the corpus of his early writings."[6] The essay was written between 1790 and 1792, while

---

[6] Günter Meckenstock, *Deterministische Ethik und kritische Theologie: Die Auseinandersetzung des frühen Schleiermacher mit Kant und Spinoza 1789–1794* (Berlin: Walter de Gruyter, 1988), p. 52. (Meckenstock is also editor of vols. I.1–3, 12 of *KGA*.)

Schleiermacher was working as a tutor at the estate of Count Dohna in Schlobitten, East Prussia. The original plan was for Schleiermacher to accompany the eldest son Wilhelm zu Dohna to Königsberg, where he was beginning his university studies in political science (and where Kant was entering his twilight years as professor of philosophy). Instead, he remained at the Count's estate, working as tutor for the three younger sons. Unpublished and unfinished (the essay breaks off in the third section; four sections were planned), *On Freedom* appears to build on three other short pieces, remaining fragments of which are also included in the first volume of *KGA* (I.1, 129–34, 135–64, 213–16).

This essay represents yet a further parting of the ways with Kant. In his Preface to *The Critique of Practical Reason*, Kant declares that "the concept of freedom . . . constitutes the *keystone* of the whole structure of a system of pure reason, even of speculative reason . . . Freedom is real, for this idea reveals itself through the moral law" (5: 3–4). Schleiermacher, however, denies the reality of freedom in Kant's absolute libertarian sense, opting for a variant of "the deterministic solution of the Leibniz–Wolff school" (*KGA* I.1, 129) – a solution no doubt suggested to him by Eberhard, his professor at Halle.

In his writings on ethics, Kant is primarily concerned with *practical* freedom – "the independence of the power of choice from *necessitation* by impulses of sensibility" (A 534/B 562). This independence has both a negative sense (freedom *from* determination by external causes) as well as a positive sense (freedom *to* legislate for oneself how to act). However, Kant also held that the possibility of practical freedom presupposes *transcendental* freedom,

the faculty of beginning a state *from itself* [*von selbst*], the causality of which does not in turn stand under another cause determining it in time in accordance with the law of nature. Freedom in this signification is a pure transcendental idea, which, first, contains nothing borrowed from experience, and second, the object of which also cannot be given determinately in any experience (A 533/B 561).

Schleiermacher, like many others before and since, rejects Kant's metaphysically extravagant notion of transcendental freedom. At the very beginning of the surviving portion of his *Notes on Kant: Critique of Practical Reason* (probably written in 1789), he writes: "transcendental freedom. Therefore apparently a faculty of causality without necessary connection with that which has gone before. I have therefore certainly not misunderstood him" (*KGA* I.1, 129). In its place, Schleiermacher posits a naturalized self that is wholly a creature of desire, or rather of multiple desires embedded in their own complex causal networks. Choice is determined by desire, and each choice made by the faculty of desire "must in every case be grounded in the totality of present representations and in the state and interrelations of all the soul's faculties that have been produced in the progression of representations in our soul" (*KGA* I.1, 237–8). And this naturalized self is also a unitary self. Schleiermacher (again, like many other critics of Kant) rejects Kant's dichotomous phenomenal/noumenal self: "it is pointless to divide the human being, all is connected in him, all is one" (*KGA* I.1, 241). However, this is not at all to say that it is easy or even possible for finite rational beings to track the actions of the naturalized self. Determinism does not necessarily imply predictability: "the activities of the faculty of desire change as richly and rapidly as the flux of external things can ever do. In every moment it is filled not simply with life but with superabundant life, multifariously active" (*KGA* I.1, 238).

In rejecting the Kantian concept of transcendental freedom, Schleiermacher essentially opts for a position on moral deliberation and choice that is much closer to that of Aristotle ("thought by itself moves nothing") or Hume ("reason is, and ought only to be the slave of the passions, and can never pretend to any other office than to serve and obey them").[7] For Kant, however, any and all such efforts to explain human choice as simply part of the mechanism of nature are at bottom "nothing better than the freedom of a turnspit, which, when once it is wound up, also accomplishes its movements of itself" (5: 97).

A stronger philosophical influence on Schleiermacher's thinking about free will and determinism (not to mention other topics) is Spinoza. Included in the first volume of the *Kritische Gesamtausgabe* are also three short pieces dealing with Spinoza's philosophy (*KGA* I.1, 511–58, 559–82, 583–97), which in Meckenstock's judgment were all written between 1793 and 1794. However, Albert Blackwell argues convincingly that Schleiermacher knew "Jacobi's secondhand presentation of Spinoza's

---

[7] Aristotle, *Nicomachean Ethics*, trans. Terence Irwin. 2nd ed. (Indianapolis: Hackett, 1999), VI.2 1139a35–36. David Hume, *A Treatise of Human Nature*, ed. P. H. Nidditch. 2nd ed. (Oxford: Oxford University Press, 1978), p. 415.

philosophy as early as 1787"[8] – i.e. well before he wrote *On Freedom*. In his *Ethics* (1677), one of the most radical works of the early Enlightenment, "the holy rejected Spinoza" (*KGA* I.2, 213) defends a straightforward version of determinism: "Nothing in nature is contingent, but all things are from the necessity of the divine nature determined to exist and to act in a definite way."[9] The determinism in Schleiermacher's *On Freedom* is partially fueled by indirect contact with Spinozism, an influence that intensifies in the years immediately following.

On the Value of Life

Schleiermacher's next major effort in the development of his ethical theory is a longish essay (pp. 391–472 in *KGA* I.1) entitled *On the Value of Life* (late 1792–early 1793). In its pursuit of a broad-based "reflection about all of life" (*KGA* I.1, 393), the essay can be seen as marking yet another departure from a Kantian morality of duty with its narrower focus on the question What ought I to do? and another move closer to ancient virtue ethics, in which "the fundamental question is, How ought I to live? or, What should my life be like?"[10] At the same time, in his triple emphases on "the destiny of the human being" (*die Bestimmung des Menschen*) (*KGA* I.1, 406); "serious virtue" (*ernste Tugend*), which strives "to appropriate everything within me to rationality, the crown of my existence" (*KGA* I.1, 413); and culture or formation (*Bildung*), the key process by means of

---

[8] Albert Blackwell, *Schleiermacher's Early Philosophy of Life: Determinism, Freedom, and Phantasy* (Chico, CA: Scholars Press, 1982), p. 125. See also Meckenstock, *Deterministische Ethik und kritische Theologie*, pp. 185–8. Many late eighteenth-century German intellectuals were attracted to Spinozism more as a result of Jacobi's work, *Briefe über die Lehre von Spinoza*, than by close study of Spinoza's own texts. For discussion, see Frederick C. Beiser, *The Fate of Reason: German Philosophy from Kant to Fichte* (Cambridge, MA: Harvard University Press, 1987), pp. 44–91.

[9] Baruch Spinoza, *The Ethics and Selected Letters*, trans. Samuel Shirley (Indianapolis: Hackett, 1982), pt. I, prop. 29. For discussion of Spinoza's influence on the Enlightenment, see Jonathan I. Israel, *Radical Enlightenment: Philosophy and the Making of Modernity 1650–1750* (New York: Oxford University Press, 2001), esp. pt. II.

[10] Julia Annas, *The Morality of Happiness* (New York: Oxford University Press, 1995), p. 27. As Annas notes (p. 27 n. 1), the question is "classically posed by Socrates in the first book of the *Republic*: 'It is not a trivial question . . . what we are talking about is how one should live,'" (352 d). At the same time, Kant's own debt to the virtue ethics tradition should not be underestimated. For discussion, see my "Kant's Virtue Ethics," *Philosophy* 61 (1986): 473–89; reprinted in Daniel Statman, ed., *Virtue Ethics: A Critical Reader* (Edinburgh: University of Edinburgh Press, 1997).

which humans are to achieve their destiny and "bring forth true human happiness ... among all peoples" (*KGA* I.1, 449), Schleiermacher once again reveals his deep debt to Kant.

Two additional themes deserve mention which are touched on here and pursued in greater depth in later writings:

1) The positive role of desire and feeling in human life. In our discussion of *On Freedom*, we noted that Schleiermacher rejects the Kantian idea of transcendental freedom as a rational capacity to produce a state spontaneously, replacing it with a causally determined faculty of desire. But now, without giving up the root claim that human thought and action, as part of nature, are always subject to laws of cause and effect, he also strives to overcome the duality between thought and desire: "Knowing and desiring should not be two in me, but one. Complete, constant harmony of the two ... that is humanity" (*KGA* I.1, 410). Pleasure (*Lust*) is declared to be "the driving wheel of all cognitive powers"; "the touchstone that shows me in which objects my two powers [of knowing and desiring] can unite" (*KGA* I.1, 410). In a manner strikingly similar to John Stuart Mill's later distinction between higher and lower pleasures,[11] Schleiermacher then distinguishes between "pleasure in truth" (which he also equates with "pleasure in rules" and "pleasure in laws") with mere "pleasure in objects." The former is declared to be "humanity in the highest degree," the *Bestimmung* of our existence (*KGA* I.1, 412).

2) The value of fantasy (*Fantasie*). Later in his essay Schleiermacher asserts: "we act wrongly if we fail to recognize the value of fantasy" (*KGA* I.1, 450). Those Enlightenment intellectuals who overvalue understanding (*Verstand*) and its "contribution of abstract concepts" are declared to be mere *Buchstabenmenschen* (people who go by the letter, bureaucrats) with an "addiction to theory and abstract being" that leaves them in "the land of the lame" (*KGA* I.1, 450). Several years later, these dual themes of feeling and fantasy will resound deeply in early German Romanticism, a movement in which, as we shall see next, Schleiermacher played a key role.

---

[11] John Stuart Mill, *Utilitarianism* (1861), ed. Roger Crisp (New York: Oxford University Press, 1998), ch. 2. Mill introduces his distinction between higher and lower pleasures in order to rebut the objection that utilitarianism is "a doctrine worthy only of swine" (p. 55).

Schleiermacher's ethics and early Romanticism

The years 1797–1802 marked a new and distinct phase in Schleiermacher's intellectual development, a phase fueled by his association with the early Romantic movement in Berlin. In 1796, he obtained his first post as pastor at the Charité Hospital in Berlin. Meanwhile, Count Alexander Dohna, whom Schleiermacher had tutored back in Schlobitten, also moved to Berlin. Through Dohna, Schleiermacher was introduced to Marcus Herz and his wife Henriette. Marcus Herz was a noted Jewish physician (Dohna was one of his patients) who had also been one of Kant's best students earlier in Königsberg. (In 1770, Kant "chose Herz to be respondent at the defense of his inaugural Dissertation – an honor all the more singular in view of Herz's Jewish origins."[12]) Schleiermacher was particularly close to Henriette (false rumors of an extramarital affair circulated for many years), herself the daughter of a Sephardic physician who had been head of the Hospital of the Jewish Community. She was a beautiful woman seventeen years younger than her husband, and by 1796 had already mastered eight languages, to which she later added Sanskrit and Turkish.

During the 1790s the Herz home was the center of a salon that attracted many of the leading philosophical and literary figures of Berlin, both Jewish and non-Jewish, and Henriette herself was the guiding spirit behind it. Much has been written about both the role of the salon and women's place within it in Enlightenment culture. Here, arguably for the first time in human history, we find

the world of a critically debating reading public that at the same time was just evolving within the broader bourgeois strata . . . the world of the men of letters but also that of the *salons* in which "mixed companies" engaged in critical discussions; here, in the bourgeois homes, the public sphere was established.[13]

It was through Henriette's salon that Schleiermacher became friends with Friedrich Schlegel in 1797 (though they actually first met each other at another famous but more secretive and exclusive literary society,

---

[12] Martin L. Davies, *Identity or History? Marcus Herz and the End of Enlightenment* (Detroit: Wayne State University Press, 1995), p. 20.

[13] Jürgen Habermas, *The Structural Transformation of the Public Sphere: An Inquiry into a Category of Bourgeois Society*, trans. Thomas Burger (Cambridge, MA: MIT Press, 1991), p. 106. See also Davies, *Identity or History?* pp. 163–94.

the Berliner Mittwochsgesellschaft).[14] Schlegel, founder with his brother August Wilhelm of the short-lived (1798–1800) but highly influential journal *Athenaeum*, was the leading figure of the new Romantic movement in Berlin, a movement which, at least in its earliest and most intense phase, was already dying out in 1802.

In his *Monologues* (1800), Schleiermacher assigns a crucial role both to Henriette and her salon in the formation of his own thinking during his early Berlin years:

you, who even now surround me in sweet love ... at every moment I could exchange thoughts and life with you; where such community exists, there is my paradise ... [I remain indebted to] this beautiful period of my life, where I came into contact with so much that was new, when many things appeared to me in bright light that previously I only darkly felt and had no preparation for (*KGA* I.3, 51, 23).

The praise is surely warranted, when we consider his extremely productive literary output during this brief time period. To begin with, his contributions to the *Athenaeum* include several significant reviews (see *KGA* I.3, 63–72, 225–34, 235–48), including one of Kant's *Anthropology from a Pragmatic Point of View* – in which the text is labeled "a collection of trivialities" and criticized for, among other shortcomings, its "treatment of the female sex as an abnormality, and throughout as a means" (*KGA* I.2, 365, 369); as well as a modest number of the famous *Fragmente*, the bulk of which were written by Friedrich Schlegel (*KGA* I.2, xxxi–xxxii, 141–56). Schleiermacher's most famous *Fragment* is Nr. 364, a feminist mini-essay entitled *Idee zu einem Katechismus der Vernunft für edle Frauen* (*Idea for a Catechism of Reason for Noble Ladies*), in which he argues for liberation from the social conventions of gender, women's right to education, and the equality of the sexes (*KGA* I.2, xxxviii, 153–4).

Other important works written during this period but not published in *Athenaeum* include *Versuch einer Theorie des geselligen Betragens* (*Attempt at a Theory of Sociable Conduct*), published in 1799 in the *Berlinisches Archiv der Zeit und ihres Geschmacks*. In the opening sentence, Schleiermacher proclaims: "Free sociability, bound and determined by no external end,

---

[14] See Günter Birtsch, "The Berlin Wednesday Society," in *What is Enlightenment? Eighteenth-Century Answers and Twentieth-Century Questions*, ed. James Schmidt (Berkeley: University of California Press, 1996), pp. 235–52.

is demanded aloud by all educated human beings as one of their first and noblest needs" (*KGA* I.2, 165). In his later ethics this concept of free sociability (*freie Geselligkeit*) is assigned a key role as a distinct form of moral community; "completely separate . . . from the state" (as well as from the church and other fundamental institutions such as universities); a community of friendship and inquiry that "goes directly from individual to individual" but which "dies away as soon as it attempts to organize itself according to external characteristics" (*WA* II, 367, 366, 367). The personal roots of Schleiermacher's theory of free sociability, often viewed as one of his most original contributions to ethics (indeed, he has even been called "the theorist of salon culture"),[15] clearly lie in Henriette Herz's salon.

Another important piece, also published in 1799, is *Briefe bei Gelegenheit der politisch theologischen Aufgabe und des Sendschreibers jüdischer Hausvater. Von einem Prediger außerhalb Berlin* (*Letters on the Occasion of the Political-Theological Responsibility and Petition of the Jewish Housefathers. From a Preacher outside Berlin*) (*KGA* I.2, 327–61). In these *Letters* Schleiermacher argues for full civil rights for Jews and recommends the establishment of a reform sect within Judaism. And in 1800 he publishes anonymously *Vertraute Briefe über Friedrich Schlegels Lucinde* (*Confidential Letters Concerning Friedrich Schlegel's Lucinde*), in which he defends both the autonomy of art ("I know of no immorality at all in a work of art other than when it fails to do its duty to be outstandingly beautiful, or when it goes beyond its boundaries, in short when it's no good" [*wenn es nichts taugt*]) (*KGA* I.3, 190) and a Romantic interpretation of erotic love.

Schleiermacher's most famous work during his early Berlin years is of course *On Religion: Speeches to its Cultured Despisers* (1799) – a defense of religion against secular Enlightenment critics who sought to reduce religion to a handmaiden of ethics or natural philosophy: "Religion's essence is neither thinking nor acting, but intuition and feeling . . . religion is sense and taste for the infinite" (*KGA* I.2, 211, 212). However, from the standpoint of Schleiermacher's ethics, it is the *Monologues* of 1800 that constitutes "the chief work of the young Schleiermacher, for in it he has condensed a thirteen-year process of ethical reflection."[16]

---

[15] Davies, *Identity or History?* p. 166. See also Gunter Scholtz, *Die Philosophie Schleiermachers* (Darmstadt: Wissenschaftliche Buchgesellschaft, 1984), p. 124; *Ethik und Hermeneutik*, p. 25.

[16] Kurt Nowak, *Schleiermacher und die Frühromantik: Eine literaturgeschichtliche Studie zum romantischen Religionsverständnis und Menschenbild am Ende des 18. Jahrhunderts in Deutschland* (Göttingen: Vandenhoeck & Ruprecht, 1986), p. 230.

Several key motifs now emerge that link this work both with his earlier as well as later ethics. First, a strong stress on individuality constitutes yet another break with Kantian ethics. Schleiermacher's "highest intuition" in the *Monologues* is the insight "that each human being is meant to present humanity in his own way, in his own mixture of its elements, so that humanity reveals itself in every manner, and so that everything can issue from its womb and become real in the fullness of infinity" (*KGA* I.3, 18). Those (like Kant and Fichte, and even the Schleiermacher of ten years earlier) who are allegedly "content to have found only reason" and who "throw themselves before duty" overvalue universality and undervalue particularity – they have not yet "risen to the higher standpoint of the formation [*Bildung*] of particularity and ethical life [*Sittlichkeit*]" (*KGA* I.3, 17, 18). And in doing so they fail to grasp what is most vital in human life. At the same time, Schleiermacher (unlike certain late twentieth-century postmodernists) is not casting universality completely aside on the ground that it is merely "an arduous campaign to smother the differences and above all to eliminate all 'wild' – autonomous, obstreperous and uncontrolled – sources of moral judgment."[17] "What I am searching for," Schleiermacher emphasizes, "is individuality and its relation to humanity" (*KGA* I.3, 26). Universality and particularity are both core values in Schleiermacher's ethics, and in his later work he tries to carve a clear space for each.

But what does the Romantic Schleiermacher offer in place of the stern ethics of duty? Here his ethics of individuality begins to sound like a (19)60s love-in: "Love, you power of attraction in the world! No individual life and no formation is possible without you, without you everything must melt into a crude homogeneous mass! . . . For us you are the alpha and omega" (*KGA* I.3, 22). And because Kantians fail to appreciate individuality, they are also unable to grasp the significance of the primal force of love, on which all else depends: "for them law and duty, uniform action and justice are sufficient" (*KGA* I.3, 22).

An additional theme touched on in the *Monologues* that takes on a central role in Schleiermacher's later ethics is what he calls "the twofold vocation of human beings on earth" (*KGA* I.3, 19). Beginning in his 1812–13 lectures, Schleiermacher repeatedly characterizes ethics as the historical process by which nature becomes the organ and symbol of reason

---

[17] Zygmunt Bauman, *Postmodern Ethics* (Oxford: Blackwell, 1993), p. 12.

(see, e.g., *WA* II, 254, 259, 561–3). In the *Monologues*, he refers to this organizing and symbolizing activity as the two ways by means of which humanity comes into possession of "its great body," the material world – "nurturing this body in order to sharpen its organs, or mimetically and artistically forming it into the imprint of reason and mind" (*KGA* I.3, 11).[18]

Grundlinien einer Kritik der bisherigen Sittenlehre

Schleiermacher's next major work in ethics is *Outlines of a Critique of Previous Doctrines of Ethics*, which he published in 1803, after the intense flame of the Berlin Romantic group had already begun to fade and he had accepted a position as court preacher in the small town of Stolpe, near the border of Poland. His longest (346 pp.) work thus far, its style is also radically different from the Berlin Romantic writings. Now the same author who only ten years earlier had criticized the *Buchstabenmenschen* for their addiction to theory himself expresses a strong craving for system: "the real to which ethics relates must be presented . . . as a system" (*WA* I, 250). Similarly, the announced critique of previous doctrines of ethics (which in effect serves as a foil to his own system of ethics) must have a "scientific form": "*for each actual science, as ethics after all wants to be and shall be, there is no other critique except that of scientific form [wissenschaftliche Form], and the presentation of such a critique will be attempted here*" (*WA* I, 10).

The conceptual structures by means of which Schleiermacher here investigates previous ethical theories definitely set the tone for his own future work in ethics. He is now firmly convinced that there are three formal ethical concepts, "namely, the concepts of duties, virtues, and of goods" (*WA* I, 128) and that in a systematic ethical theory all three will be recognized as "equally necessary" (*WA* I, 74; see also 312). Also, his own preference for an ethics that is not *beschränkend* (limiting, restrictive) but rather *hervorbringend* (productive, creative, bringing forth) becomes evident. Ethics is not simply about constraining desires, but is rather a process through which "totally unique and new" creations are brought forth into the world (*WA* I, 54). And, again, ethical theory needs to find a way to do justice to both universality and particularity: "the call of

---

[18] Cf. Horace Leland Friess, *Schleiermacher's Soliloquies: An English Translation of the Monologen, with a Critical Introduction and Appendix* (Chicago: Open Court, 1926), p. 146. See also Birkner, *Schleiermachers Christliche Sittenlehre*, p. 39; and John P. Crossley, Jr., "The Ethical Impulse in Schleiermacher's Early Ethics," *Journal of Religious Ethics* 17 (1989): 12.

Schleiermacher's earlier [*Monologues*] to bring the universal and the individual together without dominating or subordinating is extended to the *Critique* as a task for the future."[19] Finally, Plato and Spinoza once again stand out as Schleiermacher's own heroes in the history of ethics (see, e.g. *WA* I, 68–9), and much of the sting of the *Critique* is aimed at Kant and Fichte. Kant's doctrine of ethics, for instance, is declared to be "throughout more juridical than ethical, and has throughout the look and all the marks of a social legislation" (*WA* I, 65). And Fichte's doctrine of ethics also has "actually the same character; with Kant it only emerges more strongly" (*WA* I, 65).

Brouillon zur Ethik

In 1804 Schleiermacher received his first academic appointment, joining the theology faculty at his alma mater, the University of Halle. His next major work in ethics, and the one that immediately precedes the lectures translated below, is *Outline for Ethics*, a set of lectures delivered in the winter semester of 1805–6, during his second year at Halle.[20]

The *Outline for Ethics* has been described as "the first attempt at an *explicit* and *positive* presentation of Schleiermacher's systematic conception of ethics."[21] However, many aspects of this conception were strongly hinted at in earlier works as well – e.g. Schleiermacher's conviction that an adequate ethical theory requires a pluralistic integration of doctrines of good, virtue, and duty, rather than the one-sided programs favored by both ancient and modern theorists. But one key theme that emerges more clearly at this point in his writing career is the view that ethical theory properly conceived concerns not the philosophical intrusion of formal, ahistorical principles of conduct into human life, but rather the broad-based normative study of human life (individually as well as collectively and institutionally; locally as well as globally) as it actually develops

---

[19] John Wallhausser, "Schleiermacher's Critique of Ethical Reason: Toward a Systematic Ethics," *Journal of Religious Ethics* 17 (1989): 29. See also *WA* I, 111–12.

[20] *WA* II also contains a shorter text (39 pp.) entitled *Tugendlehre 1804/05* – Schleiermacher's ethics lectures from the winter semester of 1804–5 (see p. xiii). This text presents only a part of the larger system outlined in the *Brouillon*.

[21] Eilert Herms, "'Beseelung der Natur durch die Vernunft': Eine Untersuchung der Einleitung zu Schleiermachers Ethikvorlesung von 1805/06," *Archivio di filosofia* 52 (1984): 50. See also Herms's earlier book, *Herkunft, Entfaltung und erste Gestalt des Systems der Wissenschaft bei Schleiermacher* (Gütersloh: Gerd Mohn, 1974), esp. pp. 168–75, where the 1803 *Grundlinien* is described as Schleiermacher's key work before his move to Halle in 1804.

through history. By 1805, Schleiermacher is definitely an advocate of a strongly anti-formalist program in ethics, one concerned more with the *is* than the *ought* of human life.

In the *Brouillon zur Ethik*, this more material or immanent conception of ethics occurs in the opening lecture, where Schleiermacher bluntly asserts that "ethics is the science of history, that is to say, the science of intelligence as appearance" (*WA* II, 80; see also 88). In the later lectures translated below this theme is developed further in a variety of ways – for instance, in the dual claims that "the study of history provides the illustrations [*Bilderbuch*] to ethics, while the doctrine of morals provides the formulae [*Formelbuch*] for the study of history" (*WA* II, 549); and "the doctrine of morals contains the beginnings of reason, in which, in just the same way, the manifestations of reason are rooted, the whole course of which goes to form history in the widest scope of the term" (*WA* II, 536). The intent is thus not to collapse ethics into history, to re-read history moralistically, or to construe moral norms as mere shifting historical products. Rather, according to Schleiermacher's mature conception of ethics, the task of ethical theory is to "supply the categories of understanding for human-historical life";[22] while recognizing that there is always an ineliminable gap between theoretical categories and real life.

For many readers, this more material, immanent conception of ethics naturally brings to mind Hegel's philosophy, particularly its infamous notion of "reason in history" – namely, the claim that "the only thought which philosophy brings with it [to the study of history] is the simple idea of reason – the idea that reason governs the world, and that world history is therefore a rational process."[23] Like Hegel, the mature Schleiermacher advocates a concrete ethics of *Sittlichkeit* over an abstract morality of *Moralität*; a philosophical ethics committed to "*the comprehension of the present and the actual*, not the setting up of a *world beyond* which exists God knows where."[24]

Nevertheless, there is at least one basic difference between Schleiermacher's and Hegel's ethics. Schleiermacher's ethics, so to speak, contains

[22] Birkner, *Schleiermachers Christliche Sittenlehre*, p. 37.
[23] Georg Wilhelm Friedrich Hegel, *Lectures on the Philosophy of World History. Introduction: Reason in History*, trans. H. B. Nisbet (New York: Cambridge University Press, 1975), p. 27.
[24] Hegel, *Elements of the Philosophy of Right*, ed. Allen W. Wood (New York: Cambridge University Press, 1991), p. 20. See particularly §135 on the *Sittlichkeit*/*Moralität* distinction.

more normative space – there still remains an *ought* along with the *is*. For Schleiermacher (but not for Hegel), the job of ethical theory is

to draw the image of a humanity as it should be; an image that when it is first suggested in history is out of focus and imperfect. Ethics is thus at the same time image and corrective of reality. As a theory of the history of that which is still incomplete but also situated on the right path, it stands between the positions of Kant and Hegel.[25]

One prominent example of the greater normative space in Schleiermacher's ethics is that he would never endorse Hegel's notorious claim that "the state is the actuality of the ethical idea [*die Wirklichkeit der sittlichen Idee*]."[26] On the contrary, Schleiermacher reminds readers in his 1812–13 *Lectures* that one of the chief defects of the ancients was their view that the state "encompassed the whole of the ethical process" (*WA* II, 337; see also 555). On Schleiermacher's view, the proper tracking of "the ensouling [*Beseelung*] of human nature through reason" (*WA* II, 87) requires a plurality of autonomous cultural and institutional spheres.

Schleiermacher's mature ethics

The works considered thus far may be grouped together as Schleiermacher's early works in ethics. (He was only in his mid-thirties when he began delivering the *Brouillon* lectures in 1805.) But the following year marks another key shift in Schleiermacher's life. In fall 1806 Napoleon's troops occupied Halle; in October the university was shut down. In 1807 Schleiermacher moved back to Berlin, where he soon began to take a

---

[25] Scholtz, *Die Philosophie Schleiermachers*, p. 121. See also ch. 2 ("Ethik als Theorie der modernen Kultur. Mit vergleichendem Blick auf Hegel") of Scholtz's *Ethik und Hermeneutik*.

[26] Hegel, *Elements of the Philosophy of Right*, § 257. See also §§ 258, 260. Although Schleiermacher was instrumental in bringing Hegel to the University of Berlin, where they were colleagues from 1818 until Hegel's death in 1831, their relationship was often acrimonious. However, their ongoing quarrel can at least be said to have contributed to one of the history of philosophy's more memorable put-downs. Commenting on Schleiermacher's conception of religion as the feeling of absolute dependence, Hegel wrote in 1822: "If religion grounds itself in a person only on the basis of feeling, then . . . a dog would be the best Christian, for it carries this feeling more intensely within itself and lives principally satisfied by a bone. A dog even has feelings of salvation when its hunger is satisfied by a bone" ("Vorrede zu Hinrichs Religionsphilosophie," in *Werke*, ed. Eva Moldenhauer and Karl Markus Michel [Frankfurt: Suhrkamp, 1970], II, 42). For discussion, see Terry Pinkard, *Hegel: A Biography* (New York: Cambridge University Press, 2000), pp. 445–7, 498–502; Richard Crouter, "Hegel and Schleiermacher at Berlin: A Many-Sided Debate," *Journal of the American Academy of Religion* 48 (1980): 18–43; and Jeffrey Hoover, "The Origin of the Conflict between Hegel and Schleiermacher at Berlin," *The Owl of Minerva* 20 (1988): 69–79.

leading role in discussions for a new Prussian university. In 1808, he published *Occasional Thoughts on Universities in the German Sense: With an Appendix Regarding a University Soon to be Established*, and as a result quickly became a key voice in the actual planning of the university.[27] In 1809 Schleiermacher was appointed professor of theology at the new university, as well as a member of the philosophical and historical sections of the Berlin Academy of Sciences. He retained both of these appointments until his death in 1834.

Dates and style of the lectures

The text below (here translated into English for the first time) consists of lectures delivered by Schleiermacher at the University of Berlin. The first half or so of the text definitely dates from the winter semester of 1812–13; the German editors assign a probable date of 1816–17 to most of the remaining material. Additionally, when Schleiermacher lectured on philosophical ethics again in 1824, 1827, and 1832 he re-used these earlier lecture notes, adding occasional new comments in the margins of his texts. These later comments appear in our text as footnotes.

Although Schleiermacher repeatedly announced his intentions to publish his mature ethical theory, this plan was never realized. None of the following lectures were published during his lifetime; indeed, they were not published in complete form until early in the twentieth century (in volume II of *WA*). The closest that Schleiermacher's contemporaries came to seeing a published form of his mature ethical theory were the six *Akademieabhandlungen* that he read before the Academy of Sciences between 1819 and 1830.[28] However, the Academy's *Yearbook* in which these Addresses were eventually published had a small readership, and

---

[27] For discussion, see Terence N. Tice and Edwina Lawler, "Dedicatory Preface," in Schleiermacher, *Occasional Thoughts on Universities in the German Sense*, trans. Terence N. Tice and Edwina Lawler (Lewiston: The Edwin Mellen Press, 1991), p. ii. The German text is reprinted in *KGA* I.6, 15–100. See also Jean-François Lyotard, *The Postmodern Condition: A Report on Knowledge*, trans. Geoff Bennington and Brian Massumi (Minneapolis: University of Minnesota Press, 1984), pp. 31–7.

[28] The six Addresses are reprinted in *WA* I, 347–494, and were originally published between 1820 and 1832. The most important one is "On the Difference between Natural Law and Moral Law" (*WA* I, 396–416; read 1825, published 1828), in which Schleiermacher argues that both types of law are fundamentally descriptive rather than prescriptive. In "On the Difference," Schleiermacher also reinterprets Kant's categorical imperative as a hypothetical imperative: "If you want to be rational, then act so" (*WA* I, 405).

each Address is more an academic treatise dealing with a specific issue than a systematic presentation of a complete theory. In other words, the following *Lectures*, warts and all (they abound in cryptic formulations)[29] are extremely important documents: they are the closest we will ever get to a full picture of Schleiermacher's later ethical theory.

Basic concepts and themes in the lectures

Schleiermacher's mature ethics constitutes an ambitious effort to integrate many of his earlier intellectual influences in moral philosophy – e.g. Kant, ancient Greek (particularly Platonic) thought, early Romanticism, and Spinoza – as well as transformative experiences in his personal life such as the salon culture of Berlin. Because many of the key themes in his *Lectures* are in effect more detailed expositions of ideas first presented in earlier writings, much of what follows should sound familiar.

Ethics as a descriptive and historical science

First, ethics according to the mature Schleiermacher is more a descriptive science than a normative one. The task of ethics, he announces early in the Introduction, is "to encompass and document all truly human action" (*WA* II, 246). Granted, the word "truly" does imply *some* normative orientation (actions which are not "truly human" are not part of the proper purview of ethics), and we will try to get a clearer sense of the content of this normative dimension in a moment. But it is the enormous descriptive scope of his conception of ethics that first strikes the reader. Indeed, Schleiermacher regards it as a virtue of his approach that eventually "every empirical element [*alles Empirische*] will find its place" in his presentation of ethics (*WA* II, 274). On the other hand, Kant's "so-called pure doctrine of morals" is dismissed as "an empty thought" (*WA* II, 548). Kantian rationality, Schleiermacher warns in his first Introduction, posits an a priori ought as the characteristic feature of the ethical, "without concerning itself with what exists" (*WA* II, 246).

---

[29] In addition to the fact that these *Lectures* were not prepared for publication by their author, their very nature as lectures may explain part of their difficulty of comprehension. In a letter written when he first began lecturing on ethics at the University of Halle in 1804, Schleiermacher states: "You can imagine that I only note the main propositions and lecture freely for the rest of the time, and I will continue doing so" (letter to von Willich of 30 October 1804, as cited by Birkner, "Einleitung," *Ethik 1812/13* [Hamburg: Felix Meiner, 1981; rev. 2nd ed., 1990], p. xvi).

Part of the normative content of ethics is hinted at in Schleiermacher's root conviction that ethics is "the action of reason" on nature (*WA* II, 541). "Truly human action," in other words, is to be understood as action that is guided by reason. In stressing the impact of reason on and within nature, Schleiermacher seeks to overcome what he sees as the objectionable gulf between "ought" and "is" in many previous ethical theories: "The propositions of ethics ought not . . . to be commands, whether conditional or unconditional, but inasmuch as they are laws, they must express the true action of reason upon nature" (*WA* II, 545). But reason of course cannot instantly act on all aspects of nature: it is, at best, a long and gradual process as recorded in human history. Ethics for the mature Schleiermacher is thus also defined as "the science of history" (*WA* II, 251). Insofar as rational human action is a subset of human behavior, the subject matter of ethics can be viewed as a subset of the larger subject matter of history.

Nature as organ and symbol of reason

Ethics is the study of the action of reason on nature, in the broadest sense of the term "nature." Reason acts on human nature (shaping our talents and capacities) via the process of what Schleiermacher calls "gymnastics," on organic nature via agriculture, and on inorganic nature by way of "mechanics" (*WA* II, 276). A further specification of this broad historical process is obtained in Schleiermacher's dictum that the natural world, when viewed from the perspective of ethics, is "the organ and symbol of reason" (*WA* II, 254). In its organizing function, reason is involved in forming or shaping nature in accordance with its own principles: "making the world moral." In the broadest sense, we are talking now about the activity of human culture and its transformative impact on the natural environment. This aspect of Schleiermacher's ethical theory is consonant with the basic spirit of much practical philosophy in the German idealist tradition: the primary task of ethics is to create a moral world; to bring the real closer to the ideal. In its symbolizing function, reason is involved in marking or signifying nature so that nature becomes a symbol of reason. Here the arts and sciences play crucial roles. And because the arts and sciences are themselves aspects of human culture, at bottom these organizing and symbolizing activities of reason "are merely two different aspects of the same thing" (*WA* II, 254; see also 564). Nature as organ of reason refers more to the formative process of reason as it is acting on nature, while nature as symbol of reason refers to the completed process. They are thus two sides of the same coin: "both functions are essentially bound up together in every complete act" (*WA* II, 293).

Doctrines of goods, virtue, and duties

As we saw earlier, in his normative ethics the mature Schleiermacher is committed to a pluralistic program that integrates doctrines of goods, virtue, and duties. None of these doctrines is reducible to the others, and each has a necessary role to play in any adequate theory of ethics. At the same time, the doctrine of goods is more overarching than the other two and thus has a certain priority over them. Only the idea of the highest good "can stand alone" – "the moral process finds its complete depiction" in this idea, while the doctrines of virtue and duties refer back to the doctrine of goods "and are incomplete in themselves" (*WA* II, 256). As used by Schleiermacher, the term "good" refers primarily to the end or goal of moral activity (the broadest and most ambitious sense of which would be the eventual union of reason and nature – "the making moral of the whole of earthly nature" [*WA* II, 547]); "virtue" to the power or force in human beings from which moral actions flow ("reason in the human individual" [*WA* II, 375], albeit reason which has also become disposition and skill [*WA* II, 378]); and "duty" to those principles of action necessary for the realization of the highest good. For Schleiermacher, the cardinal virtues are wisdom, love, prudence, and steadfastness (*WA* II, 379); while the four major divisions of duties are duties of right, duties of profession or vocation, duties of love, and duties of conscience (*WA* II, 412).

Universality and particularity

In addition to reason's organizing and symbolizing activities, a second key distinction concerns what is universally like or identical, and what is individually unique or differentiating. With this feature of his theory Schleiermacher seeks to balance Kantian concerns with universality, fairness, and impartiality on the one hand with the Romantics' stress on individuality, tradition, and local community on the other. Ethical activity concerns both that which has "validity for everyone" (*WA* II, 279) as well as the uniqueness of each human personality – "a personal sphere which is absolutely nontransferable" (*WA* II, 289). The attempt to do justice to the real demands of both moral universality *and* particularity constitutes one of the outstanding achievements of Schleiermacher's later ethics. However, as was also the case with the organizing and symbolizing functions of reason, neither identity nor particularity stands entirely alone: "Particularity is not in another domain to identity; on the contrary they are both in the same one, so that in reality they are always interrelated, to a greater or lesser extent" (*WA* II, 286).

Four spheres of ethical activity

Within the extremely broad scope of reason's action on nature, Schleiermacher highlights four specific spheres or provinces of ethical activity. Each sphere corresponds to a quadrant created by the crossing of reason's two major antitheses or axes – the organizing/symbolizing axis and the universality/particularity axis. The four spheres are thus: (1) the organizing/universal quadrant, (2) the organizing/particular quadrant, (3) the symbolizing/universal quadrant, and (4) the symbolizing/particular quadrant. Corresponding to each of the four spheres are specific types of activity that help reason realize its domain-specific aims. For the organizing/universal sphere, he draws attention to economic activities of labor, commerce, and exchange, as regulated by basic principles of justice. Corresponding to the organizing/particular sphere are personal assets such as talents and property (particularly one's home), as well as activities that further relationships in the private sphere such as friendship and hospitality. Activities pertaining specifically to the third sphere (symbolizing/universal) are language and science (in the traditional broad German *Wissenschaft* sense of the term: natural and social sciences, as well as humanities). And in the fourth sphere, the symbolizing/particular quadrant, he sees the activities of feeling, art, and religion as playing key roles.

Four types of moral institution and community

Finally, associated with each of the above four fields of moral praxis are domain-specific institutions and forms of community designed to promote reason's different goals. Corresponding to the first sphere (organizing/universal) is the state;[30] to the second (organizing/particular), free sociability; to the third (symbolizing/universal), universities and research institutes; and to the fourth (symbolizing/particular), the church.[31] Each of these types of institution and community is to be understood as an autonomous and independent site of moral self-realization. Universities and churches, for instance, must remain free from state interference. And the intimate and informal modes of communication fostered in the salons of free sociability will die away as soon as one tries to organize such communities along bureaucratic or institutional lines.

Assessing Schleiermacher's ethics

We began by noting that many German scholars have singled out Schleiermacher's ethical theory as his most outstanding philosophical achievement. And one may hope that the above tour of his ethics provides some support for this conviction. But it should also come as no surprise to readers that his ethics, from the beginning, has generated an ample arsenal of criticisms. Although the extremely broad and descriptive swath cut by his ethics will come as a relief to those who feel that the insular battles of much modern ethical theory have resulted in an unfortunate disciplinary isolationism that has divorced philosophical analyses of ethics from those areas of life as well as scholarship that can bring content to the abstractions of theory, it is this same breadth of scope, when combined with a stubborn resistance to transcendental norms and their justification, that has led many critics to question the cogency of Schleiermacher's program. The result, or so say the critics, may be exemplary as an exercise in the philosophy of culture or philosophical sociology, but it does not pass

---

[30] Schleiermacher's placement of the state on the side of reason's move towards universality should not lead readers to infer that he envisages one world-state eventually replacing the present plurality of independent states. In the *Lectures* he writes: "Particularity in common is the basis of the state"; "if we posit the state as necessarily conditional upon national unity, we are also positing an essential plurality of states" (*WA* II, 336–7). Rather, it is shared, transnational principles of justice that will (hopefully) allow the plurality of states to coexist peacefully and collectively to make moral progress. For discussion, see Birkner, *Schleiermachers Christliche Sittenlehre*, p. 42.

[31] Here too (see previous note), the fact that Schleiermacher places the church on the particularity side of reason's activity should not lead us to infer that he sees no universalizing tendencies within religion. Birkner writes: "while a universal state and a universal language are unthinkable to Schleiermacher, matters stand differently with the idea of a universal religion and church" (*Schleiermachers Christliche Sittenlehre*, p. 43). While Schleiermacher does not pursue this theme in any detail in the following *Lectures*, he does note at the very end that "the church is within the state but as something that transcends its boundaries" (*WA* II, 484 n.).

muster as an adequate normative ethical theory. Somewhere within the myriad institutions, communities, and yearnings of *Bildung*, the task of justifying moral norms has been forgotten.[32] Others, particularly those who like their philosophy straightforward and clear, will no doubt be put off by the overly programmatic, extremely abstract, and occasionally cryptic tone of these *Lectures*. And certainly Schleiermacher's overoptimism concerning reason's presence and influence in human life, not to mention his questionable assumption that reason's ultimate goal is complete mastery and domination over all of nature (attitudes which of course mark much of the practical philosophy of the modern and late modern periods), should be factored in to any critical assessment of his mature ethics.

But let us end on a positive note. Broadly speaking, Schleiermacher's ethical theory represents an under-explored and singular option within the amazingly rich and creative tradition of German Idealism – a tradition which itself is arguably "the most successful and comprehensive formulation and assessment of the nature and legitimacy of modernity."[33] The strong and multifaceted pluralism of Schleiermacher's ethics – as evidenced not only in his attempt to integrate ancient Greek concerns with virtue and the good with modern conceptions of duty and justice, but also in his clear recognition of both the universal and individual dimensions of ethics and the related need for autonomous forms of moral institution and community, each of which plays a unique role in humanity's often tragic, sometimes comic efforts to create a moral world – should certainly speak to a contemporary audience that has grown weary of the reductive platitudes of academic ethical theory. On these and other points, Schleiermacher has much to teach us.

---

[32] For examples of such criticism, see the references cited in Birkner, *Schleiermachers Christliche Sittenlehre*, pp. 46–7; and Scholtz, *Die Philosophie Schleiermachers*, pp. 115, 119–21.

[33] Robert B. Pippin, *Modernism as a Philosophical Problem: On the Dissatisfactions of European High Culture*, 2nd ed. (Malden, MA: Blackwell, 1999), p. 9. For general discussion of German Idealism, see Karl Ameriks, ed., *The Cambridge Companion to German Idealism* (New York: Cambridge University Press, 2000).

Chronology

1795–1802	Schleiermacher among Romantic circle in Berlin with the brothers A. W. and Friedrich Schlegel, Dorothea Veit, Henriette Herz
1796	Schleiermacher appointed chaplain at the Charité Hospital in Berlin
1797	Schleiermacher and Friedrich Schlegel become friends at the salon of Henriette Herz; Schelling publishes *Ideas for a Philosophy of Nature*
1798–1800	Publication of the journal *Athenaeum*, vols. I–III, literary organ of the Berlin Romantics
1799	Schleiermacher publishes *On Religion: Speeches to its Cultured Despisers*
1799–1800	Schleiermacher publishes various reviews and *Fragmente* in the *Athenaeum*
1800	Schleiermacher publishes *Monologues*; Schelling publishes *System of Transcendental Idealism*
1803	Schleiermacher accepts position as court preacher in Stolpe, East Prussia
1804–6	Schleiermacher appointed professor of theology and university preacher at Halle
1804–28	Schleiermacher publishes German translation of Plato
1806	University of Halle overrun by Napoleon's troops
1807	Schleiermacher returns to Berlin; Hegel publishes *The Phenomenology of Spirit*
1809	Founding of the University of Berlin by Wilhelm von Humboldt with Schleiermacher as secretary to the founding commission
1809–34	Schleiermacher at the University of Berlin as professor of theology, and member of the philosophical and historical sections of the Berlin Academy of Sciences
1810–34	Schleiermacher is preacher at the Holy Trinity Church in Berlin
1812–13	Schleiermacher lectures on ethics for the first time at the University of Berlin; birth of Kierkegaard in Copenhagen
1814	Death of Fichte at University of Berlin
1815	Congress of Vienna settles the Napoleonic wars
1818–32	Hegel at the University of Berlin

1819	Schopenhauer publishes *The World as Will and Representation*
1821	Hegel publishes lectures on *Philosophy of Right*
1821–2	Schleiermacher publishes first edition of his systematic theology, *The Christian Faith* (*Glaubenslehre*)
1831	Death of Hegel, from cholera
1832	Death of Goethe
1834	Death of Schleiermacher, 6 February

Further reading

The standard new German edition of Schleiermacher's writings is the *Kritische Gesamtausgabe* (*KGA*), edited by Hans-Joachim Birkner with Gerhard Ebeling, Hermann Fischer, Heinz Kimmerle, and Kurt-Victor Selge (Berlin: Walter de Gruyter, 1984–). Forty volumes are planned (in five divisions); ten have been published thus far. An earlier German edition that contains several of Schleiermacher's ethics writings discussed in the Introduction (including the *Ethik [1812/13]*) not yet reprinted in *KGA* is *Werke. Auswahl in vier Bänden* (*WA*), edited by Otto Braun and Johannes Bauer (Leipzig: Felix Meiner, 1910–13; reprint ed. Aalen: Scientia, 1967). *WA* is a good, compact edition for those with specific interests in Schleiermacher's ethical theory. More recently, Felix Meiner (in its well-known Philosophische Bibliothek series) has re-issued two important sets of ethics lectures contained in *WA* II: *Brouillon zur Ethik* (*1805/06*) (Hamburg, 1981); and *Ethik* (*1812/13*) (Hamburg, 1981; rev. second ed., 1990). (Note: *WA* II pagination is printed in parentheses at the top of each page in each of these volumes.) Both texts are edited by Hans-Joachim Birkner. The present translation of *Ethik* (*1812/13*) is based on Birkner's text.

Many of Schleiermacher's early works on ethics have recently been translated into English for the first time. A partial translation of his first philosophical work, "Notes on Aristotle: *Nicomachean Ethics* 8–9" appears in *Theology Today* 56 (1999): 164–8. See also Michel Welker's accompanying essay, "'We Live Deeper than We Think': The Genius of Schleiermacher's Earliest Ethics," *Theology Today* 56 (1999): 169–79. The following works all appear in the Schleiermacher Studies and Translations series sponsored by the Edwin Mellen Press of Lewiston, New York:

On the Highest Good, translated, annotated, with a scholarly postscript by H. Victor Froese, no. X (1992); *On Freedom*, translated, annotated, and introduced by Albert L. Blackwell, no. IX (1992); *On What Gives Value to Life*, translated by Edwina Lawler and Terrence N. Tice, no. XIV (1995). (Note: this title is rendered as *On the Value of Life* in the Introduction.) Additionally, the following volumes in the New Athenaeum series, also sponsored by the Edwin Mellen Press, contain English translations of several of Schleiermacher's shorter ethical writings discussed above: *Schleiermacher on Workings of the Knowing Mind*, edited by Ruth Drucilla Richardson, vol. V (1998), includes a translation of Schleiermacher's critical review of Kant's *Anthropology from a Pragmatic Point of View*, first published in *Athenaeum* 2.2 (1799), as well as of two of the short fragments on freedom that form part of the background of *On Freedom; Friedrich Schleiermacher's "Toward a Theory of Sociable Conduct" and Essays on its Intellectual-Cultural Context*, edited by Ruth Drucilla Richardson, vol. IV (1995). (The title of this piece is rendered as *Attempt at a Theory of Sociable Conduct* in the Introduction.) Finally, Mellen Press has also published an English translation of Schleiermacher's *Occasional Thoughts on Universities in the German Sense: With an Appendix Regarding a University Soon to be Established*, translated by Terrence N. Tice and Edwina Lawler (1991).

Richard Crouter's well-known translation of *On Religion: Speeches to its Cultured Despisers* is a volume in the Cambridge Texts in the History of Philosophy series (Cambridge University Press, 1988). A complete English translation of the *Monologues* is contained in *Schleiermacher's Soliloquies: An English Translation of the Monologen, with a Critical Introduction and Appendix*, translated and edited by Horace Leland Friess (Chicago: Open Court, 1926). A more recent translation of parts II and III of the *Monologues* appears in *The Early Political Writings of the German Romantics*, edited and translated by Frederick C. Beiser (Cambridge University Press, 1996).

There is a huge German secondary literature on all aspects of Schleiermacher's philosophy. What follows is a select list of recommended works that deal specifically with various aspects of Schleiermacher's ethical theory. For additional references, see Birkner's extensive bibliography in *Ethik* (*1812/13*). Birkner's own monograph, *Schleiermachers Christliche Sittenlehre im Zusammenhang seines philosophisch-theologischen Systems* (Berlin: Alfred Töpelmann, 1964) is still probably the best place to start.

Gunter Scholtz's two books, *Die Philosophie Schleiermachers* (Darmstadt: Wissenschaftliche Buchgesellschaft, 1984) and *Ethik und Hermeneutik: Schleiermachers Grundlegung der Geisteswissenschaften* (Frankfurt: Suhrkamp, 1995) are also both highly recommended. Three more specialized monographs dealing with Schleiermacher's early ethics are Eilert Herms, *Herkunft, Entfaltung und erste Gestalt des Systems der Wissenschaften bei Schleiermacher* (Gütersloh: Gerd Mohn, 1974); Kurt Nowak, *Schleiermacher und die Frühromantik: Eine literaturgeschichtliche Studie zum romantischen Religionsverständnis und Menschenbild am Ende des 18. Jahrhunderts in Deutschland* (Göttingen: Vandenhoeck & Ruprecht, 1986); and Günter Meckenstock, *Deterministische Ethik und kritische Theologie: Die Auseinandersetzung des frühen Schleiermacher mit Kant und Spinoza 1789–1794* (Berlin: Walter de Gruyter, 1988).

The English-language literature on Schleiermacher's philosophical ethics pales in comparison with the German, but it is growing. Richard B. Brandt's *The Philosophy of Schleiermacher: The Development of his Theory of Scientific and Religious Knowledge* (New York, 1941; reprint ed. New York: Greenwood, 1968) is still the most detailed examination of Schleiermacher's philosophy in English. The author (1910–97) later became a noted American moral philosopher, most closely associated with rule utilitarianism. Albert L. Blackwell, in *Schleiermacher's Early Philosophy of Life: Determinism, Freedom, and Phantasy* (Chico, CA: Scholars Press, 1982) explores some of Schleiermacher's early ethics, particularly issues raised in *On Freedom*.

At present there are no English-language books devoted to Schleiermacher's ethics. However, the following essays each examine different specific aspects of his ethical theory. Brent W. Sockness provides a clear and informed guide to several of the early writings in "Was Schleiermacher a Virtue Ethicist? *Tugend* and *Bildung* in the Early Ethical Writings," *Zeitschrift für Neuere Theologiegeschichte* 8 (2001): 1–33. John Wallhausser examines the 1803 *Outline of a Critique of Previous Doctrines of Ethics* in "Schleiermacher's Critique of Ethical Reason: Toward a Systematic Ethics," *Journal of Religious Ethics* 17 (1989): 25–39. George N. Boyd discusses issues raised in the 1825 Academy Address ("On the Difference Between Natural Law and Moral Law") in "Schleiermacher's 'Über den Unterschied Zwischen Naturgesetz und Sittengesetz,'" *Journal of Religious Ethics* 17 (1989): 41–9. John P. Crossley, Jr. examines parts of Schleiermacher's later ethics in "Schleiermacher's Christian Ethics in

Relation to his Philosophical Ethics," *Annual of the Society of Christian Ethics* 18 (1998): 93–117. In "The Ethical Impulse in Schleiermacher's Early Ethics," *Journal of Religious Ethics* 17 (1989): 5–24, Crossley looks at ethical issues raised in the *Monologues* and *On Religion*. Finally, for an informed discussion of Schleiermacher's social and political philosophy, see Jeffrey Hoover, "Friedrich Schleiermacher's Theory of the Limited Communitarian State," *Canadian Journal of Philosophy* 20 (1990): 241–60.

A good English-language biography of Schleiermacher is Martin Redeker, *Schleiermacher: Life and Thought*, translated by John Wallhausser (Philadelphia: Fortress Press, 1973). For suggestions on literature dealing with other aspects of Schleiermacher's work, see the "Further Readings" sections in Crouter, ed., *Schleiermacher: On Religion* as well as in Andrew Bowie, ed., *Schleiermacher: Hermeneutics and Criticism and Other Writings* (Cambridge University Press, 1998).

Note on the text

The contrast in font size here follows the German edition and reflects Schleiermacher's intention in his ethics lectures to present a "compendium," with a few main theses set forth in each section followed by elucidatory comments. See the note by Hans-Joachim Birkner, ed., in the Meiner edition (Hamburg, 1990), pp. xvi–xvii. In the interests of internal consistency, headings and subheadings have occasionally been modified in line with the scheme set out in the index of the German edition.

Translator's note

Schleiermacher builds up the very dense texture of the *Philosophical Ethics* by creating patterns and oppositions out of a limited number of key terms. One central pairing is the opposition between *bilden* and *erkennen* (later replaced by *bezeichnen*). Both these terms are problematic for the translator, particularly *bilden*, the primary sense of which is *to form*: it is necessary to translate *bilden* and its cognates with terms such as *form*, *formative*, *formation*, but it should always be borne in mind that the important secondary sense of *educate/education* can never be far from the reader's mind. The related term *anbilden*, which Schleiermacher uses in the sense of *form onto* or *form further*, has been rendered with the less syntactically awkward *inculcate*. The noun and adjective formed from *erkennen*, *Erkenntnis*, and *erkennend*, can readily be translated *cognition* and *cognitive*, but to render the verb as *cognate* is rarely appropriate in the context, so it appears in this translation as *recognize*.

A further opposition which creates some difficulties for the translator is that between *Organ* (*organ*) and *Symbol* (*symbol*). Schleiermacher extends their meaning into the verbs *organisieren* and *symbolisieren*, whose primary sense is *organize* and *symbolize*, but it is important to realize that they also carry the meaning *turn into an organ* and *turn into a symbol*.

Between the first version of the *Philosophical Ethics* and the later one, Schleiermacher evidently came to use different words for certain concepts which remain essentially the same. One example of this is the way he moves from the term *relativ* to the more unusual adjective *beziehungsweise*. In certain cases, however, it is difficult to be sure whether a new term is intended to convey a particular, subtle nuance, and so I have chosen to err on the side of precision by flagging up these terms, even where my translation runs the risk of appearing slightly stilted as a result. Notable examples of this are the interplay between *Ethik* (*ethics*) and *Sittenlehre* (*doctrine of morals*); and between *eigenthümlich* (*particular*) and *besondere*, which I have rendered *especial*, although this, like the equally problematic term *bestimmt*, often simply means *certain, particular*. Since the cognates of the latter term (*bestimmen* and *Bestimmung*) carry the sense, in Schleiermacher's text, of *determination*, *bestimmt* has usually been rendered as *determined*.

I should like to acknowledge the help I have received over some particularly intractable words and phrases from my colleagues, Professor W. E. Yates (Exeter) and Dr. Almut Suerbaum (Somerville College, Oxford).

Louise Adey Huish

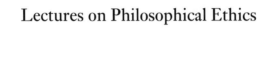
Lectures on Philosophical Ethics

Ethics 1812/13: Introduction and doctrine of goods

Introduction

I   Transition from critique to real depiction

1   The communication of a single distinct science cannot have any proper starting-point.

2   The individual science cannot have at its head a proposition which is immediately certain.

3   Even when deducing it from a higher science it can only be understood in conjunction with other knowledge which stands in opposition to it.

4   The establishment of this opposition can appear only as opinion.[1]

5   Every science has a number of shapes. The very act of beginning creates a basis for one such shape, and yet it contains knowledge only inasmuch as it is comprehended historically in conjunction with the others. The history of the sciences cannot exist without the sciences themselves, however, which gives rise to a circularity.

6   We already know something of every science by virtue of common life and common critique.

7   This influence cannot be to the good where ethics is concerned, because of the unfavorable phenomenon whereby a number of approaches

---

[1]   *Marginal addition:* Since the highest science is only in the process of becoming, and the sufficient deduction of the individual sciences will only be possible once it is perfected, the individual science must begin in imperfection in order to come into being.

Everything [is] imperfect and diverse, and so various forms are posited etc., in such a way as to show how they can be comprehended historically with a diversity in which each refers to the others. In contrast to the necessity of such [perfect] knowledge, the actual beginning is arbitrary, with an order which fluctuates, or hypothetical, as if the highest knowledge were not yet constructed.

The former is vulnerable to the unfavorable influence of what we know from common life and common critique.

start from very different assumptions but end with the same results, thus [suggesting] either error or scientific inconsistency.

8 Eudaemonistic ethics are hypothetical in the individual instance, because a purpose can be achieved in various ways, which in reality are in opposition to one another, while only one of them may be chosen. At most, therefore, they are an exposition of inclination: in the individual instance on technical grounds, and as a whole, because choice is based on inclination.

9 The Kantian form of rational ethics posits guiding thoughts to any action and can therefore only correct or perfect; it cannot, even were one to submit to it entirely, construct out of nothing.

10 Without concerning itself with what exists, Kantian rationality posits the ought, as the characteristic feature of the ethical, in contrast to the physical. However, [for Kant] even in the physical domain appearance is never adequate to the concept, and in fact ethics must presuppose that the object of ethics, the force from which individual actions proceed, exists and is identical with what ought to be.

11 Both approaches are limited also in a material respect. Without any construction they presuppose much that arises only with acting. However, right behavior in given circumstances and the form that shapes these circumstances must be one and the same thing.

12 Ethics must therefore encompass and catalog all truly human action.

13 At this higher level the opposition between reasonableness and happiness disappears.

14 Ethics must contain a form for all life's occurrences which is able to express its highest character.[2]

15 As far as a scientific treatment of the subject is concerned, the most appropriate formula is clearly that of reasonableness.

16 We might provisionally define ethics, therefore, as the life of reason, the necessary antithesis of which is acting upon nature.

17[3] We may not substitute personality for reason as the object of ethics because the action of the individual and the action of a group cannot be considered in isolation; thus, in a theory of human action, the opposition of personality must be superseded, and this leaves nothing but the life of reason in an organization.

[2] *Marginal note to 12–14 (1816):* Omitted.   [3] *Marginal note:* Omitted.

18 If the life of reason is conceived as acting upon nature, then ethics is conceived at the same time as the science that was opposed to it, namely physics.

II *Deduction of ethics by dialectical reasoning*

19 Lemma 1 of dialectic. Every kind of knowledge is narrower in scope the more it is determined by a diversity of opposites, and broader in scope the more it is the expression of higher and simpler oppositions.

20 Lemma 2 of dialectic. Absolute knowledge is the expression of no opposition whatsoever, but only of absolute being, which is identical with it.

21 Lemma 3. As such, however, it is not a definite form of knowledge in finite consciousness, that is, not one which may be expressed adequately in a plurality of concepts or propositions, but only the basis for and source of all particular forms of knowledge.

22 Lemma 4. All particular forms of knowledge, and therefore also their systematization, i.e. the real sciences, exist in the form of opposition.

23 Lemma 5. The totality of being as a finite entity must be expressed by means of a single highest opposition, because otherwise it would not be a totality but an aggregate and knowledge of it would have no unity, but would be chaotic.

24 Lemma 6. All finite being in the narrowest sense, i.e. every life, is an image of the absolute and thus an interaction of oppositions.

25 Lemma 7. Real knowledge in its totality is therefore the development of this interrelatedness of all oppositions under the power of both terms of the highest opposition.

26 Lemma 8. There are thus only two real sciences, which must incorporate all subordinate disciplines.

27 Lemma 9. The sense of opposition is inborn in the form of soul and body, the ideal and the real, reason and nature.

28 Lemma 10. Ethics is thus the depiction of finite being under the power of reason, i.e. viewed from that aspect where, in the interrelatedness of oppositions, reason is the active principle and reality that which is acted upon; physics is the depiction of finite being under the power of nature, i.e. where reality is the active principle and the ideal is what is acted upon.

29 Lemma 11. In finite existence, just as in finite knowledge as a depiction of the absolute, opposition is only relative. In their perfected state ethics is physics and physics ethics.

30 Lemma 12. Thus, as we progress towards this destination, the life of the ideal is an acting upon the real and the life of the real is an acting upon the ideal.

III Ethics considered as a process of becoming

31 In the face of this identity every science is incomplete: it is conditional upon the state of the others and has disintegrated into diverse shapes.

32 Ethics is directly conditional upon physics, inasmuch as its depictions of reality must be based upon the concept of the object to be considered, that is, nature.

33 And indirectly inasmuch as science is conditional upon disposition, which in its turn is conditional upon our domination of nature, which is dependent upon cognition of nature.

34 At no time therefore is ethics better than physics; the two must always run parallel.

35 As long as science is incomplete it will also exist in diverse forms, none of which can have universal validity. What is scientifically uncertain must reveal itself in a diversity of appearances.

36 The form taken by incompleteness may be one-sidedness of viewpoint. Here very frequently a false sense of certainty and the least appropriate respect for other points of view.[4]

37 It may also take the form of an insufficient thinking-through, both in relating backwards to causes and forwards to consequences. Here very frequently an apparent arbitrariness in the face of a robust reality in matters of detail, and very frequently a hidden feeling of uncertainty.[5]

38 Or else a coexistence of certainty and uncertainty in equal measure. Here very frequently a straightforward approaching of the goal and, as a result of the clearcut divergence of certainty and doubt, the most accurate evaluation of others.

39 Reason is to be found in nature, and ethics does not depict any action in which it arose originally. Ethics can only depict the possibility of penetrating and forming nature to an ever-increasing degree, of spreading

---

[4] *Marginal note:* 8–10 belong here.   [5] *Marginal note:* 11 and 12 here, also 17.

as broadly as possible the unification of reason and nature, taking as its starting-point the human organism, which is a part of general nature in which, however, a unification with reason is already given.

40 It is also not within the scope of ethics to depict the perfect unification of reason and nature, because for that to take place such isolated shapes must already have come to an end.

41 Ethics has therefore to depict a sequence, where each element consists of a unification which both has and has not taken place, and whose exponent expresses an increase in one factor and a decrease in another.

42 The ethics of imperatives addresses only the side of the equation where unification has not taken place, and therefore cannot express the gradual disappearance of this factor.

43 Consultative ethics addresses only the side of the equation where unification has taken place, for only then can it be a matter of indifference whether this is to be expressed in the form of reason or of sensibility.

44 A complete account must therefore supersede the opposition of the two forms.

45 Since all knowledge of reality is the imprint left in the ideal by finite existence, there cannot be any form other than depiction or narrative.

46 Physics and ethics, given their interdependence and the fact that they are opposed only in the proportional relationship of their material, can only have one and the same form.

47 Since there can be no real anti-reason, in which case there would also have to be an anti-God, the opposition of good and evil can only express the positive and negative factors in the process of gradual unification, and therefore can nowhere be better understood than in the pure and complete depiction of that process.

48 Since the opposition between freedom and physical necessity indicates in its product these two factors, which are based predominantly a) in reason and b) in nature; and in action points to something that expresses a) the inner character of the person who is acting and b) its coexistence with an external factor, that opposition can only clearly be understood by contemplating the way in which reason and nature coexist in totality.

49 Since the opposition between freedom and moral necessity is principally concerned with the discrepancy between an individual and a whole of which he is a part, where the extent of unification in the individual represents freedom, and that of the whole necessity, it can also only be

correctly understood by means of a depiction which shows how the development of an individual and of a whole are mutually dependent.

50 Ethics, as the depiction of the way in which reason and nature coexist, is the science of history.

51 Just as ethical development in its entirety consists not only of a practical side, but also of a theoretical one, in the same way ethics is not merely a matter of action in the narrow sense of the word, but also of knowledge as a form of action.

52 Just as natural science renders both the fixed forms and the fluid functions of nature comprehensible, and reduces each to an aspect of the other, in the same way ethics explains both the fixed forms of moral existence, family, state, etc., and the fluid functions, or their various moral capacities, and reduces each to an aspect of the other.

53 Just as ethics is not the intuition of reason in itself, which would be absolutely simple and therefore a part of absolute knowledge, but instead is the intuition of reason which has become nature in a plurality of functions in the form of oppositions, in the same way it is not the intuition of the individual aspects of an appearance, which might indeed be subsumed under the universal but cannot with any certainty be constructed from it.[6]

54 [Ethics] is a realistic form of knowledge, in that it is not absolute, and a speculative one in that it is not empirical.

55 The distinction between pure and applied ethics is false in this form, which is borrowed from mathematics, but is rooted in the matter itself.

56 Ethical principles in their complete determination cannot be applied to anything belonging outside the domain of ethics.

57 Anything constructed in ethics contains the potential for an infinite number of manifestations. Besides interpreting these empirically, there arises a need to link the empirical more closely with speculative depiction, namely to judge the individual manifestations as depictions of the idea, both in their extent and in terms of their particular limitations.

58 This is the essence of criticism, and there is therefore a cycle of critical disciplines which build on ethics.

59 To the extent that the individual and his moral capacity is comprehended in the production of a given phenomenon, he is placed among particular oppositions and particular natural conditions, and there is a particular need to survey how these are to be regarded.

---

[6] *Marginal note:* Omitted.

60 This is the essence of technology, and there is therefore a cycle of technical disciplines which proceed from ethics.

61 The most telling examples are: the state, political science and statesmanship, art – all forms of moral production may be seen as art – aesthetics, practical instructions for the arts.

62 As a form of knowledge which is indeed speculative and yet at the same time realistic, ethics is concerned neither with pure reason in opposition to nature, nor with pure nature in opposition to reason.

63 However, in general it rests on and is brought into community with the absolute through a form of opposition; for the side of the opposition that is orientated towards the real, no one member exists without the other, while for the side orientated towards the absolute, everything represents the absolute in the identity of the existing [members].

64 The higher critical process, which demonstrates the presence of the absolute in everything which is demonstrably real, transposed onto the level of totality, is a mediation between knowledge of reality and absolute knowledge.

65 Now, given that pure nature and pure reason do not occur in ethics, everything which does occur there is reasonable nature and natural or organic reason.

66 Given that relative identity is to be depicted in the form of becoming, one pole of depiction is a minimum of becoming, the other a maximum of becoming.

67 Ethics begins with a minimum of becoming, that is, by positing a nature in which reason is already present, and by positing a reason in which nature is already present, where the interrelatedness in each form can be traced back to an earlier phase of the same thing.

68 Since nature in the next lowest stage in the identity of the ideal and the real is animal nature, the fundamental intuition of ethics is of human nature in a form such that nothing purely animal can be found, and therefore nothing is merely material any more.

69 What essentially differentiates the human from the animal can be demonstrated first of all in the operation of the senses of perception and feeling, but equally it is also to be assumed in the subordinate functions of animal and vegetable life.

70 Just as reason is not to be posited as a separate entity, apart from its existence in nature, because each individual entity, in relative opposition to the whole, forms a coexistence of receptivity and spontaneity in life, so the

original positing of reason in human nature means that it is submerged in the receptivity of nature in the form of understanding and in the spontaneity of nature in the form of will.

71 *[Inadvertently omitted by Schleiermacher.]*

72 Each appearance of reason in this form is, however, to be posited as something which has come about, that is, as presupposing that previously it was present to a lesser degree, thus never merely as the capacity for reason, but as a capacity which only comes about with and through the activity of reason.[7]

73 Because the identity of reason and nature only appears in ethics in the form of becoming, the maximum is only a minimum of separateness between reason and nature.

74 In the relative opposition [put forward in no. 63] nature appears on the positive side as the organ and symbol of reason – which are merely two different aspects of the same thing – and on the negative side as the task, that is, as raw material.

75 The ethical process is thus to be extended in every direction until the raw material dwindles to a minimum.

76 The original ethical positing of reason in the form of understanding and will within a nature which is originally organic and symbolic is its positing in the human individual.

77 It is a fault of disposition to posit this beginning as a general formula and to posit reason as definitively personal, as is revealed through the argument that a) in terms of the individual nothing truly emerges as the organ or symbol of reason and b) in terms of the whole the essential distinction between physics and ethics is superseded by placing reason wholly under the power of nature.[8]

78 Only individual beings are to be posited as the original organs and symbols of reason; the action of reason on nature, on the other hand, is the action of the whole of reason on the whole of nature; the ethical process is only complete when the whole of nature – by means of human nature – has been appropriated organically or symbolically to reason, and the life of individuals is not a life lived merely for those individuals, but for the totality of reason and the totality of nature.

79 To place reason at the service of personality in the ethical process is at one and the same time to subordinate intuition to feeling, to accept

---

[7] *Marginal note to nos. 68–72:* Omitted.   [8] *Marginal note to nos. 74–7:* Omitted.

knowledge only as a means to pleasure, and, by superseding the equality in the opposition of reason and nature, to draw the absolute on to the side of reality, i.e. it leads to materialism.

80 The depiction of the ethical process, in which it is posited that reason and nature are ultimately at one, thus posits the totality of everything which is in the process of an ethical becoming as ultimately at one, i.e. the various functions of nature and the various orientations of reason becoming one with those functions as an organic whole.

81 Since reason only exists in the form of personality, the opposing view will only be superseded by showing that reason, completely united with personality, is the elemental force which produces the ethical process in its total perfection.

82 In personality, the action of reason is conditional upon place and time. If an action is absorbed by its spatial and temporal determinants so that it is an absolutely isolated occurrence, then in each action the totality of the moral process is negated. In this form too, reason must therefore be depicted as equal to itself, and it must be demonstrated that the totality of the moral process is posited in every action by virtue of its reasonableness.

83 Everything which has become moral is a good, and the totality of that [process] a single entity, hence the highest good. The objective depiction of the ethical is therefore the depiction of the idea of the highest good.

84 Every function of human nature raised to the power of reason is a virtue, and hence the first part of an indirect depiction is the doctrine of virtue.

85 It is because an action can only be understood in the context of the totality of a life, raised up out of momentary limitations, that it corresponds to the concept of duty; thus the other part of indirect depiction is the doctrine of duty.

86 Historically these forms have always coexisted without any consciousness of distinction, in such a way, however, that in antiquity the idea of the good dominated most and duty receded most, whereas now the idea of the good has almost completely disappeared and the concept of duty dominates even the concept of virtue.

87 Only a depiction concerned with the idea of the highest good can stand alone, because here production and product are identical, and so the moral process finds its complete depiction.

88 In the doctrine of virtue the product does not appear but is merely implicit, invisible. It is merely reason in human nature, or – what amounts to the same thing – human nature raised to the power of reason.

89 In the doctrine of duty only a system of formulae is put forward directly; the product does not appear any more than a curve appears in its function.

90 These two last-named depictions thus refer back to the first and are incomplete in themselves.

91 Their genesis rests in a need. The doctrine of virtue is a polemic against that point of view which subordinates reason to personality; for where the latter views man as a system of inclinations, the former presents him as an organism of virtues, and is thus polemic.

92 The doctrine of duty is also founded on a need – since in every individual that false notion also rumbles and might disturb the smooth course of the ethical process – to be able to find one's bearings at any given moment.

93 The historical transition from the objective form to the most subjective is not a regression, simply because the first attempts of that kind were not carried through, nor could they have been. – Active progression within the ethical process had first to furnish the material for this.

94 The form which concerns itself with virtue proceeds from technical interest, in that it demonstrates what someone must be like who is to work successfully within the ethical process.

95 The form which concerns itself with duty proceeds from critical interest, in that it distinguishes what is to be regarded as ethically real from what is ethically empty.

96 The form which concerns itself with virtue was therefore the natural product of a productive age, just as the form which concerns itself with duty was the work of an empty, contemplative age.

97 Every instance where reason is at one with nature, and thus every virtue, too, must also appear in the depiction of the highest good.

98 The essence of duty, namely that in every moral action as such we find a relationship to the totality of the process, must also appear in the objective depiction, because every organic term can only be posited in its relationship to the totality, and together with it.

99 The continued existence of these subordinate depictions alongside the superior one thus points to the limited state of the discipline, i.e. the

necessity of examining for their own sake the limited forms of being taken by reason in nature.

100 The doctrine of virtue, in that it is the depiction of the reasonable personality orientated towards the outside world, is the depiction of the moral microcosm.

101 The doctrine of duty, in that it is the depiction of the reasonable moment, is the depiction of the infinitely small, of the element in the moral process.

102 The depiction of the moral as the highest good is parallel to the depiction of nature as the totality of forms.

103 The doctrine of virtue is parallel to its depiction as a system of forces, which has also arisen out of a technical interest and in which the world is also posited only implicitly.

104 The doctrine of duty is parallel to its depiction in the form of a totality of movements, which is also the product of a passive view, and in which the specific nature of those forces also ultimately disappears.

105 The doctrine of virtue can only be understood inasmuch as it demonstrates that every moral form exists only through the totality of all virtues.

106 The doctrine of duty [can be understood] only inasmuch as it demonstrates that every moral action as such has an influence on the totality of all moral forms.

107 The depiction of the highest good by its very form makes no claim to ascetic usefulness; the other two do not possess it either.

108 The depiction of the highest good must necessarily come first and the others follow.

The highest good

Introduction

1 The ethical process is set in motion once the ideal principle has been given to the real as inherent in the form of perfect consciousness, that is, as cognition and hence reason.

2 The minimum of original unification with which it starts off is that to be found where nature is the organ of reason, i.e. that by which reason acts on the rest of nature.

3 Now, inasmuch as the process is only one of broadening and heightening the original unification as a result of the activity of reason, it is thus only complete when the whole of nature has become the organ of reason by means of reason, and the activity of reason is the organizing principle.

4 However, inasmuch as reason has no existence other than as cognition, its action on nature and its unification with nature is only the molding of nature by means of cognition.

5 Inasmuch as reason in nature is only to be found in the form of life, and every life, given that it is both a relative being-posited-in-one's-own-right and a being-posited-in-community, is merely an interaction and sequence of taking-things-into-oneself and taking-things-out-of-oneself-and-putting-them-down; the being of reason also comes under this opposition, so that the molding of cognition is on the one hand more receptive, cognition in the precise sense of the word, and on the other hand more productive, hence depiction, which coincides with § 70 of the Introduction.

6 The two main functions of reason, the organizing function and the cognitive function, are not separate in reality, but in fact every act is subsumed *a parte potiori* under one or the other, for through the forming of the organ cognition is strengthened, and with every instance of cognition a new organ is posited. Thus with each depiction there is cognition, and each organ is also a symbol.

7 We must look at each in isolation, however, by means of abstraction, though not unconscious abstraction, in order to arrive in due course at a state of intuition which is all the more perfect and lively.

8 Since both are bound up together in reality, any scientific depiction would give no real priority to either, in that organs are only formed by use and cognition can only occur when mediated through organs.

9 Since nature is the organ of reason from the very beginning, though this can only be so in the form of personality, and personality rests on the opposition between the general and the particular, the entering of reason into this opposition was an aspect of the unification and its essential form from the very beginning.

10 In reality the two terms of the equation – that reason is inherent in human nature as a general principle, and inherent in the individual as a particular characteristic – cannot be separated. For without the character of generality, being cannot be something reasonable, and without the character of particularity, action cannot be something natural; in each

case then one would appear to come to the fore, while the other was forced into the background.

11 In abstraction they must be separated, but subsequently the opposite character must be stamped on each as a subordinate quality.

12 The former opposition modifies the latter as form upon material, and thus there is an organizing action with a predominantly general character and one with a predominantly particular character, and likewise a cognitive action.

13 Since the opposition of general and particular is mediated across a gradual scale, this holds true for all gradual scales given by nature in this respect.

14 Just as the particularity of personality is put in place by the original presence of reason in nature and given as a minimum, so the formation of the personality into particularity is merely the unattainable maximum; at every given stage, however, we assume a difference between personality and particularity.

15 Because personality, abstracted from particularity, contains only spatial and temporal limitations, which would overcome the fundamental nature of reason, personality must, through its actions, be both posited and superseded.

16 In the form of time this can only occur by means of oscillation, and this takes place, as demonstrated in § 5 above, and § 70 of the Introduction, in the way cognition passes over into depiction and the organ into a symbol.[9]

17 The character of particularity is not bound up with personality, for identity is also only a matter of persons, and there are particularities which are identical in a plurality of persons; on the contrary, this opposition of the identical and the particular is to be found in the form of finite being, which can only be given in the interaction of unity and plurality.

18 The fact that every activity of reason is limited in space and time in the form of individual consciousness – a limitation for which personality in itself is responsible – would prevent what is acted upon being there for reason in itself, i.e. for the totality of the ideal principle in the form of cognition, if it were not for the fact that personal consciousness is also

---

[9] *Marginal note:* N.B. It will be necessary to make some rearrangements here, probably also modifications with ref. to [para.] XVI.

endowed with the consciousness of the unity of reason in the totality of persons, and thus the activity of reason would always stand in relation to an absolute community of persons.

19 The unity of every activity of reason thus rests in a duality of moments, in one of which [the presence of] personality is posited, while in the other – following the analogy of taking-things-in and setting-them-down in physical life, and by virtue of the way in which this act emerges into the community – personality is superseded again for the duration of the act.

20 In reality the two moments are never separated, and only in their coexistence do they give a single act; but acts undoubtedly exist in which one or the other aspect is dominant.

21 In the activity which forms the organs this duality is to be found in the coexistence of organizing and symbolizing, and in cognitive activity in the identity of cognition and depiction.

22 Here too, precisely because of this relative dominance [of one factor or the other], a perfect scientific depiction can only be conveyed by means of a prior abstraction.

23 In reality, too, the two characters of identity and particularity are always intimately connected. For even the greatest particularity exists on the basis of identity, either in the elements or in their combination, for without such a basis there could be no communication. And even where an act is identical in all essentials, it has its aspect of particularity, even if this exists merely as a minimum, with what is thought and what is posited in each.

24 Thus the whole of morality could be depicted under each of these separate headings, in the process of which, it is true, all the others would have to take their place in the depiction, but with what is in opposition present only in truncated form, which is precisely what forms its one-sidedness. Morality as culture, the political perspective; morality as knowledge, as theory, the perspective of antiquity; morality as genius, the artistic perspective; morality as lawfulness, the legal perspective; morality as perfection and bliss, the French perspective; as sociability and sympathy, the English perspective.

25 Now, since no term in these oppositions can be understood without the other, and yet our intuition of each one individually cannot be completed without resorting to abstraction, it is necessary to begin with a general

overview which remains within the context of the whole, and once we have prepared the ground for a lively intuition [of our subject] we may pursue each individual aspect further.

Part I   General overview

§ 1 [10] Our starting-point must be the organizing function since, relatively speaking, and even though a minimum of unification is already given, it represents the entry of reason into nature.

§ 2 It is true that the original organic system may everywhere appear to us a given; however, just as the individual himself comes into being by means of an ethical act, this too we can only regard in itself as the result of activity on the part of reason.

§ 3 Practice [*Übung*] is the particularly human factor, apparent from the very beginning, in the way the organs evolve, by means of which the organs continue to evolve even when, in physical terms, decay is already setting in again; in animals, on the other hand, perfectibility is restricted to the domain of physical growth.

§ 4 The relative opposition between human nature, given as body, and the rest of nature, given as raw material, is gradually superseded in the process of forming the organs.

§ 5 Inasmuch as neither the earth itself nor anything on it exists for itself, that process is not limited to the earth alone; on the contrary, the forces and influences of other heavenly bodies are also drawn into it.

§ 6 However, inasmuch as human nature is only a product of the earth and the earth itself a product of the cosmic system, neither the former nor the latter can become an organ.

§ 7 The limit of the organizing function is that of cognition, for the unity of the earth and of the other heavenly bodies becomes an organ through being recognized, and to the extent that it is recognized.

§ 8 Our existence is given only in the form of consciousness, and we may therefore posit cognitive activity as an original feature of it, but even that original form of consciousness can only be regarded, according to § 2, as resulting from the activity of reason.

---

[10] *Marginal addition 1827:* Symbolizing function more representative of the end. If the process were complete everything would be a symbol and nothing would need to be an organ.

§ 9 In its broader sense the original human form of cognition is the definite separation of subject and object and thus of feeling and perception, in which the human being becomes I to himself and what is outside himself becomes a diversity of objects; whereas we do not attribute either true self-consciousness nor a true knowledge of objects to the animals.

§ 10 The absorption of the object in self-consciousness is the original act of freedom, perpetually renewed, while the absorption of self-consciousness in the object is that of surrender.

§ 11 The way in which objects are referred to the individual personality in the act of perception, which predominates in any sensory encounter, is only a way of directing us onward towards genuine cognition (by virtue of the original correspondence between human nature and general nature), and only in this capacity to direct us onward is it human and moral. True cognition, however, is the grasping of the individual entity in its relation to the totality, that is, in the identity of general and particular, so that when personal reason becomes one with an individual thing, we are given at the same time the identity of the whole of reason with the whole of nature.

§ 12 The continuation of the process in terms of extent is the division of the confused object and subject, inasmuch as they can come into contact with one another.

§ 13 Now, since many objects can become subjects as a result of the organizing function, a subject must for its part also be able to become an object.

§ 14 [11] The limit of cognition lies only in those most immediate organs, psychic as well as physical, which are nothing other than organizing activity itself and which in themselves, therefore, do not come to consciousness.

§ 15 Given that the two functions form a complete circle, and each is limited by the other, we see how necessary it is for the two to be identical in every act.

§ 16 In terms of its existence in the form of personality, the identity of reason is represented by the community of persons.

§ 17 In terms of the totality of persons, the way in which peculiarity adheres to reason, existing in nature in the form of particularity, is represented by the impossibility of transference from one to the other.

§ 18 The character of identity adheres most closely to the organizing function in its external operations, in the formation of external natural

---

[11] *Marginal note:* § 14 ought to be phrased more by analogy with 6.

objects for the purposes of reason according to a schematism. For, by virtue of its nature, whatever is formed in this way is available to everyone who can deal with this schematism.[12]

§ 19 To the extent that they are also formed according to a general schematism, the immediate organs also yield results which are available to all those who know how to use them.

§ 20[13] The impossibility of transference is indicated physically on the organs themselves, given that they are integrating components of existence, by the fact that they cannot leave the domain of the person without being lost.

§ 21 Thus the character of identity is manifested in the organizing process through a general schematism, and whatever bears the marks of this forms a sphere of common usage (= commerce) in which individual entities determine their claims for themselves, according to ability and need.

§ 22 Since those objects which have been formed according to § 18 have also already been formed by the organs as integrating components of the person (§ 20), they too must bear traces of particularity.

§ 23 The more this character comes to the fore in those things which have been formed, the more they will resemble the immediate organs (§ 20).

§ 24 The character of particularity manifests itself in what has been organized through the relationship to the unity of all the organs in the person, and whichever are the dominant traces from among the elements of understanding and will, sense and limbs will form for each one the sphere of his proper characteristics.

§ 25[14] The character of identity in the cognitive function manifests itself in the requirement which accompanies its acts, namely that any individual

---

[12] *Marginal addition 1827, against § 15–§ 18:*
Demonstration of what is identical and what is particular.
General.
As the process is carried out it will lack unity unless something of each point participates in every part of the process, and vice versa.
The impossibility of transference forms the limit of community. Where one is, the other is not; but this must be superseded in order for the process to be complete everywhere. It is thus a condition of morality that, taken from another viewpoint, the one could at the same time be the other, and this must be realized in the pre-formation of nature, as a basis [for the rest].
With particular reference to the organizing principle.
The process of forming and educating is only a moral one to the extent that it has a schematism of this kind, with a basis in the natural forms. – All formative activity is only moral to the extent that the tendency to such schematism is present.

[13] *Marginal addition 1827:* As integrating components of existence, those natural objects which have been formed acquire the same character.

[14] *Marginal note 1827:* In the symbolizing sphere a) Identity.

could only carry out that act in precisely that way and could only achieve precisely that result, and thus under the same conditions would be obliged to come up with an action which is identical in every respect to that of the other person.

§ 26 This character is to be found first and foremost in all acts where reason manifests itself as a system of ideas or as a combinatory capacity within a schema of oscillation between the general and the particular.

§ 26 *[N.B. Schleiermacher erroneously writes § 26 twice.]* It is also to be found in the domain of the empirical, although here it is assumed that at the same time there is an identical formation of the organs as in § 19.

§ 27 The totality of the existence of reason in nature thus characterized forms the sphere of objective cognition or knowledge.

§ 28 [15] Every act of cognition, even if it is objective, is bound up in reality with a self-consciousness that has been stirred into activity, so that without this we regard such an act as a mechanical imitation rather than something generated from the very beginning.

§ 29 Self-consciousness that has been stirred into activity is always the expression of the characteristic way in which all the functions of reason and nature are at one in any particular existence, and is thus a kind of cognition which is special to each individual and non-transferable, from which each person excludes all the others.

§ 30 The totality of the existence of reason in nature thus characterized forms the sphere of subjective cognition,[16] of moods and emotions.

§ 31 [17] What has been formed according to the general schematism, as in § 18, can only support the activity of reason as an organ [of reason] to the extent that it is connected with an individual personality; thus it only becomes an organ to the extent that we posit the existence of a personality, and in doing so all other personalities are excluded to exactly the same extent; this isolation must be superseded.

§ 32 It is superseded by the reverse of this process, to the extent that matters are taken out of the sphere of personality and placed in the sphere of community.

---

[15] *Marginal note 1827:* b) Particularity.

[16] *Here the following words were crossed out:* or of feeling.

[17] *Marginal addition 1827:* Organization; unification of what is personal and what is held in common
  1. Formal a) quantitatively.

§ 33 Both are essentially identical, in that every individual is himself an organ of reason in general in his own existence, but in each individual act one factor will predominate over the others just as it does in every relative opposition.

§ 34 For the person engaged in such appropriation himself, this will be superseded by the accompanying consciousness that he is always in a process of working for the community; but it is only resolved for the totality if such appropriation is essentially conditional upon such work.[18] The positing of personality in these terms is [what we term] right.

§ 35[19] Since what has penetrated the sphere of the particular and formed it (23, 24) acquires the character of non-transferability belonging to the original organs, nature which has been formed in this way is completely cut off from unity with all reason except for what is posited within that particularity, a limitation which must be completely superseded.

§ 36 This can only happen by surrendering it to reason in general as an object for the cognitive function, since only when it is mediated through what has been formed in this way can reason, modified by particularity – i.e. the special way in which all the functions of reason are at one in the individual –·be recognized.

§ 37 For the individual engaged in formative activity, this superseding is brought about through the endeavor which accompanies the act of formation to give what has been formed symbolic value, i.e. to make it a recognizable sign of the formative power of reason. For the totality, however, it is only brought about by the fact that the forming of spheres belonging to particularity is conditional upon the formation of a cognitive community for those same spheres.

§ 38 The whole process of formation is simply an integrating component of the moral in the identity of these two moments.

§ 39 In instances of isolated appropriation the purely human character gets lost and takes on the form of violence, i.e. non-recognition of personalities outside the self.

§ 40 In instances of isolated surrender it is dissipated in the form of flabbiness, i.e. the failure to posit one's own personality.[20]

§ 41 Both involve a contradiction, however.

---

[18] *Marginal addition 1827:* Could one not just as well say: for feeling and for cognition?
[19] *Marginal addition 1827:* See marg[inalia] to § 17. From 31 onward: *Ways in which each character is conditional upon the other* b) qualitatively.
[20] *Marginal note:* N.B. 39 and 40 would be better placed later, with 79.

§ 42 [21] The way in which identical appropriation is conditional upon the surrender of self to the community creates the state of right. The way in which particular appropriation is conditional upon surrendering oneself to intuition creates that of sociability.

§ 43 [22] To the extent that a piece of knowledge is first generated in a personal consciousness, the rest of reason is excluded, and so there must be a means whereby it can get out of personality into the community.

§ 44 Objective knowledge becomes external through speech.

§ 45 For the individual engaged in cognitive activity himself the identity of the two is there from the beginning, since a moment of cognition only arises as a form of internal speaking, which is always already differentiated from external speech.

§ 46 Since, however, a moment of cognition can only be fixed by bringing it into connection with all the others, and this can only take place by leading it through the lively domain of speech, this identity is also present for the totality.

§ 47 The identical nature of positing and superseding personality is to be found in the essentially identical nature of generating and communicating cognition.

§ 48 This domain thus encompasses not only the more rigorous domain of science but also every instance of empirical communication in everyday life.

§ 49 [23] Self-consciousness which is sealed up inside personality is not an ethical act, because here reason stands under the power of nature; it can only become an ethical act by means of a reaction which supersedes that self-consciousness.

§ 50 It must become external in the form of cognition, in the same way as something objective does; as something particular, however, it can only enter a community of objective cognition.

§ 51 The way in which self-consciousness becomes external to further the cognition of others is through depiction, and the morality of self-consciousness rests on the identical nature of the state of excitation and its depiction.

§ 52 This domain encompasses not only the rigorous domain of art, where everything objective is, after all, only the depiction of what is subjective,

---

[21] *Marginal note 1827:* 2. Material a) symbolizing.
[22] *Marginal note 1827:* α) Knowledge.
[23] *Marginal note 1827:* β) Self-consciousness.

but also all those more formless communications of life lived in a state of excitation.

§ 53 [24] Since everyone engaged in formative activity according to the general schematism does that forming, after all, through the medium of his own particularity, and since in every thinking individual his own particularity participates in the process of thought, so that, in the same way, perfect particularity is not formed from the outset as an end in itself but, on the contrary, its genesis rests on an identical process of formation, and every state of emotion and excitement is only brought about by those things which at the same time touch us by their objective representation, the domain of what is identical can only be something particular as well, and particularity can only be something identical as well.

§ 54 Thus the reality of the relative opposition is based on the fact that there is not community per se and particularity per se, etc., but a common particularity and a particular community, a particular form of knowledge and an identical state of excitation and particularity of excitement.

§ 55 [25] Since personality, in positing itself, does so with its whole being and thus also with its tendency to supersede itself, and in superseding itself also does so with its tendency to posit itself, [26] every positing must therefore be a positing which supersedes, and every superseding a superseding which posits. The same is thus also true of the whole domain of common possession and possessed community, all property sociable[27] and all sociability property-forming, all cognition language-forming, all language cognition-forming, everything which shapes the emotions depictional and all depiction capable of moving the emotions.

§ 56 Since the whole moral process does not originate with the entry of reason into nature, but on the contrary reason is found already existing in nature, there cannot be any beginning to the entering into one another of the elements in the oppositions either; on the contrary, they must be found to be present from the beginning, and this given must form the basis of the ethical process.

---

[24] *Marginal note 1827:* Unification of what is identical and what is particular.

[25] *Marginal note 1827:* Summary of oppositions.

[26] *Marginal addition 1824:* Since both activities run parallel both in the domain of identity and of disparity, a twofold measure is required.
Derivation determines the common element in particularity. Climatic adjustment determines the particular element in community.

[27] *Corrected from:* depictional.

§ 57 The original interrelatedness of the functions is given in the identity of soul and body, i.e. in personality itself, which we must therefore (H[ighest].G[ood]. Intro. 2) also be able to regard as a result of the ethical process.

§ 58 The way in which personality itself is the result of the ethical process must be the basis on which the identity of positing and superseding personality rests.

§ 59 Personality is a result of the ethical process in the sense of something generated in the community of the sexes; and this is where we find the original identity of positing and superseding personality.

§ 60 Everything which is demanded in § 55 is in actuality posited in the family and through the family.

§ 61 The basis on which all interrelatedness of the identical and the particular rests must be an original interrelatedness of the identical and the particular which is to be found in the soul and the body.

§ 62 If identity and particularity were absolute, all human beings would form a single homogeneous mass in relation to the community; particular community and common particularity, however, can only reside in the plurality of separate spheres.

§ 63 Relevant to these spheres are the minimal or natural conditions of climatic differences, races and tribes, and individual folk traditions.

§ 64 In this gradation from the family upwards, everything demanded in § 54 is posited.

§ 65 As far as contemplation of the individual is concerned, and as long as that contemplation remains in the abstract, only personality itself may serve as a basis; if we are to turn our gaze upon living reality we must take as our starting-point the condition imposed by nature posited in § 59 and § 63.

§ 66 The state is a possessed community and a common possession (§ 55) and is attached to folk tradition in the immediate particularity of its organization.

§ 67 Academic associations are language-forming cognition (§ 55) and are attached to the identity of the spheres.

§ 68 Free sociability is sociable property (§ 55) and encompasses various circles, the widest of which appears to be limited only by the historical nature of formation, since it is only mobile and immobile tribes that do not enter into sociable relations with one another.

§ 69 The church is a particularity of the state of excitation and of depiction because in fact the highest level of feeling is religious feeling and also the summit of all art is also religious art. It is hardest to determine in what way it is conditioned by nature.

§ 70 It is clearly apparent that it is much easier to fix the natural aspect of the relative spheres, which are characterized by a predominating identity, than their particularity.

§ 71 The family contains the germ of all four relative spheres, which only start to diverge the further they spread.

§ 72 Individual states, languages, etc. are themselves persons in a higher sense of the word; only through their community, therefore, can the totality of reason be depicted.

§ 73 This community cannot be generally comprehended, however, in any higher, definite form than that of the unity of the human species. For this very reason, however, the existence of reason and nature also appears in it as a particular form, and totality can only be depicted in the plurality of the heavenly bodies.

§ 74 Each of these spheres is regarded, moreover, in a one-sided way as encompassing everything that is moral, just like the formulae which underlie them (see H[ighest] G[ood], Intro. 24). There is a certain sense in which each contains all the others; the state, to the extent that they all have some external existence, the church, to the extent that they all rest on a certain disposition, science, to the extent that they must all have an identical medium, free sociability as a general way of creating bonds and because all individual states etc. must only stand in a relationship of free sociability to one another.

§ 75 To restrict the depiction of the individual to those great forms of state, church, academic associations and general sociability would be to provide ideals without allowing us to contemplate the living process of becoming.

§ 76 It would not be any more appropriate, however, to give an exhaustive depiction of every state of becoming and each individual bodying-forth of those great forms, because such a depiction would then contain historical material too. It should only include the principle of diversity in its interpretation and should leave the rest to the critical disciplines.

§ 77 In this way everything that is empirical will find its place in our depiction, and this indicates progress within the moral process; we must, however, look at what it is that cancels it out, or evil in general.

§ 78 The obvious disparity between the non-existence of good and the existence of evil, which cannot be found if the process of unification is considered as a single unity, can readily be comprehended if that process is split into disparity of function and opposition of characteristics. The non-positing of a moral element in one function, which is posited in the same subject in the other, is evil.

§ 79 This is just as true of the non-positing of something in the cognitive function which is posited in the organizing function, as the other way round. The same goes for opposing characters and moments.

§ 80 To posit evil in the conflict between the will of an individual and the general will is an incorrect formulation, because all progress within a moral whole must proceed from the conflict of individuals.

§ 81 To the extent that the existence of the individual consists of a series of moments in the form of oscillation, it is possible not to posit something at one moment which was posited at an earlier moment, and this non-positing is also evil to the empirical conscience which represents the average of moral consciousness in a series of moments.

Part II Detailed exposition

I The organizing function

1 Considered in very general terms

§ 1 The organizing function can only be comprehended in terms of the cognitive function. Just as all taking-things-into-oneself and taking-things-out-of-oneself-and-putting-them-down should retain their connection to the idea, this same orientation is stamped on the organic actions, both as individual moments and in combination, and they are only purely human to the extent that the process of becoming encompasses this character.

§ 2 Considered from the point of view of an analogy with what is purely animal, its essence consists, therefore, in successively raising the organic function to the power of the idea.

§ 3 If we regard the organic function as receptivity and spontaneity, that essence is thus the formation by reason of all sense and all talent, by means of which everything which is posited in reason as a possibility of its existence in nature acquires its organ.

§ 4 Since personality is only the starting-point for unification and organization should, by a process of appropriation, also move out from personality to be disseminated over external nature, [personality] is thus to be regarded as raw material; seen from this point of view it explains the mythical representation of chaos.

§ 5 What is inorganic in external nature belongs by virtue of its opposition most directly to the organizing function, in that it has both the capacity and the need for formation; what is organic, on the other hand, belongs to the cognitive function, in that it is already formed, and only in a subordinate capacity and regardless of its original sanctity to the formative function, in order to bring the lower level into an ancillary relationship with the higher one.

§ 6 Just as what is celestial can only be organized inasmuch as it is an earthly force, but according to its being can only be recognized, and only the being recognized can be used in an organizing way, in the same way what is earthly may be used as an organ most particularly in terms of its being recognized.

§ 7 The rational formation of the direct senses and talents, starting with the understanding and the will, which in terms of their form are also organs, is *gymnastics* in the broadest sense of the term.

§ 8 Here we can intuit directly the identity of the organizing and cognitive functions, since in terms of their form the understanding and the will can only be formed when what is material in cognition and depiction is produced at the same time.

§ 9 To the extent that the involuntary physical organs are almost too distant from the center of higher life to be raised to the power of the idea, they form the extreme end of gymnastics.

§ 10 The forming of inorganic nature to be the tool of sense and talent is *mechanics* in the broadest sense of the term.

§ 11 Just as mechanics interacts with the cognitive function, because only what has been recognized can be formed, in the same way it interacts with gymnastics, because only direct organs which have been formed can themselves form indirect ones, and also because in their turn indirect organs promote the formation of the direct ones.

§ 12 By virtue of its most general element, a possible designation for the formation of lower organic nature into a relationship of service to higher nature, is that of *agriculture*.

§ 13 The sanctity of organic nature is not opposed to the destruction of individual beings, provided that this is linked to active participation in the preservation and refining of the species.

§ 14 Where the relationship of the individual to the species has not yet been recognized, then either fear extends to individual beings, or else the sanctity of organic nature has not yet come to consciousness.[28]

§ 15 All things, whether organic or inorganic, may be used in an organic way when they are *put together* in the form of an *apparatus* or *microcosm*, since the universal, in all its gradations, may be contemplated in such details.

§ 16 This term [in the proposition] also interacts with the two previous ones and shows us the identity of the organizing and cognitive functions; (as dependency of the former?)[.]

§ 17 If we take away the intensive orientation towards a content of reason, all those things which are necessarily bound together by it then fall apart; 1) an opposition arises between formation of the direct organs (education) and that of the indirect ones (inculcation); in terms of personality each individual, the more he inclines to the one, believes he is able to find in it a substitute for the other, an opposition which produces the athletic and dissolute lifestyles; 2) formation of those functions, skills and dexterities which tend more to external things and of those intellectual capacities which tend more to what is inward all take on a particular character, and for the wellbeing of the personality an excess of the one can provide a substitute for the other.[29]

§ 18 If the extensive orientation is taken away, the intensive one contracts to nothing and reason is there in nature with nothing and to no purpose. Indeed, even the formation of the understanding and the will becomes something inconsequential, because they too are now something external; and if we posit them, we cannot maintain a distinction between what is the human being himself, and what is posited as being outside the human being.

---

[28] *Marginal addition:* For this reason, cannibalism is the most extreme barbarity.

[29] *Marginal addition 1824:* in which one side can produce a substitute for the other. True in terms of form. But the hidden spiritual power is then something negative, the tendency to remain within the activity of reason despite all deficiency and obstacles. But this itself is one which dwindles almost to nothing. This is the most vulgar way of thinking, which, however, in the domain of formative activity, the state, reduces the human being to nothing and in the domain of cognitive activity cannot yet make its voice heard in empirical knowledge but already has a limited existence in the ethical sphere, which is also nothing.

§ 19 The polemic against nature conducted by the Cynics and Stoics is directed at that falling apart in which, certainly, the predominance of the external function becomes ponderousness and dependency and man loses himself in things. The polemic of withdrawal, however, becomes aridity and passivity, and it, too, is unable to draw the cognitive function out towards the real and the empirical.

§ 20 The modern polemic, which attributes to culture a lack of cognition and a cowardly spirit, is directed at the disintegration into [a multiplicity of] skills, where the higher consciousness of the masses is lost in mechanical transactions, and at the pleasure content which is all that remains, and which demands to be saved by any possible means.

§ 21 Mechanics and agriculture encompass, as their result, everything that we call wealth. Regarded objectively, this is something that ought not to be despised. It can only be the object of polemic when the result is desired without the activity, or when each individual only values wealth inasmuch as it is bound up with their own personality, which is the subjective aspect.

§ 22 All polemics against culture are related in some way to the pleasure content upon which emphasis is laid. As an excluding tendency, however, this is so little in accordance with nature that with any transaction, even the most superficial, a pure pleasure always develops in it wherever there is not complete dullness and perversity.

§ 23 Since activities and capacities may be split into infinity just like the task itself, each talent, no matter how trivial, will be the expression of a moral activity if it is carried out in that spirit and with interest, even if there is only a vague consciousness of its connection with the whole; if this condition does not hold, on the other hand, the most significant talent will only be the expression of an immoral activity.

2 Considered under opposing characters

3 a) With dominant identity

α) In general

§ 24[30] The character of identity finds expression in schematism, namely in the fact that just as a piece of objective knowledge is posited as having

---

[30] *Marginal note:* Transference and assemblage.

validity for everyone, in that it is itself posited, every formative activity is to be posited as being the same from everyone's point of view and as being considered the same by everyone.

§ 25 It follows from this that everything that bears the traces of this schematism is to be regarded as formed, starting with the person himself and continuing through all his works, and is therefore not available to be drawn upon as raw material either.

§ 26 The inclination to proceed skeptically in this regard is an indication that one is caught up in personality; reason in the personality must seek itself outside the personality also and trust lovingly in the possibility of renewed recognition.

§ 27 The acknowledgment of this, to the extent that it excludes what has been formed from the process of formation, is the basis of all *right*.

§ 28 Furthermore it follows that reason in personality considers a talent which is called by the same name to be the same in other individuals as it is for him, and thus posits that every organ could also be used from the point of view of reason just as the organs of the individual could also be used by others. To the extent that it supersedes all exclusive referring back to the personality, this requirement is the basis of all *community*.

§ 29 Just as both concepts, right and community, follow from the same thing, so each is conditional upon the other, in that the former refers to the continued existence of what has been formed, the latter to the action of continuing formation, in that nothing is formed without formation and there is no formation which does not presuppose something formed.[31]

§ 30 As the depiction of the existence of reason in nature, each person is conditioned externally (i.e. above and beyond that internal principle which makes for particularity) by the various influences of the external powers, and at every point of moral activity this conditioning is something given, with the result that it can have more of an effect on one side than on another.[32]

§ 31 When formative activity is related to the personality, there must be an endeavor to supersede this conditioning, because the needs of any

---

[31] *Marginal addition 1827:* § 29. b. Both acknowledgment and community begin in the system of direct organs. This system is only appearance, relatively raw material, primarily there to develop the organizing activities of others, and is only posited by them. Their perfection is only achieved, however, in practice, that is, in activity, which cannot be related to the sphere of personality, which has yet to arise, but only to reason in itself, and is thus posited as a common good.

[32] *Marginal note:* Differences in identity; how they are distinct from what is particular.

given person are dispersed uniformly across all areas. If formative activity is related to the totality of reason, that conditioning (seen as the natural determination of the individual organ) becomes a schematism imposed on the organ; this is the foundation of the *division of labor*.

§ 32 This division carves a course through all the domains of culture, and is strongest in the domain of the apparatus, where individual talent appears as amateur enthusiasm and idiosyncrasy; it is weakest in the domain of gymnastics, however, because each individual must attempt to come into complete possession of his organs.

Note. Natural conditioning must be posited and maintained inasmuch as the personal organism is the subject of formation; but it must be superseded or limited inasmuch as it is the object of formation.

§ 33 Every person is partly a representative of reason and partly an organ of reason. To the extent that, as a representative, he aspires to the division of labor, he must be sure, as an organ, that he will be preserved by the collective activity of reason.

§ 34 To the extent that the equilibrium between need and skill is transcended by the division of labor, its preservation is thereby endangered.

§ 35 The products of the predominant activity must be able to leave the circle of personality and the means of preservation to enter it.

§ 36[33] If we also take into consideration the opposition between formed and formative organs, itself only relative, then the division of labor is conditional upon the possibility of *exchange*; exchange in its turn is conditional upon the transferability [*Ablösbarkeit*] of things and the possibility of using the organic capacities of the one to promote the purposes of the other.

§ 37 When exchange is conditional in this way, we find in it the identity of right and community. Reason, and hence the individual as the representative of reason, can acknowledge personal right only to the extent that everything can once more come to the point of exchange; and the individual, as the organ of reason, can surrender something to the community only to the extent that he receives something back from it with the acknowledgment of the totality. Thus in individual matters, too, someone can only surrender something to the extent that he either receives

---

[33] *Marginal addition 1827:* § 36. b. Since in the division of transactions the organizing capacities become still more relative because practice is restricted to one aspect only, a community of the organs in all aspects is also posited.

something similar in return or else acknowledges that surrender is necessary for an objectively reasonable purpose.

§ 38 Just as all possibility of transference rests on the identity of the schematism, so the reality of how far we should acknowledge an action which originated not in a particular human being himself but in another individual to be an essential element in the process, rests on *persuasion*.

§ 39 The reality of the transference and the extent to which the individual should reduce the circle of his personality, rests on [the idea of] equivalence, which is only fully realized in the concept of *money*.

§ 40 Money and goods are correlates, and money is only money to the extent that it is not goods. If, then, money has almost always been realized historically using only the noble metals, the reason for this does not lie in a direct value which they possess in the cultural process; it must be sought elsewhere, perhaps in the combination of rigidity and light, or in some other factor.

§ 41 Money and persuasion are also correlates and money is thus only money to the extent that it requires no persuasion to regard it as an equivalent.

§ 42 Metallic currency and bills of exchange as a means of compensating for the uncertainty produced by distance: these are the culmination of the concept of money. Paper money, or language as money, already constitutes a falling off from this point.

§ 43 Since every person is always both representative and organ, all commerce is based on both money and persuasion, but in differing proportions.

§ 44 Given that A is permitted to enter B's personality circle in return for an equivalent of some kind, he passes responsibility on to B for all further actions concerning the thing he has passed on, and as far as B is concerned this involves no persuasion on A's part except that he, B, should not be *persona turpis*.

§ 45 [The level of] persuasion increases on one side, the more certainty is diminished [on the other] because the service offered in return is deferred.

§ 46 Given that B persuades A to be directly active, as an organ, in a deed which can only exist in the totality of the formative process through the action of B's personal circle, no money is required other than as compensation for the activity which A was meanwhile not performing in his own personality circle.

§ 47 Every act of giving from one's own property without money and without persuasion is immoral and may only be defended as common charity a) on the assumption that one person's circumstances have been straitened by the division of labor to another's advantage, or b) on the assumption that one receives an equivalent through the totality. Charity is to be regarded merely as a transaction.

§ 48 Anything proceeding only from the standpoint of money is polluted by more than a minimum of persuasion; anything proceeding only from the standpoint of persuasion is polluted by more than a minimum of money. (Confidence tricksters and bribery.)

β) In the oscillation of personality

§ 49 Taking something into the personality is taking possession, putting it outside oneself is renunciation.

§ 50 In the growth of personality, reckoning from the beginning of the cultural process onward, we may posit a predominance of taking possession, because the personal spheres have little contact with one another.

§ 51 In the adult state we may posit an equilibrium, determined by the measure of possible activity which is required to preserve each personality in the identical integrity of its circle.

§ 52 Empirically speaking, this equilibrium can only appear in the oscillation of expansion and contraction of one personality in relation to another; the closer the approach to this equilibrium, however, the more perfect the cultural state. Here, too, there is a relativity in the various branches.

§ 53 Everything which has been found up until now is found in the relationship of each individual personality to reason in itself or to the totality of personalities; that is, then, in steady dissemination across the whole earth, the total domain of the cultural task.[34]

§ 54 To the extent that the positing of culture as a personal sphere and as a common good (§§ 29 and 37) are identical propositions, and to the extent that everyone regards as their own action the positing of each personal sphere, while each one regards as his own action the positing

---

[34] *Marginal note (1816?):* direct and indirect, strong and weak, on the particular province of each one.

of everything that has been formed, even in his own sphere, as common good, there exists a state of contractuality.[35]

Note. Each individual action of contract and exchange must first be based on such a state because without it any offer of this kind is unthinkable.

§ 55 The relative opposition between the individual sphere and the common good becomes firstly more tense and then gradually comes apart. There is first community without possession here and possession without community there, before property and community become quite separate, and reciprocally binding.

§ 56 Now, since these various states of development exist simultaneously on earth, it is impossible for the state of contractuality in one to be identical with all the others. A narrower sphere is required, where this state is uniform, a sphere which can convey its relationship to the totality.

§ 57 In the gradual transition from the imperfect state of contractuality to the perfect one, there is nothing to be found which would cause this sphere to narrow and the incomplete external form to close.

§ 58 Since the form of the cultural process necessarily varies in accordance with climatic variations, one person cannot think of himself as a live element in the relationship to all the others which is created by the division of transactions, but only mediated through a sphere which is identical in form, the determining principle of which is, accordingly, only to be found in the factor of particularity.[36]

§ 59 Contractuality thus only finds completion in the state, and the positing of the latter and the completion of the former are identical.

§ 60 Money and persuasion are the motives for every contract; and they are also what the state hinges on, for the latter is the condition of legislation, the former the condition of administration.

§ 61 The basis of persuasion is in a mass of identical notions, and here formative activity is dependent on cognitive activity.

§ 62 From the viewpoint of each individual this mass must gradually diminish on all sides, so that he cannot think of himself as existing in the same relationship of persuasion to everyone else.

§ 63 The gradual diminishing is a chaotic process and some effort is necessary to organize it by means of an opposing principle, i.e. to posit a

---

[35] *Marginal note (1816?):* Even contractuality is not yet the state.
[36] *Marginal note (1832?):* Only an unequal relationship which presses [?] on the natural limits.

narrower sphere within the broader one which once again can only be a particular community.

§ 64 The sharp cutting edge of money has its basis in the certainty that it will be accepted, something which we cannot possibly assume to be true for the whole earth.

§ 65 Here it would seem that a sphere whose limits have been marked out quite arbitrarily is sufficient (in the same way that many regard the state when they relate it to the safeguarding of property); but one is always driven to seek the reason why something has been marked out in one way and not in another, a reason which can once again only be found in the domain of particularity.[37]

§ 66 Everything that we have found is thus incomplete in itself, and awaits a perfection which can only be achieved by combining the identical factor with the particular one.[38]

b) With that of particularity

α) In general

§ 67 The character of particularity is that element in the formative activity of a subject which means that it cannot be the activity of another subject, and in the formed organ which means that it cannot be the organ of another subject.

§ 68 Particularity is not in another domain than identity; on the contrary they are both in the same one, so that in reality they are always interrelated, to a greater or lesser extent. Thus in all formative activity and its results, particularity is simply the relationship to difference between one subject and another.[39]

§ 69 If I were to be confronted only by the identity of the schematism in a given organ, there would be nothing posited in it which would allow me

---

[37] *Marginal note (1832?):* Money, too, constitutes only an arbitrary and impermanent limitation.

[38] *Marginal note:* Deferred once (the Academy's doing).

[39] *The following marginal notes (1816?) are to be found against §§ 68 and 69:*

1. Connected with non-transferability and the assemblage is the placing next to one another of unequal formative principles and their following on from one another.
2. Dependency must not develop out of identity.
3. From this: closing off = house, opening up = hospitality.
4. Particularity in own harmony. Not often in the individual, therefore, and individual property can consist of identically formed [elements].
5. Negation of division and exchange.

to recognize it as not mine, and this confusion would cause all personal spheres to be superseded. In the same way, if I were to be confronted only by what is not transferable, that is, by strangeness, in something which has been formed, nothing would be posited in it which would allow me to recognize it as something formed.

§ 70 The minimum which must be posited here as having been originally present is thus difference posited with every detail between this one human organism and all the others which exist to a higher power than that of the purely animal.

§ 71 We may posit the difference between one animal and all the others which are designated by that same lowest concept as a product of external influences acting on individual functions; its personality is thus essentially an incomplete one.

§ 72 In a human being, it is true, this difference is also a relationship of individual talents to one another, not rooted in external influence, however, but in an inner principle which always reproduces the same vital relationship, even without such external influences, or despite them.

§ 73 Here, then, particularity has its basis in a certain harmony of talents.

§ 74 This is expressed in every complete action as well as in every combination or transition from one combination to another.

§ 75 The original given factor to which activity, characterized in this way, adheres, is temperament, which, in the course of its commerce with objects, develops into a system of inclinations.[40]

§ 76 However, as particularity in formative action [develops into] the particularity of reason, and activity is related to the ethical process of formation, temperament is raised to the level of character and the system of inclinations to the level of genius, and the coexistence of the two becomes the perfection of moral individuality, from the organizing point of view.

§ 77 What is inculcated from external nature takes on the characteristics of the inculcating organs, and cannot therefore be the organ of another without being transformed either into identical schematisms or into another particularity, that is, without the first formation being destroyed. It is accordingly appropriated to become property in the narrow sense of the term, and does not belong in the domain of exchange.

§ 78 This character belongs predominantly in the sphere of exchange, if it inhabits a thing only incompletely; its relationship to the originator

---

[40] *A marginal note (1816?) identifies §§ 75 and 76 as* "not belonging" *here.*

remains, however, inasmuch as it bears the mark of his particularity, and the domain in which a thing may be exchanged becomes ever more limited, the more clearly apparent its particularity.

§ 79 To the extent that house and home denote the domain where particularity is dominant, nothing that belongs to it is available for sale, and this constitutes the moral immovability of possessions.

§ 80 When particularity is not present to the degree we demand, we describe this as vulgar and routine.

§ 81 Beauty and art are to be found in all areas of culture to the extent that particularity manifests itself.

§ 82 In production which is characterized by particularity there is no division of labor. For no one can want any one of the functions not to reveal its relationship to the totality of all his functions, and no one can want to allow his particularity to be produced partly by others.

§ 83 If we turn our attention to action, particularity is also the basis of everything which belongs in the domain of identity.

§ 84 If we turn our attention to products, universality is the basis of all individuality, which grows out of it only gradually; therefore, universality always forms the largest mass.

§ 85 Even though the individual, as an organ, strives for a personal sphere which is absolutely non-transferable, nevertheless, as a representative, he cannot want to emerge from community with the formative activity of all.

§ 86 However, the more the opposition of the two characters in activity causes them to become separate entities, the more difficult it is for this community to remain a community of commerce.

§ 87 Since what has become organized initially approaches reason of its own accord to be an object of cognition, and since particularity is an inexhaustible source for cognition to explore, it is impossible, when the domain of particularity is opened up to reason for the purpose of cognition, for reason to proceed as far as the desire for exchange.

§ 88 The morality of individual property is conditional upon hospitality, and hospitality in this sense is conditional upon that morality.

§ 89 The identity of both is the essence of sociability, in which the highest forming activity of the person is united with the self-consciousness of reason in the form which underlies that activity.

§ 90 Since what proceeds initially from hospitality is simply the acknowledgment of the particular sphere, the interest of reason is at first perfectly satisfied by the fact that the particular sphere shows itself to be productive for the sphere of commerce.[41]

§ 91 This occurs in two ways: 1) on the one hand because the development of particularity itself enhances an individual's existence, so that this also has an influence on his identical activity; and on the other because, the more his organs are formed in a particular way, the more he can achieve with them in every domain.

§ 92 And 2) because the observation of particularity stimulates particularity in others in its turn, in that they imitate individual processes and apply them to their own more or less highly developed particularity.

§ 93 In this way the two spheres of formation develop an equilibrium, in that the sphere of particularity needs the other as a basis, but then has a powerful effect on it in its turn.

β) In the oscillation of personality

§ 94 If appropriation is only moral when it is identical with communication, this identity must be present in every individual deed, corresponding to that duplication of moments, whereby personality is posited – that is, broadened – by means of appropriation, but absorbed, by means of communication, into reason in itself and thus in relative terms superseded, so that communication is to be regarded as renunciation.

§ 95 The identity of the two moments cannot be an identical emerging of the two in time, because no one can produce this one-sidedly; it can only be an identity of consciousness and inner action, so that every appropriation can be related to communication, and every communication related to appropriation.

§ 96 Youth, the time when character is formed, is a predominance of appropriation over communication, in the gradual, individual emergence of particularity from identity.[42]

§ 97 Old age – when the possibility of formation has been superseded but life continues nevertheless in the personal sphere through activity intended purely to maintain – is a predominance of communication, given the diversity of those for whom that property has been unlocked.

---

[41] *A marginal note (1816?) similarly identifies §§ 90–3 as* 'not belonging" *here.*
[42] *Marginal note (1816?) against §§ 96–8:* Do not belong here.

§ 98 The summit of life, when the individual is conscious of the unity inherent in his particularity, is where equilibrium comes to the fore and there is a rapid alternation between appropriation and communication.

§ 99 Since the morality of the process always consists in the identity of the two terms of the opposition, so the opposition itself develops in the process, as its character evolves out of what is opposed to it.

§ 100 As long as particularity exists only in individual traces, in an inorganic form, so to speak, there is only a minimum of appropriation and at the same time of hospitality.

§ 101 Emerging hospitality, without the appropriation commensurate with it, is merely an empty, anticipatory form, based on presentiment, which only allows a homogeneous mass to pile up.

§ 102 Emerging appropriation, without the communication commensurate with it, is the hoarding of secrets, and is the basis of every system based on caste; it can only be maintained at all at a subordinate level of the cultural process.

§ 103 As tension increases in the opposition between appropriation and communication, where the perfection of this character is to be found, an equilibrium also develops between the domain of this character and the one which opposes it. (§§ 91, 92.)[43]

§ 104 Since, according to its genesis, the personal sphere of particularity is dependent on the personal sphere of identity, the one can only be completed in a way which has general validity under the same conditions as the other. (See § 56–63.)[44]

§ 105 Since the state of sociability probably only consists in the identity of appropriation and communication and in the mutuality of communication, but, given the coexistence of all states of development of particularity, the one who falls behind cannot understand the one who has progressed, while the latter has no interest in considering the sphere of the one who has fallen behind, then sociability is restricted to a sphere where states have developed in the same way.[45]

---

[43] *Marginal addition 1827:* The stages of formation are not posited here as a definite differentiating principle, but are superseded by the fact that two stages which were originally similar are also similar at other times.

[44] *Marginal addition 1827:* The maximum of difference in intensity also supersedes acknowledgment, in relative terms; hence servitude or rather serfdom (for a lawless state is impermissible). This a great tool of development.

[45] *Marginal note 1827:* Basis of slavery?

§ 106 Since the non-transferability of particularity also extends to representation, which forms the basis of any formative action, and since the intuition of activity cannot be anything but a reconstruction of that representation, then in reality the state of sociability is limited, either by a direct affinity between particularities or by the community of a large mass of identical representations.

§ 107 Since each person, as a representative, is only a fragment, i.e. each talent is only directed towards a certain part of the natural side corresponding to it, while particularity can only be recognized from actions, then the state of sociability is also limited by the affinity of inclinations.

§ 108 All of this shows that, in the relationship of one person to all others, the state of sociability is not completely determined, but requires a partitioning and determining principle derived from somewhere else.

II The cognitive function under the condition of mere personality

1 Considered in very general terms

§ 109 In their relative opposition, one function can only be comprehended in the light of the other.[46]

§ 110 Just as the formative function represents more the act whereby reason seizes nature and enters it, so to speak, so the cognitive function represents more the act whereby reason exists in nature and manifests itself there.

§ 111 If it is nevertheless true that reason also manifests itself in formative acts, this is so to the extent that all seizing subsequently involves being, and every formative act begins with cognition; taken altogether both functions are essentially bound up together in every complete act.[47]

§ 112 The full extent of where reason is to be found are the two aspects of the organic system, the receptive and the spontaneous, inasmuch as they are organs, i.e. not merely to the extent that they have first been formed.

---

[46] *Marginal note 1816:* N.B. Since I am defining the term "consciousness" here, § 50 of the Introduction will probably have to be altered accordingly and shaping in formative activity designated in the same way.

[47] *Marginal note 1812:* At the end of this lecture hour – perhaps something is missing, but certainly nothing essential.

§ 113 Since no aspect of the ethical process has a beginning in absolute terms, we must posit a minimum of cognition as originally present,
assuming however that it is the result of the cognitive function, from
which it follows that there is some reason-content in most actions that we
may posit in the proximity of what is animal.[48]

§ 114 The raising of this minimum to the power of cognition is already
posited in the definite way in which objective and subjective confront
each other, because here an opposition is already developing out of a
unity.

§ 115 If, in order to find out how far this process extends, we go beyond
what has originally been given and posit the animal and rational factors
as separate, the cognitive process is absorbed into two formulae: reason-
content passes over entirely into organic action, and everything in organic
action is permeated by reason-content.[49]

§ 116 The latter seems more to describe the common character of each
action – what makes it human – but at the same time it describes the highest
perfection, in that every organic action is an analytically infinite one.[50]

§ 117 The former seems more to describe the perfection of the process,
but at the same time it describes its common character, because a totality
of all relations, and hence also a connection to the complete system of
ideas, is posited in every objective unity.

§ 118 If we posit as a minimum that which is closest to the animal form,
containing only a minimum of reason-content, then at the other extreme is

---

[48] *Marginal addition 1827:* 38. 1. Minimum of reason is already a definite divergence of objective and
subjective, raising us above what is internal.
2. If we turn our attention to the reason-content, everything is implicitly present, but not in
organizing action and thus not in reality, 117.
3. What is real is the interaction which is achieved in the entirety of all instances of contact. –
The more organs, the more instances of contact are developed, and so in itself the function has no
limit.

[49] *Marginal addition 1827:* 39. According to the goal of intensity, the intention of which is that
everything in the organic action should be permeated by reason-content.

   1. Something is permeated as soon as something definite is posited. Animals never reach this
   point.
   2. The action is thus permeated as a single entity, but to reassure during this process is to inhibit
   the process. What is diverse in the action should also become something definite, and so the
   task is infinite.
   3. It is really only complete when everything has been brought into the opposition of objective
   and subjective, and thus related to a definite proposition.

[50] *Marginal addition 1827:* 40. Since in consciousness unity and multiplicity are bound up together,
each must be separately present in consciousness. This follows from the above – explanation
provided by 119, 120, 122.

that which contains a maximum of ideational content and only a minimum of organic action.

§ 119 Without organic content of any kind, reason-content could not be the system, but only the principle, i.e. it could only be given as an absolute unity and could not therefore feature in the process of cognition.[51]

§ 120 As absolute unity, the deity is not present in our cognition as a real act, but is present as a tendency, as it were; as a real act, however, it can only be bound up with an organic minimum.

§ 121 Without ideational content of any kind, sense-content cannot be present in us as a real act, because in this case it would only be infinite finite diversity.

§ 122 Mass, as absolute diversity, is not present in our cognition as a real act, but is present as a *terminus a quo*, from which all positing of unity proceeds.

§ 123 The element in real cognition which relates to absolute diversity as a *terminus a quo* and which depicts pure quantity in it, is the *mathematical*.

§ 124 The element in real cognition which relates to absolute unity, and is therefore the highest form in knowledge, is the *transcendental*.[52]

§ 125[53] The element in it that depicts the coexistence of reason-content and the organic, depending which is posited as the predominant one, is the ethical and the physical.[54]

§ 126 Both of these, therefore, inasmuch as they have an organic content, are only complete knowledge inasmuch as this is mathematically known. As the ancients said: There is only as much knowledge as there is mathematics.[55]

---

[51] *Addition (1824? 1832?), subsequently crossed out:* Reality is only [to be understood as] a bound opposition, thus what is set in opposition to it must also be described on its own.

[52] *Marginal addition 1827:* Mechanization in infinite divisibility, 123, 124.

[53] *Additions (1827), subsequently crossed out:* 42. From 120, 124, 125, simply in *reality*, ethical and physical division does not belong here at all. 43. The opposition between physical and ethical not to be developed here, but simply incorporated.

[54] *Marginal addition 1827:* 42. In all real consciousness what is good is only what is transcendentally and mathematically determined (125–128).
Note. 1. There are not two different powers. 129, 130.
2. All error comes from being overhasty.
3. The transcendent and the mathematical as border zones. 132, 133.

[55] *Marginal addition 1827, subsequently crossed out:* 44. There is only as much empirical certainty as there is mathematical certainty; only as much speculative certainty as there is transcendental certainty. 126.
(Or does this belong to schematism? It certainly does, at least when expressed in this way. In that case: There is only as much that is moral ...)

§ 127 Both of these, having a reason-content, are only knowledge inasmuch as this is also transcendentally known, i.e. inasmuch as it is dialectical and religious.

§ 128 In reality, therefore, these areas are not at all separate; for when one makes an object of either quantity in itself or absolute unity in itself, the task can only be resolved by means of a series of individual actions, in which there is immediately an element of reality, and so it acquires a share in what is opposed to it.

§ 129 As we found this process to be a continuum, designated by a single formula, starting with the analogy with what is animal and going as far as the most complete possible shedding of what is organic, then no opposition is posited here between science and life.[56]

§ 130 This opposition can only be a subordinate one, moreover, since according to § 116, there must be elements of what is unpermeated and unconscious in every action up to the point of absolute perfection, and according to § 117, in every action, even those in closest proximity to the animal, reason-content is present in its totality.

§ 131 The four domains do not form a series in such a way that the two which are at the ends have a closer affinity to the formative function, as is the case there with gymnastics and apparatus; on the contrary, it is held directly within each one of them.

§ 132 [57] The mathematical and the transcendental are, however, all-encompassing and themselves without limits, and each individual posits them as valid even for what is inaccessible to our real cognition.

§ 133 [58] What is real is, however, limited by the organic aspect of our function; what cannot be given to it directly can also only be recognized mathematically and transcendentally.

§ 134 From the point of view of the infinity of undetermined diversity, the cognitive process is a positing of unity within it; only in this way can definite cognition come about.[59]

---

[56] *Marginal note:* Any opposition between science and life can only appear at a very subordinate stage.

[57] *Marginal addition (1816? 1824?):* Monday. Extensive and intensive orientation, each conditioned by the other, hence truth and error, skepticism and conviction. (Error mostly just ignorance.)

[58] *Marginal addition 1827, subsequently crossed out:* 45. In all moments the extensive and the intensive conditional upon each other. a) the intensive is conditional because all relations must be exhausted. b) the extensive is conditional . . .

[59] *Marginal addition (1827?):* Everything which is good is in the sum total of all predominance of the one over the other; 134–138.

§ 135 From the point of view of existence at rest, of the system of ideas in reason, it is a positing of diversity proceeding from them, in that, every time a unity of reason is posited in the diversity of space and time, one is also positing that this is susceptible of infinite repetition.

§ 136[60] If one side is considered in isolation – and it is only a fiction that the two exist separately – there arise two opposing one-sided phenomena, the a priori one and the a posteriori one, or, in scholastic terms, the nominalistic and the realistic, which aim to produce all cognition from one side only, excluding the other side altogether; in fact, however, neither can take even the first step towards doing so without invoking the other. For there is no unity without an intellectual element, and no reality in action without a sensory one.

§ 137 In every real act, however, one apprehends predominantly either the sensory or the intellectual aspect, and in doing so posits (*ad* 1) a single unity containing the possibility of a general plurality and (*ad* 2) a general unity containing the possibility of a single plurality.

§ 138 In real cognition, the pure identity of the two sides is not posited as something which is in existence, but only as something which is coming about through the steady tipping of the balance from one side to the other.

§ 139 It is necessary to achieve an equilibrium between the two sorts of unity as they develop in the course of activity, an equilibrium which appears as the positing of identity and difference between the two.

§ 140 The diverse forms are thus: positing of the individual and positing of the general, ascent from the individual to the general and descent from the general to the particular.

§ 141[61] Since, however, in reality itself there is no separation between the sides themselves, but only differentiation, these forms are not separated and therefore – as has also been established dialectically – any real positing occurs only in ascent and descent, and any ascent and descent only in positing.[62]

§ 142 The cognitive process is a series which continues in an *extensive* direction, to the extent that the formula considered in § 117 is only depicted in its totality when it runs through the infinity of diversity.

---

[60] *Marginal addition (1816? 1824?):* Tuesday. § 134–138. Here too, then, skepticism and certainty, truth and error.

[61] *Marginal addition 1827:* 44. At each point there must be as much skepticism with regard to both series as is still missing. 142–146.

[62] *Marginal addition 1832:* The expressions "skepticism" and "conviction" already refer to identity. More general terms should be chosen – absolute perfection and fluctuation.

§ 143 It is a series which continues in an *intensive* direction, to the extent that at the level analogous to that of the animal everything is related to personality, and this relationship should be absorbed into a relationship to reason in general.

§ 144 All cognition, therefore, simply constitutes a result from a particular degree of raising the process to the power of reason, one point at which truth and error coexist.

§ 145 The simple positions, in which the relationship to the organic function dominates, are so closely attached to each other that they can never be completely eliminated, and traces of error are still to be found on truth.

§ 146 Equilibrium is achieved here in all areas by means of conscience, which posits in a felt lack of satisfaction that intensity is incomplete. This is the real ethical root of skepticism.

§ 147 The process can only be completed in an extensive direction by the totality of persons, so that a) while it is true that each person produces a great deal that has already been produced by others, b) at the same time each person has points in his or her sphere which do not lie in that of others.

§ 148 [63] In each individual consciousness, therefore, we may posit an extensive progression in a temporal series of individual acts.

§ 149 In order to distinguish the two moments here, the content of the individual acts themselves, and the formula for connecting them in a sequence, it is first necessary to determine what constitutes the unity of an act.

§ 150 The view which clings exclusively to the organic side will not recognize any unity other than that of the infinitely small and so endeavors to depict everything as association; in this way, however, it never arrives at the point where the act is completed. [64]

§ 151 The view which clings exclusively to the intellectual side will not recognize any unity other than that of the idea, and regards all analytic operations merely as elements of a general position, but misses the way in which the great masses of knowledge, posited as a unity, have developed.

---

[63] *Marginal addition (1816? 1824?):* Wednesday. Analytic and synthetic progression conditional upon each other. Forcible separation immoral ... [?] Progression of the objective depends on feeling.

[64] *Marginal addition 1827:* 45. The vital connection between each act and all the others is, then, that every synthesis is analytic and every analysis synthetic. 147–154.

§ 152 The true depiction of the process is only to be found in the combination and mutual limitation of these one-sided constructions.

§ 153 Nothing can be regarded as a complete action in which only a mass is posited without any particular unity; and one cannot regard anything as having unity of action, only multiplicity, if one finds, in a unity which has already been posited, that there are oppositions and multiplicities.

§ 154 For this reason two different ways of progressing are posited: synthetically, from one unity to the other; and within a single unity to the diversities which are posited in it, that is, analytically.

§ 155[65] A third possibility arises from the intensive orientation (§ 143), which endeavors not to abandon a position until cognition has been raised to the highest possible power.

§ 156 A new duplication develops out of the distinction (§ 147) between what has already been posited and what has not yet been posited, in that one can strive on the one hand for personal consciousness to be filled up, without distinguishing between old and new, or on the other hand one can strive for whatever has not yet been posited for reason altogether.

§ 157 These diverse combination formulae are as important as the positions themselves.

2 Considered under opposing characters

§ 158[66] Both characters and the difference between them are to be considered, in terms of the content of the positions themselves and also the formula which describes how they are connected.

§ 159 Since in real human cognition perception and feeling, or the objective and subjective aspects, definitely diverge, it is evident that, inasmuch as we posit every intuition as something pure, we posit it also as isolated from anything which might be genetically present from the previous act upon which it builds, or from the admixture of any subjective element; and inasmuch as it is a simple position, as having also the character of identity associated with schematism, that is, as being the same in all cases and having universal validity. On the other hand, if one is not content to rest at the assumption that consciousness represents not individual being

---

[65] *Marginal addition 1827:* 46. The coexistence of skepticism and certainty is moral in the way it reverts to everything that came earlier in what occurs later. 155–157.

[66] *Marginal addition 1827:* Perception is predominantly based on identity, feeling on difference. 158–159.

but being as organ and component of a greater sphere, every feeling, in its completeness, is posited as having the character of particularity, which then determines the material element of both characters in general.

§ 160 [67] Now, since the form in which cognition comes about at all is that of progression, the relative opposition of characters must be present here too.

§ 161 All analytical progression, by means of which the totality of subordinate unities is posited in any given unity, carries within itself the identity of schematism, i.e. the demand that everyone who takes a given step must also reproduce all the others and arrive at the same bottom line.

Any synthesis can only make such a demand inasmuch as it is posited within an analysis. On the other hand, if particularity seeks to meddle with the analysis, it leads only to confusion.[68]

§ 162 Purely mathematical analysis constitutes an exception here, since it is not in fact true analysis, because what is merely infinitely divisible does not present us with any definite unities. The greatest degree of invention is therefore to be found in mathematical analysis.

§ 163 All synthetic progression from one unity to another which lies outside it expresses particularity, i.e. it is different in each person, depending on the relations between the various orientations within him, both in general and at any given moment, according to his talents and inclinations.

§ 164 Mathematical synthesis constitutes an exception here: it is not a true synthesis because the infinitely divisible does not present us with any kind of separation; thus the synthetic process is entirely mechanical here. *Note:* The domain of pure mathematics is not receptive to the opposition between the analytic and the synthetic.

§ 165 Just as there is always a correspondence between material and form, so here too feeling is always the principle of the synthetic process. For in a particular kind of cognition one is conscious of oneself in a particular state, depending on the relationship between the individual act as it coexists with others which are stimulated simultaneously and the task of cognition in general, as posited in each individual and posited in a particular way.

§ 166 The objective position or intuition is always the principle of the analytic process, for everything which is subordinate can only be posited from, and in relation to, what is in the first position.

---

[67] *Marginal addition 1827:* Analysis is predominantly based on identity, synthesis on difference. 160–166.

[68] This paragraph copied into the margin from elsewhere.

3 a) Identity of schematism

[α) In general]

§ 167[69] Each person is a unity of consciousness that is complete in itself. Thus, when reason produces a moment of cognition, it is produced as consciousness only for that person. What is produced under the character of schematism, however, is posited as having validity for everyone, and so in any one person being does not correspond to its character.

§ 168 In addition to such producing, therefore – and posited as being identical with it – what is produced must also emerge from the precincts of personality into common ownership.

§ 169 The morality of this aspect of the process thus lies in the identity of *experience* and *communication*, and this identity forms the domain of *tradition*, which is the form in which the totality of this side of the process appears, conditional upon personality.

§ 170 Note 1. Experience refers just as much to the transcendental aspect of knowledge as to the empirical aspect, in that there too one must no

---

[69] *Virtually the entire margin on this page is covered with additions to § 167 ff., dating from different years.*
Addition (1816? 1824?): Tradition is safekeeping and discovery. Safekeeping is memory and the written word. Discovery is observation and experiment, a concept that also includes the speculative. Experiment is possible only in the intensive [domain].
Addition 1832: Safekeeping = comprehension and communication not subordinate to discovery. If one separates the two, morality is superseded. Safekeeping and discovery found in both moments of personality, erudition and pedagogical virtuosity. Memory is a necessary condition of communication with what is external and what is internal. A natural condition is not without moral activity, however.
The moral aspect derives from interest in the object and interest in communication.
The more general the memory, the more the moral aspect recedes.
Since consciousness consists essentially in two moments, the purpose of memory is essentially its construction.
Memory and the written word in opposition.
For life in general the written word is analogous to money. (Anti-Plato.)
But communication through the written word alone, if it is not lively and dialogical, always becomes death.
(We would apparently have no need of memory if we were holding the subjects of our communication in our hands at the time and could think ourselves back to the point where there was a primary identity of stimulus and arbitrariness. But communication is only an act of assemblage.)
Addition 1827: 49. The domain of knowledge develops out of the identity of discovery and communication.
The immorality of discovery without communication. Communication without discovery is merely mechanism. Discovery = observation and experiment, communication = memory and tradition, tradition is the spoken and written word.
Addition 1824: Teaching and learning (the same thing) already included in the basic outlines. This perhaps not quite right[.] 1824.

doubt make a distinction between the individual temporal representation and what is eternally posited in reason.

§ 171 Note 2. In reality, the identity of experience and communication may be anything from fine detail to coarse outline, depending on whether we consider an instance of cognition to be complete in various respects and whether we consider it to be communicable in a variety of respects.

§ 172 Note 3. In the case of § 147a, the urge to communicate has already been satisfied by consciousness of the identity of the experience, so that a particular act of communication would be an empty one. In the case of § 147b, the moment of cognition would be empty if it were not communicated as quickly as possible, so that each individual could process the material in his own way.

§ 173[70] In addition to the particularity which must also be taken into account here by virtue of the influence of combination, each person is also a fragmentary depiction (see § 30); thus here too a *division of labor* is the only ethical form.

§ 174 Note 1. Since the coherence of cognition is in fact an internal one, it is possible for everyone to feel a need for some kind of cognition, even where this is rendered difficult by its conditional nature; but it is true that the equilibrium between need and skill is further superseded by real division. See § 34.

§ 175 Note 2. Someone may be relatively incapable of seizing an object directly, but highly capable of reproducing the process of cognition undertaken by someone else, which is the basis for saying that communication can be a true completion.

§ 176 Cognition, in this form of the tradition, rests on the possibility of transferring something from one consciousness to the other. This is conditional upon the fact that the act, as something internal in origin, becomes external: something which appears to the person bringing it forth to be an *expression*, but exists for everyone else as a *sign* by means of which – by virtue of the identity of the schematism – he is able to recognize what is internal, or the original act.

§ 177 Just as the totality of all acts of cognition, as the depiction of ideas, forms a system, then given that they correspond to it, the signs must also form a system.

---

[70] *Marginal addition 1827:* It is in the identity of common good and virtuosity. (N.B. Relationship to the formative activity of the same name.)

§ 178 What is internal in consciousness can only become something external in the variety of the organism, and that external thing which corresponds to an individual act can only exist in the organism in the form of movement.

§ 179[71] This system of organic movements which are both expression and sign of acts of consciousness, construed as the capacity for cognition with the character of identity found in schematism, is *language*.

§ 180 Note 1. Wherever human beings are to be found in a true community of cognition, language emerges as *sound language*, based on an organic system of its own but with no further definite meaning.

§ 181 Note 2. *Sign language*, as language (i.e. depicting the identity of schematism), is only to be found in an imperfect state, as a surrogate, a) where communication is organically inhibited by sound language; b) in earliest childhood, when, because representation is still in an imperfect state, expression and sign are similarly imperfect, and require duplication to supplement them; c) when people who are in possession of different languages are together.

§ 182 Note 3. In the same way, however, that the latter will always be in the process of attempting to produce a common sound language at the same time, so too the child, from the point where perception and feeling distinctly diverge, is in the process of producing articulated speech. If he appears to acquire language earlier than this in the form of receptivity, this relates only to the particular language spoken around him; the spontaneous urge to speak at all occurs at the same time.

§ 183 Note 4. Since the basis of all observation, considered through the stages of development, is this: that the child's perception only really becomes objective at the same time as he acquires language, so in each individual, too, the complete formation of representation is the same thing as the formation of the word. The latter designates only the degree of formation of the act at which it is sufficiently mature to be communicated. Internal speech gives permission for external speech, as it were, and desire for the latter is posited at the same time as the former.

§ 184 When the need arises in one person to be allowed to communicate, this cannot take place at the same time as another person's production. A means must therefore exist of holding the acts of the cognitive process

---

[71] *Marginal note:* N.B. Language already appears in the basic outlines.

in place over the moment of production, just as it does for those of the formative function, and the means of doing so is *memory*.

§ 185 The desire to keep hold of a certain individual act is always related to communication; herein lies the moral aspect of memory.

§ 186 Note. No one actually needs memory for themselves. Each time it is needed, the result must come back in exactly the same form as it did the first time, to the extent, that is, that the representation was complete at the original moment of production, i.e. it achieved a certain identity of the transcendental and the empirical.

§ 187 In communication, language in itself is there more for results, memory more for combination; however, just as there can be no unity in the act without combination and vice versa, so there can be no language without memory and vice versa.

§ 188 Note. To the extent that memory alone constitutes the unity of the empirical subject, it is as much a force of love as a tendency to communication. For, as far as reason in itself is concerned, separation in space means the same as separation in time.

§ 189 Internal speech is the language of memory; the written word is the memory and tradition of language, by means of which it is first posited as entirely objective and communication is made independent of the time of production.

§ 190 Here, then, the *minimum*, which is always given, but which must also be regarded as a result of the ethical process, is the simultaneity of thought and internal speech, and of the combining and holding fast to the identity of the subject.

§ 191 This is also precisely the formula, applied to the domain as a whole, which allows us to comprehend the notion of *completion*. For 1. thinking which cannot be expressed is necessarily unclear and confused, in that complaints as to the inadequacy of language belong only in the domain of particular cognition; 2. a combination not immediately accompanied by an echo which fixes it in place will only bear imperfect traces of the character of identity.

§ 192 Note 1. A new instance of cognition also demands a new form of expression, it is true; but this must always appear to reside within the language already, and pure cognition and the finding of an expression for it will always be identical.

§ 193 Note 2. The fact that, in the speculative domain, one new linguistic creation so rapidly gives way to another, does not prove that language is not appropriate to higher intuition, but only that there is a necessity not so much to cling to unities as to grasp everything as a matter of combination. § 194 Note 3. For every combination which is not held fast in memory, reproduction will be necessary, and there will always be some new element to prove that the previous one was incomplete. Every combination which has been developed to the point of complete analysis is automatically imprinted on the memory, because it is at one with the direct concept of the object itself.

§ 195 Note 4. Speaking without thinking, i.e. speech which does not correspond to any act of cognition, is either not communication but merely a rehearsal of the act of comprehension itself, such as one finds with children, or else it employs empty formulae and hence appears trivial. When, however, language loses something of its simplicity and truth, the whole of communication becomes uncertain, since every individual not only has his own coherence but also shares coherence with all things in the act of usage.

β) In the oscillation of personality

§ 196[72] In every completed act there is the simultaneity of both moments. Even internal speech already contains some superseding of personality in that, even as the thought is placed in language, it is also posited as a common good.

§ 197 The apparent inequality of the two moments, which comes to the fore in the great epochs of life, arises from the fact that childhood is dominated by incomplete acts, while in advanced age the communication which predominates is simply an after-effect; pure equilibrium is achieved when one reaches the summit of life.

§ 198 In the same way, in every individual great mass, pure equilibrium is achieved only at the culmination-point; as the whole comes into be-ing communication is relatively restrained; later, repeated depictions are mere after-effects, inasmuch as they no longer contain any kind of inten-sification, and denote the aging of the operation.

§ 199 The state of the tradition in its perfection is one of symmetry, where each person receives cognition from language and sets cognition down in language.

---

[72] *Marginal addition 1827:* 51. Here, too, culmination in two focal points; maximum of discovery is the maturity of youth; maximum of communication is the youthfulness of age.

§ 200[73] This is not possible in one person's relationship to all the others, 1. because in those points of the intensive orientation where one is distant from the other there can be no interest in one individual for the views of the other, and the latter will possess no key to the thoughts of the former.

§ 201 Since no thing exists which can be understood as a unity other than in the totality of its relations, yet this unity must be differently shaped depending on whether man's position vis-à-vis nature is a different one, then at opposite points varying systems of cognition are also to be found.

§ 202 Since communication is based on a mass of identical movements, where, however, the natural position also modifies the linguistic tools, one and the same movement cannot always have the same meaning, but on the contrary the masses of what is identical must gradually diminish.

§ 203 What has been found up to now, therefore, is also only incomplete and requires a determining principle in order to depict unity through plurality, but this cannot be located in the mere form of personality.

b) Particularity

[α) In general]

§ 204 Since what is produced with this character holds true only for the individual person, it can only be regarded as having been produced by reason:

Firstly, to the extent that the particularities of cognition form a system (and hence cannot be regarded as occurring in isolation, by chance): a system in which reason appears as having become nature.

Note. Every instance of particularity therefore rests on the presupposition of all the others.

§ 205 Secondly, – so that this totality is also present to reason in the form of consciousness – to the extent that the particularity of cognition is communicated as far as possible, namely through intuition.

§ 206 This community of particularity of cognition, just like that of formation, is *sociability*, but in a more direct and internal form.

§ 207 Falling within its scope are definite self-consciousness = feeling, and the truly synthetic combination described in § [163].

---

[73] *Marginal addition 1827:* 52. Distance is a gradual lessening without definite crossing-points.

§ 208 These two elements are not separate in reality. For every feeling is the result of external influences on the unity of the internal principle, and every association is the result of the internal principle [penetrating] the objective in its indeterminate diversity. The two stand in the same relation, then, as passion and reaction, which are always found together.

§ 209 It is not only the transition from one act of cognition to the other which belongs to the synthetic process, but also that from and to formative acts, in that these are always preceded by an act of cognition as a prototype, so that both functions encompass each other, and the cognitive function encompasses the formative one.

§ 210 No division of transactions can take place in the production of particularity, for each particularity should permeate the person entirely, and each person stands in complete connection to the universe; there is indeed limitation present here, but it cannot be deliberate.

§ 211 The possibility of sociability rests on the possibility of bringing particularity to intuition; this can only be through a mediating term which is at the same time both expression and sign.

§ 212[74] Every definite excitement of the sensibility is accompanied by tone or gesture as a natural means of expression.

§ 213 Note. Tone is present here not as word, but as song, and gesture is not present here as an indirect sign of the concept, but as a direct one; through both what is purely internal becomes external in a natural and necessary way.

§ 214[75] Since, however, feeling alone is not a sufficient designation for this entire domain, a sign must also exist for synthetic combination.

§ 215 What should actually be depicted here, however, is not the individual, real act, for only two things together, following on from each other, are real; but the law which informs them as it relates to a particular instance.

§ 216 This law is quite simply the general formula for the relative value of each individual thing for the individual person.

§ 217 The way in which every feeling eventually concludes in action in order to maintain a state of affairs or dissolve it – even though we also

---

[74] *Marginal addition 1827:* 53. Feeling is to combination as gesture and tone are to art. 212–236. On art, 215 onwards. Question of whether self-depiction can ever be completed in a single work of art.

[75] *Additional material (1816), relating to § 214 ff., has been entered against § 204 ff.:*
Tuesday. 1. Feeling and the combinatory principle are one and the same thing. For self-consciousness steps in between one moment and the next, because otherwise one act could not be distinguished from the next. The two can only be distinguished as self-consciousness which is the same as itself and self-consciousness which has been determined by the object.

describe life itself as art, precisely inasmuch as all action is [a means of]
expression – this is expression, but only of a very imperfect kind.

§ 218 Hence every definite excitement, considered in its spontaneous
aspect, is accompanied by a forming of fantasy [which constitutes] a representational act.

§ 219 Note 1. This follows from the simple expression of feeling. For if
gesture and tone are posited as a sequence and, however obscurely, were
previously thought and conceived of, then they themselves [constitute] a
representational forming of this kind.

§ 220 Note 2. Fantasy is a synthetic capacity, on all levels. One's personal
sensibility is fantasy, and reason is also fantasy. In every domain, however,
synthetic combinations only belong to representational fantasy to the
extent that they do not seek to become analytic.[76]

§ 221[77] Just as in earliest childhood gesture and tone manifest themselves,
and it is only through them that the particular character of the external

---

2. Depiction of the combinatory principle cannot be a simple gesture, but is an expression of the
law in a certain case, where the individual case is secondary, the law the most important thing.
This is *art*. Science becomes art when this is dominant. It ceases to be art in exercises etc. Simple,
involuntary depictions become mere elements as art develops.

3. Feeling unites all four moments in each act. Quantity is the mathematical moment, pleasure
the physical one, conscience the ethical one, religion the dialectical one. All four must coexist in
perfect human consciousness.

4. The development of the religious is intensive perfection.

Wednesday. 1. Extensive perfection is in the totality of relationships. All particularities should exist,
and therefore none is evil. b) All relations should exist. Therefore also what is evil or unpleasant;
but only as points of transition.

2. Particularity is also inequality of organization for the technique of depiction, both on the side
of spontaneity and on that of receptivity.

3. Since excitation and depiction are two separate moments, they can also stand in various relations
to one another. Predominance of the drive to depict determines the relationship.

Thursday. 1. Because of the separation of the moments, not every work of art has to arise individually from a state of enthusiasm, but a life of enthusiasm must underlie the whole.

2. Against this, the claim that virtuosity or skill is everything. Even conception from a great
mythical cycle is skill, etc. But even the most superficial skill only comes through practice, and
this presupposes drive.

II. Construction of the domains of art. 1. Adaptation of direct utterances by fantasy. Mysticism and
miracles. 2. The particular formation of fantasy, a) as the imitation of nature, painting, sculpture;
b) as the imitation of history, plastic art; c) second rank, art as ... [?] of mechanics etc., linking up
with architecture.

76 *Marginal addition 1827:* By excluding the partially affected organs, we are positing primarily
spiritual self-consciousness. § 220 and following.
Just as on the organic side, here too we find the particular in all that is identical. Often true art
begins with this (statues, painting). Particular way of comprehending man and nature.

77 *Marginal addition 1816, referring to various paragraphs: Friday.* If we go one step further, then all
action, as an act of combination, is rooted in feeling, and particularity can be recognized from it,
too. Thus life strives to become art and stands in exactly the same relation to art as to science.

person develops, so too the formation of fantasy manifests itself at an early stage and from it there develops the particular character of the internal person, whose individual utterances are conditional upon the one as much as the other.

§ 222 Formation, with its specific qualities, depends on the dominating sense, with which, as a talent, it is itself identical.

§ 223 Besides those depictions relating to a definite excitement, then, there are others which relate to the permanent consciousness of the dominating organic side.

§ 224 In poetic fiction, in its earliest development, every mood becomes a story, and this is, moreover, essentially the character it continues to have.

§ 225 The various kinds of depiction thus form a system (in the place of the single system of language on the objective side) which includes everything that can be an element of one of the arts.

§ 226 Note 1. It is most improper and conceals the nature of the other arts if one regards them all as emanations, so to speak, of poetry. The painter most certainly does not see the history first, nor the landscape, but straight away sees the picture, and in the same way the poet does not need to see external figures at all.

§ 227 Note 2. At the lower levels, where one-sidedness is still dominant, the conversion of feeling into either formative action or effective action creates a state of relative opposition; anyone who inhabits the one has only contempt for the other.

§ 228 Accordingly, if the formation of fantasy as it emerges and develops is art, and the reason-content in particular cognition is religion, then art stands in the same relation to religion as language does to knowledge.

§ 229 Note 1. The word religious does not just refer to religion in the narrower sense of the word, namely that domain which corresponds to the

---

2. Each person's interest in actual art is connected with the art of life, even if this only takes the form of receptivity or taste.

3. There are different levels here too. Appropriation is the highest level, [then] response without appropriation, [then] acknowledgment without response. A complete lack of acknowledgment is impossible; but everything merges into everything else.

Addendum. Intensive advance is the development of the religious. This is conditional upon extensive advance. Only when dispersed factors are united and diversity is everywhere apprehended can the apprehension of absolute unity evolve.

Extensive is totality of contact and this is conditional upon intensive. It is religion that first drives the human being to unconditional expansion; otherwise he is content in the mass with what is traditional.

With regard to art, these two sides correspond to the two styles: religious and secular. Separated from one another entirely, these, too, degenerate.

dialectical, but to all real feeling, and to synthesis which is present in the physical domain as spirit and in the ethical domain as heart, to the extent that both transcend personality in their relation to unity and totality.

§ 230 Note 2. As the cognition of particularity is only religion in the process of becoming, its depiction can only mark the gradation of reason-content which is internally given.

§ 231 Note 3. Each individual, by virtue of his fragmentary nature, is directed only to individual branches of art, so that a division of labor takes place in the domain of depiction.

§ 232 Note 4. Thus, for the person who has no particular affinity for a given technique of depiction, its significance must often be hard to understand, and it will appear hollow.

§ 233 Note 5. If, in art, feeling is meant to compose itself and momentary expression is to become fixed and objectivized, so that art becomes the repository of all feeling and each person receives from it his communicating and communicated existence, then in each new depiction there will be something that relates to the tradition of the technique of depiction and its improvement, and it is that in particular which stands out as virtuosity.

§ 234 Note 6. This will be present in the same measure as, in the act of depiction, the moment recedes and permanent self-consciousness, in the form of consciousness of the dominant talent, comes to the fore.

§ 235 Note 7. Since feeling and depiction are essentially bound up together but cannot be brought into pure equilibrium, it is possible for the drive to depiction to prevail in such a way that the state of excitement may seem only a flimsy reason for it.

§ 236 Note 8. The technique of depiction, in its objectivity, represents the average of morality in the particular cognition of a certain mass. For this reason, the most powerful states of agitation experienced by those who are particularly prominent as artists may not be susceptible to depiction. The alphabet required is either lost or has not yet been found.

§ 237[78] A complete separation of the two moments, that is, feeling without depiction or depiction without feeling, could be posited only as immorality [*Unsittlichkeit*].

---

[78] *Marginal addition 1827:* 54. It is an immorality to separate the two completely; but only where depiction tears itself away from the moment of excitation do we find art. – N.B. Separation is where feeling is without expression, as well as where individual combination is without artistic production. – Depiction without feeling is a hollow spectacle, or else epideictic virtuosity.

§ 238 Note 1. Relation to a specific time comes to an end as relation to personality or location does. Thus morality does not reside in the momentary identity of feeling and depiction, which is only demanded at a low level, but only in the consciousness which relates that excitement to the sphere of communication and holds it in safekeeping for that sphere. Each moment is posited as something lively and continuously effective.

§ 239 Note 2. For the same reason the morality of a depiction does not reside in its proceeding directly from a moment of excitement – our normal understanding of enthusiasm – but in the internal truth by virtue of which it is related, in what is produced, to something real in that particular being.

§ 240 Note 3. If in many instances depiction initially expresses an idea, then this itself, as a synthesis, is the expression of a feeling and can never, moreover, be depicted with pure objectivity.

§ 241 Note 4. Where, however, we posit feeling without depiction, it is only possible for the external side of depiction to be lacking, since the internal side is posited also, as a matter of natural necessity. We can only assume, therefore, that the right ways and means are still being sought, and morality resides in that search.

§ 242 Note 5. Where we posit depiction without feeling, we are positing the second half of an action without the first. Now, since this is not possible, the action actually belongs to the person in whom the first half is to be found, and the agent of depiction is merely the organ of that person, by virtue of a community of organizing functions.

§ 243 All communication, the answering recognition of a feeling, takes place here only through the medium of an analogical process; just as the movement to depiction is similar to one that appears in my self, so the feeling producing that movement is similar to one that forms the basis of my self.

§ 244 This process must rest on an identity which, in this case, can only be that of the formation of the human organism, so that here, too, what is individual rests on the foundations of what is universal.

§ 245 The various branches of the system of depiction form simply a mediating mass, out of which each person receives his cognition of individuality and into which he sets his own individuality, for others to recognize.

§ 246 Note 1. Every individual has an interest in art, in the broader sense of the word, just as he does in knowledge in the broader sense;

and everything depictional actually belongs to art in just the same way as everything that is empirical actually belongs to knowledge.

§ 247 Note 2. To the extent that depiction rests on talents, each person is restricted to particular branches when it comes to external productivity, whereas receptivity must, in a certain sense, be general.

§ 248 Note 3. To the extent that, in many individuals, talents do not emerge, they appropriate the depiction of others.

§ 249[79] In this identity of feeling and depiction the whole function should be raised up from relation to personality to relation to the unity and totality of reason, so that every pleasure and absence of pleasure becomes religious in nature. Here we must make a distinction, however, between the religious [impulse] which emerges of its own accord in opposition to the dialectical, and the religious [impulse] which is contained in ethical feelings (heart) and physical ones (spirit).

§ 250 Note. By means of this connection the requirement that all pleasure should become religious loses its disconcerting quality. For it can be expressed negatively in the following terms: no pleasure ought to be merely animal or sensual.

§ 251 Both aspects should come to totality, moreover; every possible modification of feeling should make its appearance, and in this way every branch of the system of depiction should be exhausted, too.

β) In the oscillation of personality

§ 252 The inequality of individuals who are otherwise at the same level of formation is not as great as it might appear, because there is much which is not in itself depiction but merely repetition; and often, where one is inclined to conclude that lack of depiction indicates lack of feeling, the appropriation of another's depiction, which is always internal production as well, is connected with a state of powerful excitement.

§ 253 Starting from the point at which man is closest to the animal stage, the particular works its way very gradually out of the universal, out of a state where there is no division, relatively speaking, between what is identical and what is particular, a state which forms the basis of analogy.

---

[79] *Marginal addition 1827:* 55. Depiction through art mediates the relationship of revelation.

§ 254 Receptivity, taste, and spontaneity develop alongside one another and as a result of one another in the most diverse relations; taken as a whole, however, depiction always lags behind feeling.

§ 255 Advanced age generates less that is new on the side of feeling, partly because there is a general diminishing of excitability, and partly because there is a greater withdrawal from common life as the type-patterns of the age change.

§ 256 On the other hand, in a well-organized sensibility the old excitements remain preserved, and memory breaks out in depiction; in this way it gains the upper hand over feeling.

§ 257 The prime of life is characterized by precisely that equilibrium between feeling and depiction as defined above.

§ 258 Those individuals who stand at points of intensive progress far distant from one another can experience no community of feeling or depiction.

§ 259 It requires a further common point of a particular kind to know what the relationship is between internal excitability and external power in any given state of excitement; where this is not the case there is no possibility of arriving at understanding through analogy.

§ 260 Where there are significant disparities in the organism even the initial elements of simple depiction acquire a different meaning, and there can be no possibility of arriving at a common system of depictional means.

§ 261 Complex depiction is conditional upon a mass of elementary intuitions held in common and has the same subjective significance; thus the above also holds true for this.

§ 262 It will only be possible to arrive at internal sociability either to the degree that the relationship between the two sides of feeling, spirit, and heart is an analogous one, or else if the two may be separated in communication.

§ 263 Internal sociability is thus only possible in a plurality of spheres, but we are not in possession of the principle which would allow us to determine what they are and separate them from one another.

Part III   On perfect ethical forms

Introduction

§ 1 Just as what is moral is not complete in personality per se, so personality is not given per se, but is simultaneous with its manner of becoming,

namely with sexual difference and one's particular form of race and nationality.[80]

§ 2 Deduction of these determined forms, and indeed of that general
form, would be an exercise for speculative physics, not ethics. Deduction
could, however, only show us the relationship between sexual difference
and certain natural functions, and between the particular forms and the
characters of the various continents, to follow a large-scale analogy.

§ 3 If, however, we regard both these things as given, then, since reason is
to become one with nature, the question arises how this is to come about
given these determining factors, and what they correspond to in ethical
terms.

§ 4 What they correspond to cannot fall outside the scope of what has
already been discussed; on the contrary, only the entirely determined
manner of what has been demonstrated, the way in which it has been
realized, can follow from what has been said.

§ 5 The result of sexual difference and connection is the family, and this
is the original and elementary manner of being for both ethical functions
with their respective characters.

§ 6 Considered under the character of identity both functions relate more
to the more narrowly defined type of nationality; under the character of
particularity they relate more to the broader type, that of race.

On the sexes, and the family

§ 7 Sexual character is given at the same time as personality, and does not
relate solely to sexual function, but extends throughout the body.

---

[80] *Marginal addition 1816: Monday*, 22 July. Recapitulation of general outline. *Measure* as divided
identity and particularity held in common, smallest, medium, largest.
Family [has] the first right [to consideration] as common element, but we must not forget that it
is conditional upon the others.
Sexual difference is the general form of nature on earth, though we do not know whether this
is more widely the case, or whether even on earth it is restricted to certain epochs. Related to
duplication in the general form of life.
No basis in reason in itself, but quickly used by reason to blur the edges of the one-sidedness of
character. This is the ethical side of the sexual drive, which develops out of alienation.
Satisfaction develops into *marriage*. Possession of persons because each has become an organ of
reason for the other. Vague commingling could only be considered moral if commingling and
procreation had already been separated by an aberration of nature. Taken from a strictly ethical
point of view, the activity of reason would always have to be destroyed by the separation of man
and wife. There is no essential distinction to be drawn between polygamy and marriage which can
be ended by divorce, on the one hand, and sexual community on the other.

§ 8 In the physical organs, too – that is, in the way in which reason was originally embodied in nature – the distinction is recognized by everyone as given.

§ 9 Its essence follows most clearly, however, from sexual function, where we find a predominance of receptivity in the female and of spontaneity in the male. Hence:

Particular [type of] cognition:

feeling female, fantasy male; appropriation female, invention male.

Particular [type of] formation:

in accordance with custom female, transcending custom, male.

Identical [type of] cognition:

more female to absorb than to develop.

Identical [type of] formation:

female more with reference to the particular sphere, male more to pure objectivity.

§ 10 Bound up with sexual difference, on the organic side, is a drive to particular community; this is linked to the preservation of the species and arises from the gradual development of sexual difference.

§ 11 As each sex develops it becomes more alien to the other on the spiritual side as well, and this feeling is then suffocated in an urge [to escape] from sexual one-sidedness into such community, to the extent that sexual commingling and procreation are identical here.

§ 12 What is particular about sexual community is the way in which two consciousnesses momentarily become one, and two lives permanently become one as a result of the factor of procreation.

§ 13 We find sexual community ethical by the very way it is determined, in that it can encompass only two people; for in the individual act need is satisfied entirely, and, at the same time, the presupposition of the activity gives rise to another factor, cohabitation for the sake of what has been produced in common.

§ 14 The unity created by sexual community, posited together with its indissolubility, is the true concept of *marriage*.

§ 15 As long as individuality has not worked its way out, each person sees in another individual only the representative of their sex and hence feels less bound to the person themselves, but becomes bound to them by the possession of children in common.

§ 16 Even a more universal marriage of this kind becomes indissoluble as a result of the possession of children in common, and separation can only come about if something develops in the one party which makes the common raising of children an impossibility.[81]

§ 17 Where individuality is already dominant, the ethical side of the sexual drive should also be directed by a personal elective attraction.

§ 18 A false result can be given by a superficial choice, the cause of which is usually excessive weight given to the physical side, or vanity which gets caught up in trivialities and overlooks what is essential.

§ 19 Presumptuous anxiety, for which nothing is sufficiently perfect to warrant a decision, makes it impossible for a result of any kind to proceed from it. For the possibility of achieving his moral destiny must be contained in a human being's natural situation.

§ 20 The unmarried state can therefore only be excused in that class where individuality emerges, and then only because of particular circumstances and when it is not a matter of choice.

§ 21 Since every personal elective attraction constitutes a friendship, there can be as many forms of individual marriage as there are forms of friendship.

§ 22 If later, then, one arrives at the view that a more perfect marriage would be possible with another person, this should not lead to separation, both because of children possessed in common and also because of the mutual possession of persons which already exists.

§ 23 The measure of perfection in a marriage is the extinguishing of the one-sidedness of sexual character and the growing awareness of what is other.

§ 24 Vague, momentary sexual community is immoral, because it separates commingling from procreation; it is the more criminal when the

---

[81] *Marginal addition 1816: Tuesday*, 23 July. 1. Various levels of marriage. *Universality.* When the motives for marriage are *either* of the greatest nobility with regard to external factors, and without self-interest, concerned with the relationship between the individual and the whole which he represents; in negative terms, conformity to tradition, in positive terms, furthering of the common good (excuse for the marriages of princes). *Or* by comparison: of the greatest nobility with regard to beauty, i.e. with regard to the freedom and completeness of the productive force. – *Individuality.* Positive, elective choice, this time not based on comparison. Absolute agreement, ideal of romantic love, presupposes the perfection of the individual. (This alone excludes deuterogamy; in reality, then, it is not excluded at all.)
2. Diverse *forms* in universal marriage, depending on predominant relationships between the elements. Individual marriage follows the diverse forms of friendship.
Repercussions of the marriage on the parents – in negative terms: limitation of the errors to which each sex inclines and which become caricatured in life outside marriage; in positive terms, development of repressed factors § 32–35 through children. Parents and children = family. Unity of particular life, from which diversity develops. No alternation of ethical forms.

psychic aspect of the sexual drive also comes into play, and the more animal when physical attraction is the only factor.

§ 25 Satisfaction of the sexual function within the same sex is unnatural from the physical point of view alone and so cannot be ennobled by the addition of any ethical element.

§ 26 Where they occur in the masses such abnormalities point back to a morally distorted state of affairs overall, either to an imbalance in the development of the physical and psychic aspects of sexual character, or, where there has been balanced development, to the failure to coincide of the external conditions necessary for the formation of an independent life.

§ 27 This is not sufficient to justify impurity of will in the individual, for given the reciprocal relationship between individual and common existence, the healing of one must start with the other.

§ 28 Since marriage is posited as a result of the act of sexual commingling, because this acknowledges the completeness of mutual elective attraction, and because the act is thereby posited as creating a continuing relationship, the barrenness of a marriage cannot change the fact that it is indissoluble.

§ 29 Since the human sexual drive is not periodical, nature is given such enormous latitude in this respect that one can always regard barrenness as something temporary.

§ 30 Since it is unnatural, one is somewhat inclined to regard barrenness as a person's own fault, at the very least to be attributed to a distorted relationship between the organic and intellectual sides; but it is also posited as an exception within the essence of the overall freedom of nature.

§ 31[82] The extinction of one-sidedness is posited in the identity of sexual community and procreation, in the former more as sense and in the latter more as drive.

§ 32 Just as the child gradually changes from being something internal to something external, from a part of the conscious self to an object of intuition, so the capacity for intuition is conducted by the maternal instinct, which is an extension of one's own feeling, until the child becomes the mediating point of his own cognition.

§ 33 Conversely, for the father the child is originally something external, but becomes something internal because of the way he possesses the

---

[82] *Against this § and those that follow, content and order is indicated by the following marginal comments (1816? 1827?):* a) 31–35. Relationship to marriage on both sides. b) 42–46. The character of the family. c) 37–38; 47–50. Children's relationship to parents. d) 39–40. Sibling relationships. e) 41; 51–53. Family as moral person. f) 54–57. Adequacy of family, intervention of death.

mother, and hence altogether the mediating point for the activity of his feeling.

Note. The fatherland, too, is something he feels should be preserved and protected.

§ 34 Before marriage, the man lacks any urge for specific property which appears effeminate to him in his unmarried state. Its expression in marriage, however, coming from the woman's side, becomes a genuine action in common because of its relationship to the common sphere in general and to the particular aspect of the cognitive function.

§ 35 Before marriage, the woman lacks any urge for the sphere of rights, which also appears masculine (for this reason they [*sic*] attach beauty as a form of ornamentation, however superficial, to all identical production). In marriage she must acquire some understanding of it because of her understanding of her husband and the relationship to the sphere of particularity.

§ 36 As a living whole the family contains no principle of limitation on what had hitherto been considered undetermined, but only the living means of connection, without which any beginning would be purely arbitrary, since a moral beginning cannot be determined by time and place but only by an internal reason.

§ 37 The parents' identity with their children derives from the organs they originally have in common, which is where the schematism of natural formation begins; and the way in which the children develop their own particularity, which is subordinated to this, is the original way in which the individual sphere rises up out of the universal one.

§ 38 It is in the community of children and parents that their thinking about the language they have already been given develops, and by means of its particularity of thought the family becomes the repository for at least the original development of language, which the parents can understand as such, because of their original identity.

§ 39 Among all members of a family, possessed community and common possession occurs in an original form.

§ 40 The community of siblings is internal sociability in its original form. For here we find identity both of feeling – in the unity of consciousness mediated through the parents – and of direct depiction, by means of organs which have been formed according to the same type, as well as indirect depiction because of the mass of intuitions held in common which are formed by familial cognition; in this way we are given a measure for analogy. For this reason sibling love is also the highest type of internal sociability.

§ 41 The family, taken as an entity, also assumes the form of personality, in that it is a numerical unit which appears and then vanishes, and depicts the existence of reason in nature in a particular way.

§ 42 Man and wife form a particularity in common which we may depict as a sphere within which and from which individual modifications develop which are encompassed by it.

§ 43 This particularity in common is the character of the family; since the particularity of the two individuals is not strictly identical, it does not strictly constitute a unity, but a unity which bears multiplicity within it and will allow multiplicity to develop from it.

§ 44 It is true that in procreation the parents embody the pure indifference of the species, and the procreated being is the result of that indifference, differentiating itself as it pleases; but they embody the species only in the definite form of individualities which meet, and so the procreated being also takes that form.

§ 45 Just as the physiognomical expressions of the parents grow ever closer together, depicting the family character in this similarity which is never quite complete, so the children, whose features are a mixture of both parents, demonstrate a free modification of that character.

§ 46 Exceptions can thus be explained by the fact that each parent is also only a modification of his or her family character, so that a similarity to a more distant relative may often emerge.

§ 47 Since everyone occupies a higher position than the one who is universal while they themselves are individual, children never occupy a higher position than their parents, regarded as a single entity, even if in this respect particularity develops ever more strongly. This feeling is at the root of filial piety towards one's parents.

§ 48 As long as that life force which can be regarded as identical through several generations of the same family is on the increase, the process of developing particularity within that family will also be on the increase.

§ 49 In general terms, intensive progression of the ethical process within a family rests on the congenital existence of reason as a system of ideas; however, the fact that those family members who follow after are immediately put in possession of the given estate [*Zustand*] rests on tradition.

§ 50 And so, even when the children occupy a higher position than their parents in intensive terms, they attribute this to their parents, seeing it as their doing; this constitutes the other factor in filial piety.

§ 51 The lasting nature of the family's external personality depends on whether the family character dominates personal particularity within it or vice versa; both of these forms are given at the same time as the fact that the individual consists of these two factors.

§ 52 If personal particularity dominates, then once the children have dispersed and the parents are dead, the soul of the previous person ceases to be, and the body, that is, the complex of acquired organs, loses its value and goes back into circulation as relatively raw material. This is the democratic character of the short-lived family.

§ 53 If family character dominates, then even when the children have dispersed this identity remains with them as a firm bond and their lives appear to them to be more a continuation of the lives of their forebears. Hence piety and attachment to the things which have been formed within the family prevail. This is the aristocratic character of the long-lived family.[83]

§ 54 In every family, taken as a unity, we may posit an adequacy for the ethical process. Initially in the parents themselves, as long as they are in their prime, during which time the children appear merely as *annexa*; then in both at the same time, as the children come into their prime and the parents continue in their maturity (here what is organic is more to be found in the children, what is spiritual more in the parents still); and finally in the children alone, for whom, however, the parents have now become history and are beginning to die away.

§ 55 Given these assumptions, death is an authorized natural event; all the more so when this decline of the organs coincides with the consciousness that one no longer fits into the whole of the formative process. When this happens first, we see the sad side of old age.

§ 56 The apparent immortality of the individual within the family is the undetermined reappearance of the same type in different generations.

§ 57 The rise or fall in the recurrence of exceptional individuals has its basis partly in the excellence of the family character itself and partly on the life force of the larger mass to which the family belongs.

---

[83] *Marginal addition 1816: Opposition between families* of aristocratic and democratic nature, which must necessarily exist alongside one another. All nobility gives rise to fossilization, all democracy to anarchic movement. 56–57 also belong here.

§ 58 The adequacy of the family is only present once it has been posited; it is not adequate, however, at the time of its genesis unless one assumes that the founding members are the product of a single family and hence siblings.

§ 59 If marriage is to rest on elective attraction and if sibling love is the original type of friendship, then there would appear to be no objection to the marriage of siblings.[84]

§ 60 If we assume that the human race had its origins in a single couple, this would necessarily entail marriage between siblings, and since this could not therefore be immoral, it is impossible to understand why it should subsequently have become so.

§ 61 If marriage between siblings had once been moral it would no doubt also have become the custom, and then the whole of the human race would merely have consisted of a single family type instead of an infinite diversity, internal as well as external, and any intuition of the human race as such would be impossible.[85]

§ 62 For this reason, the orientation of the sexual drive away from the family is to be regarded as a minimum of orientation, found in nature, towards the depiction of the human race as a totality.

§ 63 It is possible to conceive of exceptions in the most imperfect state of the family, where particularity is very little in evidence, so that the difference between one's sister and a stranger is hardly significant.

§ 64 For this reason, however, this movement away ought not to be posited as movement as far away as possible; the measure of it is the fact that an elective attraction hinting at a higher common particularity must be possible, namely that of nationality.

---

[84] *Marginal addition 1816: g. Friday.* The family conditioned by the other ethical forms. 1. Sexual drive essentially moves beyond the family, aversion to marriage between relatives is a natural instinct. Examples: castes and ruling houses. 59–62.

2. Marriage conditioned by folk customs and religion. Exceptions found only amongst peoples on the lowest levels, or at higher levels as the result of rare influences exercised by the general community; these must be justified by their success.

Exception of circles beyond the church and beyond Protestant and Catholic only as a result of indifferentism. Fewer exceptions here, because women are more in the church than in the state.

3. The condition of satisfaction, as soon as individuality develops, is sociability, intercourse ... [?] Always experiment and approximation to love. Morality consists a) in an equilibrium between the two sides of the sexual drive and b) in an uninhibited transition from the multiplicity of indefinite relationships to the unity of the genuine one. – This sociability is only possible at the same formative stage. To join together different stages produces a misalliance, where either external motivating factors or the physical side must have prevailed.

[85] *Marginal addition 1816:* N.B. Should a separate treatment of personality be included here?

§ 65 In a mass of families where intermarriage takes place, it is necessary to arrive at an external and internal sociability, which we will only examine here with reference to the relationship between the sexes.

§ 66 It is impossible for a sociable relationship between unmarried persons of different sexes who come from one domain of the kind described above to be quite without any bias towards love, since both parties must be in the process of seeking out a marriage partner.

§ 67 The way this bias is depicted in the relationship – to the extent that it remains merely on a general level – is the essence of what we call gallantry, or devotion to women; this also expresses the specific character of the Germano-Romantic era, however.

§ 68 The morality of such a relationship rests on the equilibrium between the two sides of the sexual drive and on the symmetry of the approach on both sides.

§ 69 A friendly relationship without love may exist between married persons of different sexes,

§ 70 and also between a married person on the one hand and an unmarried person on the other, depending on the extent to which the sanctity of marriage has been accepted by the mass and also on whether the individual case qualifies for subsumption [under this law], since the married person is then entirely excluded from the process of seeking out [a partner].

§ 71 The education of children is based on [filial] piety and because originally the formative principle lies entirely with the parents, its starting-point is in obedience.

§ 72 Within the parents, however, there is also a quest for their own developing particularity and, as this develops, an inclination to leave others be to the same extent.

§ 73 Since [filial] piety looks for the prolongation of obedience while parental love seeks to cut it short, the natural modifications of the relationship can evolve without discord of any kind until the family community comes to an end, which is precisely the basis of all morality.

§ 74 The technical aspect need only be depicted in the particular discipline of *pedagogy*, the original diversity of which proceeds from the variety of forms of the family and the variety of relationships to the state.[86]

---

[86] *Marginal addition 1816 (written in against § 52): Thursday.* Principle of pedagogy: the opposition between parental and filial love, based on the individual aspect and the universal one. 70–74. Internally something which gradually diminishes, externally having a definite limit. This cannot give rise to conflict, however, since it is not determined within the family, but in the state and the church.

§ 75 Besides parents and children, and other members of the family who live with them, the family also contains a servant body whose existence, stretching in an infinite series of gradations from the serf to the hired hand, is based partly on warlike relations, partly on diversity of race, and partly on the natural distance between parental home and family formation.

§ 76 The moral treatment of the relationship depends on the difference in formative levels, whether great or small.

On national unity

§ 77[87] When marriage joins together a mass of families whilst excluding other families, they constitute a single people.

§ 78 Marriage does not create a single people; on the contrary, it is based on real identity and is conditional upon that identity.

§ 79 Note. At the lower political level marriage can extend beyond the state, if the state is strongly biased towards expansion; this may also be the case at a high level if there is extensive free community among nations, but then it has no political significance.

§ 80[88] Real identity produces on the one hand a feeling of kinship between personal family individualities; on the other hand it appears as a uniform type of the cognitive and organizing function and a positing of this function's sphere as a common unity.

§ 81 We must posit a plurality of national unities even if only as a condition for the reproduction of families, and these can vary greatly in outward extent.

§ 82 The more kinship dominates, the smaller the unity; the more uniformity of type dominates, the greater that unity can be, because any number of small differences in this respect can be resolved by commerce.

§ 83 Identity of type in the cognitive function and the formative function cannot be completely separated; it does not follow, however, that where

---

[87] *Marginal addition 1816:* Monday 29 July. Second measure: national unity, balance between particularity in common and in particular, i.e. community which is divided off from the others. In acknowledgment, marriage already demonstrates the activity of reason, rooted in feeling, which can be regarded as a more and a less and as an opposition. Marriage gives rise to restricted commerce and the identity of schematism.

The larger and smaller units, horde and people, are already present in this double view: the latter are already at the level of commerce when the former are still at the level of marriage.

A turning to the formative function = state; to the symbolizing function = knowledge.

[88] *Marginal note 1813:* N.B. Just as a person develops out of a family, so the family must develop out of the greater unity, in order to be its equal.

it predominates the one could not form a smaller unity and the other a larger one.

On the state[89]

§ 84 A mass of families which has joined together to form a unity of type in the formative function is originally a *horde*; in this condition it is dominated by uniformity among those who exist alongside one another.

§ 85 The essence of the *state* consists in the opposition which emerges between authority and subjects, however this comes about, and to that extent it stands in the same relation to the horde as conscious does to unconscious.

§ 86 As a higher [form of] life by comparison with what came before, its genesis cannot be fully comprehended, neither can it usually be proved historically.

§ 87 The state can be coterminous with the horde, in which case the transition is rooted in the gradual development of consciousness, which then emerges on what is often an insignificant occasion to create the opposition.

§ 88 It can also arise if several hordes are fused together, when consciousness develops of the larger living unity which is the same in all of them and then emerges energetically at some point, though this cannot happen without some greater cause. Genesis of the state in this form will always be revolutionary.

§ 89 That the state should arise through contract is an impossibility, partly because by definition contract only exists because of the state and is essentially conditional upon the state, precisely because there is something lacking in simple contractuality which would bring it up to the level of the state; partly because such a contract would have to arise by force of persuasion, but force of that kind can never be present in the individual where there is no urgent need; where it does rise to the surface, however,

---

[89] *Marginal addition 1816 (written in against § 78):* On the state. 1. Comparison of horde and state. Only the internal opposition is new. Since it refers to the same being and doing, however, it exists only in consciousness, thus how unconscious can be relative to conscious.
Transition not given a posteriori, can thus only be reconstructed, cognition therefore imperfect. Two possible forms result, the one uniform and the other not. The former inclines towards contract, the latter towards usurpation. But it is impossible for the state truly to come into being through contract, because contract exists only within the state. The same is true for usurpation, because nothing is taken away, even from the person who becomes a subject.

the power of nature is also at work, so that the individual with his force of persuasion can only appear as a single moment.

§ 90 A state which is founded on contract, moreover, cannot last; for no force is present in the contract as such which will inhibit destructive internal movements.

§ 91 Least of all, therefore, can we ascribe a higher value to the concept of a state which has been established by contract than we can to the other. The truth of the matter is that we must be able to regard the formation of the opposition as a common enterprise. For if that opposition is a one-sided action on the part of the individual who sets himself up in authority, there remains posited within the masses a striving towards annihilation, so that what we have is merely a usurpation.

§ 92 Variation in political dignity is always a sign that several hordes have been fused together – if they are of the same kind, then the higher dignity is to be found in the one for which consciousness of the greater unity developed first; if they are not, it is to be found in the more individual one, the nobler one.[90]

§ 93 Particularity in common is the basis of the state, partly to the extent that it is also a family bond and partly because only to that extent will every individual posit the totality of the external sphere of the state as his own moral, particular sphere (that is, as absolutely holy and inviolable), for on this alone does the defence of the state rest.[91]

---

[90] *Marginal addition 1816 (written in against § 82):* Tuesday 30 July. 1. The hordes [which make up] a people also exist alongside one another, and in them too development can be either uniform or not. In the first case we find the peaceful existence alongside one another of several individual small states. Otherwise we find state existing alongside un-state (this will not last very long), or else one state in the process of becoming, while all grow together towards a greater unity, dominated by one of the hordes. The small monarchies of the *Odyssey*, which readily become democracies. The great Asiatic monarchies which appear either despotic or aristocratic.

2. Objection. Contrary to this view are a) the definition produced by antiquity; § 97, 98; the basis of which is the state as precursor of other developments, which still lie concealed within it; b) the modern, negative objection of the lawyer which arises from the question: in what way does the state help the individual? This view is destructive of the state, because it supersedes the separating principle and portrays truth as a matter of chance. Hostile contact produces the predatory state and the cowardly state which gives up any attempt at self-defence. For every state has right on its side. A people which allows itself to be conquered can say: I will let the other party decide what is right for me and defend me; that is a great expense and I do well by the bargain. From such a view we may deduce that there is a natural bias towards universal monarchy.

There might appear to be less in a state than our explanation suggests, because in small states what little commerce there is is poorly developed. That is only because division of labor has not yet been developed. It may exist before the state, or be absent even when the state is in existence.

[91] *Marginal note 1813:* Terrible experiences of recent times.

§ 94 If we posit the state as necessarily conditional upon national unity, we are also positing an essential plurality of states, and it is only their moral process in itself which forms the basis of a peaceful existence alongside one another.

§ 95 If we do not regard that unity as the basis of the state, there is no internal reason for a plurality of states, and since, if several states exist alongside one another there is the possibility of hostile relations, this must give rise to a tendency to supersede such hostility by fusing them together, i.e. if external force provides no restraint, the orientation of the state must be towards infinity, that is, towards the universal state.

§ 96 If such an association is not rooted in particularity it can only have a negative basis, namely to safeguard every person's activity, which means also those individuals who are in opposition. If the state is not merely to be some kind of criminal institution, it must attempt to supersede any grounds for disruption. But then it is itself dispensable and either people will live as hordes once again – this presupposes individual ties of some kind, however – or else in isolation, and then the goal which they will set themselves will be a point at which the ethical process cannot even begin.

§ 97 The ancients did not restrict the state to the cultural domain; to them it was an association of families which was sufficient to produce the highest good, and which therefore encompassed the whole of the ethical process.

§ 98 For them, however, everything was more under the power of nature and the other functions were in the background, religion ranking below the state and knowledge scarcely tolerated. Once they have developed to the same extent, we cannot assume that knowledge or religion could be made by means of the same opposition of authority and subject, or spontaneity and receptivity.

§ 99 Since, however, knowledge and religion also require an organization and this depends, as far as the former is concerned, on a greater or lesser degree of national unity and, as far as the latter is concerned, on unity of race at the very least, then the interrelatedness of the two functions is nevertheless safeguarded.

§ 100 If, according to the negative view, the state ought to protect personal freedom in matters of knowledge and religion as well, its positive activity may not for that reason extend beyond the cultural domain; for any way in which these two become external belongs essentially to that domain.

§ 101 In essence, the view put forward here includes legal procedures, for any organism must either assimilate foreign bodies or expel them. To transform the state into a mere legal institution, however, would be to reverse the direction of the ethical process.

§ 102 It is the state which first gives rise to the ultimate, complete form for contract and property, and determines criteria for their existence and violation which are generally valid, since in the horde the necessary external aspect is lacking, and for this reason restitution is only ever a private matter.

§ 103 It is with regard to property, indeed, that we can articulate the [central] dilemma: it can only exist through the state, because the universal validity of the term depends on the external emergence of unity, while the state can only exist through property because, in order to produce a common act (§ 91), individuals must be given to one another in external terms and therefore acknowledged in their own person, i.e. their [most] primitive property. Both [propositions], therefore, are simply two moments in one and the same act of nature.

§ 104 It is the state which first produces that full guarantee for the division of labor, money, and hence first allows the full scope of that division to emerge.[92]

§ 105 Since through division of labor each person's sphere becomes a mere fragment and he is unable to acquire a clear sense of its relationship to the

---

[92] *Marginal addition 1816:* Wednesday 31 July. Commentary. 1. Commerce first perfected in the state. For only then do true contractuality and true money come into being. Before the state, money is simply whatever goods are most sought after; it only acquires its particular character in definite expression and through the term itself, which is only possible in the state. – The safeguarding of a contract is only to be found when the whole [community] genuinely comes out in defense of the person whose rights have been infringed, i.e. in public power; before that this is an uncertain assumption. Safeguards against misunderstanding are only to be found in the authorization of language for commerce, and this is only possible in the state. – Indeed, even possession is only complete once the term has been spoken out loud and established. By this means, then, that sphere separates itself off at the same time from all other commerce.
2. Formative activity and the schematism that goes with it comes from the subjects of a state as such. But since only the authorities are familiar with the patterns which the threads make, it must extend consciousness of the relationships of the whole into all parts. Where such communication is absent, an essential element of the state has been repressed.
3. The aspiration to freedom in the subject as such can only relate to those things which fall outside the scope of reasons of state: scientific, religious, and domestic freedom. None of these is absolute, however, because the state cannot exist completely separate from the other spheres. There is no necessity for the state to grant the same civil rights to the adherents of every religion, no necessity to spare those things in the house which ought not yet to have developed a domestic existence. – Within the scope of reasons of state, the subject as such can only aspire to a lively interaction with the authorities, which amounts to the same thing as self-preservation on the part of the state. He cannot aspire to unlimited possession (116–118), only that any limitation should be constitutional.

whole, often only becoming aware of it too late by experiencing the conse-quences, a quickening insight into this relationship, and in consequence the proper directing of forces, must come from the ruling authorities.

§ 106 The formative process itself, however, must always come from the individual himself, and when the authorities act in a business capacity, they destroy the opposition again.

§ 107 Since, however, the need for many activities can only be experienced as a result of the overseeing function of the whole, both in its entirety and with regard to individual points, incitement may of course come from the authorities on this point.

§ 108 The form which is particular to the people must not appear in any part of the cultural process to be the imposition of the authorities on subjects; for since one does not command what happens of its own accord, the two elements [would] then appear to be in opposition, and what is inborn [would] appear to have been imposed from outside.

§ 109 From this it follows that the development of this particular form will come most naturally from the middle levels of the hierarchy, not to the extent that they are in authority, however, but as subjects themselves, a higher echelon of the people.

§ 110 On the other hand, it is right that what is being formed spon-taneously in the people receives from the authorities the definite shape which the people are unable to give it; in this the unity of the two sides is effectively displayed.

§ 111 Just as the opposition between subject and authority is expressed in command and obedience, so the relativity of that opposition is expressed in the concept of civic freedom, as a minimum of limitation of the subject by the authority.

§ 112 To the extent that the individual is at the same time a part of scholarly and religious organizations he is right to demand that, since the state does not engage in these processes, it should not prevent him from engaging in them himself.

§ 113 To the extent that the religious sphere is far more extensive than the state, so that the latter is immersed in a greater sphere of this kind, it must admittedly express consciousness of that fact, but not as the aspiration to dominate that sphere.

§ 114 The same is true of the specific formation of property in the strictest sense of the word. As a matter of taste, this too must be left entirely up to the individual himself.

§ 115 Since the identity of all these functions is to be found in the family and the household, any interference on the part of the authorities with what is inside the house is the most detestable thing, and its sanctity is the first requirement of personal freedom.

§ 116 If, however, the individual demands isolation from the state with something which belongs to his sphere of particularity, this is inadmissible. For, since the state's entire sphere of particularity is posited as something held in common, each individual receives his own sphere of particularity as a fief, with the state giving it the final, formal completion.

§ 117 Since everyone must have the feeling that only as a member of the nation can he engage in the process of formation, he must also desire to purchase the preservation of form, as the living force of reproduction, for the sake of the totality of the results.

§ 118 The state, which can only feel its own existence in the liveliness and the richness of the process of formation, must necessarily desire the preservation and growth of the sphere of each individual.

§ 119 In this respect, the true morality of the state consists in there being no demand for what is called civic freedom.

§ 120 The way in which the opposition between authorities and subject is expressed is the *constitution* of the state.

§ 121 Leaving aside the influence exercised by the genesis of the state, such a constitution is as diverse – where the state rests on family bonds – as the relationships of aristocratic families to democratic ones and – where the state is a whole formed by nature – as the relationships of those who are only in possession of the mechanical aspects to those who are also in possession of the intelligent aspects.

§ 122 Partly because these relationships themselves are gradually modified, partly also because the genesis of the state is only the beginning of the process of becoming and the inequality originally posited in it must even itself out to an ever-greater extent, any long-lived state must also experience changes in its constitution.

§ 123 These changes, too, are either simply the emerging acknowledgment of something that has already come about, or else they are revolutionary. They cannot be made in an arbitrary way, and still less can something internal in the state be improved on by arbitrary amendments to the constitution. Only inasmuch as a matter is already present can the supervention of the perfected form bring about improvement.

§ 124 Changes to the constitution must also be a joint action on the part of authority and subjects. For this to come about, however, they must also arise from a joint action. If they originate with the authorities and the authorities have made a mistake, this gives an appearance of tyranny; for this reason it is better for the authorities to acquiesce.

§ 125 If they originate with the subjects, this gives an appearance – until such changes become a joint action – of rebellion; and if they do not become a joint action and the subject's relationship to the authorities has been damaged by the undertaking, he can be punished as a rebel.

§ 126 The genuine civic disposition, then, consists here merely in this: if a man regards something as necessary to the general good, he should attempt to implement it even if this means staking his own existence on it. Momentary success does not always prove the morality of something; for there is much which can succeed for a moment because of its influence on the private advantage of a few individuals. Neither does momentary lack of success prove immorality. On the contrary, something may be necessary by way of preparation which can only later become real.

§ 127 The state considered as a person has an internal side and an external side, just like the individual. Its internal side is the national particularity which manifests itself in the process of formation; this remains consistent through all its various developments and the corresponding changes to the constitution, just as the character of the individual human being does.

§ 128 National particularity is represented externally through language and physiognomy. The natural outward extent of a state thus goes beyond people and soil as far as language and physical shape.

§ 129 Essentially people and soil belong together, and for this reason the soil is the first object, for everyone, of the force of attraction exercised by love, so that a people must always feel it to be theft when it forfeits some part of the soil it originally inhabited.[93]

---

[93] *Marginal addition 1816:* Thursday and Friday. 1. State is the identity of people and soil. It is rare for a nomadic people already to constitute a state.

a) The adequacy of the soil consists in the fact that essential needs can be produced *in natura*. For, even if the state ought not to exist in isolation, the feeling that it can exist in isolation is a necessary element in its freedom. Hence the need for small states to merge together into one larger state which represents a national unity; this can occur peacefully or by military means (wars of unification) and may create an absolute unity or a federal one. The need does not go beyond this, only inward.

For states engaged in global commerce which have needs in foreign zones (which are not just needs, but which reveal the universality of human nature for the whole earth), colonization develops (at least until global commerce is complete, bringing with it the certainty that not every

§ 130 Since, however, the lesser unity of the tribe and the greater unity of the nation continue to exist, subordinated to one another, either one of them can be state-forming and both can be in conflict.

§ 131 Since, in peaceful times, tribes and peoples that are related to one another and surround one another will not be able to remain strictly separated, the personal outward extent of the state may come into dispute wherever there is a tendency towards a community of peoples.

§ 132 If the determination of the extent of the state continues to oscillate, this is the condition of war.

§ 133 Among prudent peoples who have reflected on such matters, both unities can participate in the formation of the state; this gives rise to federal constitutions. These also fluctuate constantly, since it is impossible to imagine the two unities remaining in a pure state of equilibrium, and this creates an internal condition of war. If one of the unities is then completely annihilated, the federal state was merely a transitional moment. It only

source can be stopped up at the same time). Maritime connections are of course necessary to this, but now there can scarcely be an independent state without them. This is bound up with the situation of overpopulation and serfdom.

b) The determining power of the soil is an essential element in the character of the people and the natural surroundings – the two tend to merge along lines of contact, which therefore appear in one sense to be uncertain and susceptible to adjustment according to external motives. (Not, however, where one of the two falls away: no mountain border without its crossover type and crossover language.) Hence frontier wars.

Note. In any moral war there is no opposition between offensive and defensive. If there is such an opposition, there is also injustice.

2. States are diverse in terms of quality and also according to the degree of perfection they have attained.

a) Constitutional differences have a part to play in both. The constitution is partly motivated by the genesis of the state and partly by the relationship between its families, but if the [underlying] opposition is strained to the limit, a different constitution is also called for, and for this reason all states run through a whole series of them. Changes are arbitrary when they originate with the authorities and rebellious when they originate with the subjects. Even if they are only the expression of what has already come about, they nevertheless presuppose irregularities which had not been calculated for, and hence contain anarchic elements. Reformation, if the improvement is already present in the constitution in embryonic form.

b) Permanent difference is only what was a given element before the state came into being, which admittedly also modifies the constitution but has less effect on the broad outlines.

c) Difference at the point of perfection consists in the permeation of both sides. Extremes meeting, for here, too, the opposition must have molded each separate element (individual, family, corporation); 1. He must ply his trade as a part of the whole = public spirit; 2. As a subject, he must help to posit the existence of the authorities. This takes place in an unstructured way, i.e. through public opinion, and formally in representation. (Here, strictly speaking, the subject is not a part of the authorities); 3. He himself must assume authority, each individual having his part to play in implementation.

3. The relationship of each state to the others. 140–145.

constitutes a permanent type when the large and small unities alternate in repressing one another, without either being destroyed.

§ 134 Every state needs a sufficiency of soil because it ought not to be dependent [on others] for its essential needs. These essential needs increase, however, if the community of peoples gains in size. The state strives to push back its frontiers in order to acquire what is lacking; these are wars of need.

§ 135 Thus we can distinguish three different sorts of natural warfare: wars of unification which form the state, frontier wars, or wars which maintain a state of equilibrium, and wars of need which defend the state; the usual distinction, on the other hand, between offensive wars and defensive ones, is an entirely empty one.

§ 136 The internal growth of the state consists first of all in the fact that the material aspect of formative activity, and the formal aspect of the constitution permeate each other to an ever-greater extent, in that political opposition regularly institutes the necessary influence of the cognitive function on the formative one (§ 121), whilst the particular form of the cultural process determines that political opposition in its developments and modifications.

§ 137 Moreover [it depends on] the fact that political opposition develops and extends ever further. The latter, by virtue of the fact that it is instilled into every individual and each person somehow participates in the existence of the authorities; the former, because the functions of the two parts become more distinctly separate and develop in a graded sequence commensurate with the size of the all-embracing whole, which may decrease as well as increase.

§ 138 And then finally [it depends on] the fact that the cultural process will achieve completeness in finding its way into every part of the domain occupied by the state and appearing to be purely the result of national activity. The former occurs when all raw material is organized according to national structures. The latter is the case to the extent that the individual cannot isolate himself from the community by using the whole, and to the extent that chance has lost its force in the extreme multiplicity of connections.

§ 139 From the individual's point of view and as far as he is concerned, the life of the state is perfect to the extent that the duplication of nationality and personality is both separate and combined. Nationality only gives satisfaction to personality, however, inasmuch as the individual feels himself to be present in both terms of the opposition, while personality only gives satisfaction to nationality inasmuch as the individual always apprehends the existence of the whole and is subordinate to it; i.e. the individual should be neither serf nor despot.

§ 140 When states which come into contact are not in the process of mutually defining one another through warfare, they are naturally at peace with one another as long as their spheres of formation are capable of mutual acknowledgment.

§ 141 The next stage comes when the state can take the part of a citizen from another state against one of its own, which may occur partly without reference to the plaintiff, it is true, so as not to condone unlawful behavior on the part of the perpetrator; but principally on the basis of a tacit, imperfect contract that the other state would do the same thing in the same situation.

§ 142 A further stage is the extended exchange of goods on a large scale or mutual liberality with regard to objects, which is neither an imperfection in itself, nor on the other hand something which can ever be unlimited; partly because every state has things which are sacrosanct, i.e. possessions which are perfectly individualized, and partly because every state must be independent with regard to its essential needs.

§ 143 Partly if a closer affinity comes about, partly if especial situations arise, then both of these steps, taken together, may give rise to a closer connection, a closer interest felt by one state for the other, which has the character of a friendship. This is the true nature of defensive alliances.

§ 144 Neither of these situations can bear the weight of the ultimate form of contract in themselves, if both states are independent and entirely autonomous. By their very nature, therefore, they last only as long as there is a lively urge in that direction and are most reliable when concluded only for a short period of time with the possibility of renewal reserved.

§ 145 If a state holds to a contract when it is no longer to its advantage to do so, this can only occur for the sake of its credit, which is weakened when it is seen that it is unable to calculate its long-term advantage and is casual in entrusting itself to something, although compulsion in itself cannot render a contract invalid.

On the national community of knowledge

§ 146 Since this side of the process cannot be linked merely to personality either, but has no use for the family, the organization of the objective side of the cognitive process clearly falls to the same higher unity as that of the formative process. The community of knowledge is therefore the other aspect of national unity.

§ 147 Nevertheless, even if they are founded at the same level of unity (§ 83), the two organizations will not become a single entity in a single nation because, given the relative separation of the functions, there is no internal reason why the functional differences ought to coincide.

§ 148 Since the basis of marriage is a close homogeneity which cannot manifest itself in the formative function without the cognitive one, it precisely presupposes a common particularity of cognition.

§ 149 The absolute identity of schematism in knowledge exists only as a claim made by certain individuals, but we are unable to produce anything which perfectly corresponds to it.

§ 150 National particularity is a given and runs through all four domains, both in the stricter form of science, where admittedly it should be least prominent in the mathematical and transcendental domains, and even more so in [science in] the broader sense.[94]

---

[94] *Marginal addition 1816 (referring to the whole section): Monday, Tuesday and Wednesday.* 1. Here, too, common particularity is a given before opposition develops (153). The development of the opposition is the emergence into consciousness of formative activity. At the same time, common particularity becomes the combinatory principle in this.
The public only produces cognition which is dependent partly on formative activity, partly on feeling. Scholars produce with reference to the idea of knowledge.
The prestige and influence of scholars, just like that of the authorities, is dependent on public opinion. This can only be acquired, however, by descending into the public process. The English and the French superior to the Germans in this.
Again, the first production in the popular domain originates with the people; but it is only made complete, both in overall conception and in detail, through the influence of the scholars. This is directive activity.
Historical activity follows on from critical activity. A history of consciousness – coherent life in consciousness – is only to be found once there is opposition; before this everything has more the character of myth and fable.
Critical and historical activity also naturally directed towards language. This is not in itself something to criticize, only when linguistic production proceeding from life is inhibited. It ought rather only to allocate a particular domain of language to each element.
2. The opposition of the various systems proves nothing against the nationality of knowledge. They merely exaggerate necessary orientations and so must necessarily always be together, even if in varying relationship. But in every people each system has its own character.
It is no more true of academic communication between different peoples. For a) it is mostly only the material which is taken and then revised in a particular way, which is true even of mathematics;

§ 151 The attitude which a people takes towards nature is naturally conditional upon its position in nature, just as its ethical knowledge is conditional upon its social relationships, and this is reciprocal, so that each stands in relation to the other as its ideal and real aspect.

§ 152 The most powerful manifestation of this difference is in languages, which are so diverse, not only in tone but also in meaning, that this runs through all their material and formal elements, so that every language becomes the repository of a particular system of concepts and ways of combining.

§ 153 Originally, the homogeneous masses also merely live as hordes alongside one another; that is to say that in each family we find much the same tradition, without any far-reaching division of transactions or gradation of activities.

§ 154 Here, too, the unity of the organization is dependent on the awakening of an opposition; only then does the function itself emerge into consciousness.

§ 155 Since all actions will come to resemble one another all the more as the same relationship is to be found in all of them between the organic and the intellectual sides, greater community of knowledge is conditional upon the emergence of both sides into an opposition with a diversity of forms.

§ 156 Since, in the larger organization, every point must have an influence on every other, it is admittedly conditional upon the written word as a general means of communication, but this can only develop as the cognitive function emerges from the state in which it is blended with the formative function.

---

b) it is surely true that only what one people does better is positively accepted, and even then only temporarily, just as in the domain of commerce. –In our cultural domain, where it is most lively, such commerce is made considerably easier by a common scholarly language; however, even here particularity is revealed in its diverse usage.

3. Scholars who join together in an academy are united partly in a more wide-ranging way, by virtue of the division of labor, and partly more narrowly, by virtue of common production, because any great work involves all the talents.

Schools constitute the influence of scholars on the preservation of the opposition for the future generation. Where a people's schools are plied predominantly as a trade, a subordinate view dominates and scholars have less influence. – Schools must use the same methods to develop receptivity in some, spontaneity in others.

Universities are the peak of this process, tending in the direction of spontaneity. Their relativities 169, 170.

4. All external commerce is conditional upon translation. All internal commerce upon the greatest possible clarity with regard to the relationship between personal and common particularity.

§ 157 The opposition which is denoted by the terms "public" and "scholars," however, in such a way that the former corresponds to the subjects, the latter to the authorities, should not be taken to imply that scholars are people who can write and the public people who cannot write, for writing serves every interest, even those which are foreign to the cognitive function as such.

§ 158 If this opposition rests on the divergence of the organic and intellectual sides in differing proportion, this should not be taken to mean that the philosophers, in the narrow sense of that word, could be the authorities; for they would be least capable of directing the organic side and bringing it into agreement with the intellectual side.

§ 159 It is out of the question not least because in that case the constitution would have to be either civil war or despotism.

§ 160 The opposition can only be a functional one, not a purely personal one, because there is no one who, in every act of knowledge, has also posited its relationship to the whole. The essence of the scholar's function consists in this positing of the whole, which accompanies individual actions as a guiding idea.

§ 161 This does not exclude consideration of the individual. On the contrary, the function lies in this [consideration], when the individual is posited in and for the science which properly applies to him. For science is that construction of actions of a similar nature which finds the basis of its form in the idea of the unity and totality of knowledge.

§ 162 In consideration of the general per se the function is not necessary. Not when the general is viewed merely as something that has been formed from the bottom up; nor when it is considered separately from the organic side; only, then, insofar as it is treated as the principle of the individual sciences.

§ 163 Considering the opposition merely in a functional sense, but regarding the function of scholars as a unity, we presuppose that those persons who exercise this function are in lively contact with one another, to the extent that the development of science itself forms a lively unity. Such contact stands as a given alongside the written word, however, and requires no external form (except to the extent that we need to designate certain gradations between scholars and public, which are, however, always arbitrary ones!).[95]

---

[95] *Marginal addition 1832, entered against § 152: 1832.* There is a correspondence between the formation of the state and the awakening of consciousness by way of language. This gives rise to a

§ 164 The public's original activity is material and productive, and either the national type predominates, appearing to be merely a matter of convention, however, or else the personal predominates, but is only able to emerge in the form of arbitrary combination.

§ 165 The scholars' original activity is formal. It relates partly to what is produced by the given public and to that extent it is partly directive, turning production in the direction of scientific need or scientific strength, and partly judgmental, assimilating whatever is worthy of entering the living national tradition, partly rejecting, consigning to oblivion things which belong to antiquated concept formations, or which are coarse, arbitrary, or alien. With regard to both aspects, the scholars form what we call an *academy*.

§ 166 Directive activity applies to the extensive orientation of the process, judgmental activity to the intensive orientation. If we relate the latter to the concept of scientific literature, the formula to which we can reduce the function of the scholars is that they produce what is classical.

§ 167 Their function is partly to preserve the totality of the national process, that is, to ensure that the opposition between scholars and public remains permanent. This is their pedagogical effectiveness.

§ 168 Youth is [a state of] indifference [to the distinction] between public and scholars, yet it will give rise to both. The whole of their development before their going different ways, and their development as public after this point, lies in the *school* system. Under the influence of scholars, its tendency must be to keep them receptive to the influence of scholars by setting up the tradition of knowledge and the formation of skills in such a way that they have some inkling of the higher application and organization of knowledge.

§ 169 The continuing development of those who demonstrate an urge [to embrace] the scholarly function can only come about by holding up the idea of knowledge before their eyes, partly in an indirect way in everyday life and partly in a direct way, per se. This takes place in the *universities*. The more one form prevails at the expense of the other, the more we create people who either get stuck in empty introspection or who revert back to empiricism.

separation between thinking in itself and the other two things. The latter are placed outside the domain of the former. In opposition to scholars and public. This evolution does not occur in the smaller community, nor in dialect, or at least both occur at the same time, the awakening of this consciousness and of the greater unity of language.

§ 170 The dependence of these institutions on the state, historically a given factor, can be explained either as an as-yet incomplete separation of the domains of the two functions, originating with the family, where the two are as one, or else as a favoring of the state, which secures the basis of the scientific organization in order to be sure of its own influence on the formative function.

§ 171 In neither case does [the state] enter into dispute with the idea, provided in the first case that both domains can be regarded as being in a process of further divergence; and in the second case that the state does not intervene in material terms and does not attempt to determine either orientation or individual results, nor to impose on such institutions anyone who is not a recognized scholar.

§ 172 However, where the state dominates in this domain in real terms, both the formative and the cognitive functions are sick; the former because it is unnaturally extended and the latter because, if it were healthy, other free institutions of a similar kind would have to take shape alongside those which have been bent under the yoke of the state or which the state refuses to acknowledge.

§ 173 The apparently great difference between the two notwithstanding, the authority of scholars rests on the same principle as that of the [political] authorities (the latter having its definitive basis only in the force of opinion in exactly the same way), namely on the conviction [felt by] those who have an interest in the national type that it finds expression here.

§ 174 The difference is only that, considered from the outside, the scientific opposition is produced afresh, so to speak, between every individual in every action, while this does not emerge as clearly within the state, though it is essentially present there too; also that in the domain of knowledge punishment is not acknowledged as such, precisely because it only applies within that domain.

§ 175 The opposition of various systems in all branches of knowledge does not supersede the unity of national knowledge. For since it is not possible to achieve a pure, stable equilibrium between opposing views, but only an oscillation, and since each of these views denotes and promotes a necessary orientation within the process, they must coexist, and if one of them were absent, then in qualitative terms knowledge would only be fragmentary.

§ 176 Differences in national particularities cannot simply be related to differences in these systems, either, but only partly to their relative predominance and partly to a character which varies from nation to nation, which is uniformly accepted by all these systems.

§ 177 National and personal individualities are mediated through differences in *schools*, which establish intermediate points of view; these are partly general and partly concerned with particular domains of knowledge.

§ 178 The main forms, in particular the Academy, are linked to a multitude of lesser ones, partly ranging downward from the Academy towards the public and partly upward; they are intended either to popularize ideas and introduce them into common production, or else to gather raw information and prepare it for scientific revision. It is only in this way that national life is revealed in general terms in the function, and such forms will assume their own particular shape in every nation.

§ 179 In these forms national unity now covers all the conditions which were first sought above for a real community of cognition. As a family tie it contains a lively interest in all points, however different they may be with regard to its progress; as an identical type of organization it also determines the identity of the position vis-à-vis nature and the significance of the organic signs; and in that it is determined by language it subordinates personal particularity to that of the community in such a way that it cannot be an impediment to the community.

§ 180 We must admittedly posit language as a given, but under these circumstances it is only a minimum and only comes into being through the process of the function. Everything achieved there passes into language and we can reduce the whole of its results to the idea of language formation.

§ 181 Here too the mass and representative character in general proceed from the commerce in which the people engages, while the gradation of the various spheres and the [overall] classical qualities proceed from its scholars.

§ 182 Thus, as long as cognition is produced, language must also be produced (and not merely used). The closure of language in material terms presupposes that knowledge, too, has reached a point of closure, for as new opinions come into being, they also have a formative effect on language. Formal closure must be the grounds for the cessation of [acts of] combination and for the mechanization of thought, pulled by the strings of language.

§ 183 Hence the freer and less closed off language is, the more personal individuality comes to the fore in a nation; the more it is controlled, the less this is the case.

§ 184 Community amongst several national spheres of knowledge comes about because of natural frontier traffic amongst individuals and is epitomized by a mixture of languages that is local but extends over all subjects, which the force of nationality must oppose from the center and seek to repress. The predominant passivity of one nationality will express itself through the predominant influence of the other. This same effect need not necessarily arise from the skillfulness of the absorbing nation and its higher tendency to balance out diverse spheres, as long as nationality is a lively force. However, such a nation will have other ways of fighting back.

§ 185 This tendency to bring national particularity comparatively to consciousness gives rise to a community of translation, which can, however, also have a detrimental effect on the character of a language. As far as the purity of the type is concerned, it is a matter of indifference whether one imitates a contemporary foreign language or a dead foreign language.

§ 186 Finally, community comes about because each nation, regarded as a person, also contains something fragmentary and each one elaborates certain domains of knowledge but remains backward in others. Hence each people takes refuge with the people who represent virtuosity in a particular domain, but must take their own individual characteristics with them. This relationship of dependency is epitomized by linguistic mixtures in terminology. This is less influential the more empirical and individual the object, and more so, the more speculative it is.

Closing remarks on nationality

§ 187 A critical discipline which would be the equivalent of politics does not exist. Unity of form is insufficiently obvious. A far higher exercise would be that of comparing the various national systems of knowledge, from a position above all individual speculation and for this very reason purely critical in nature, but for the time being that is out of the question.

§ 188 A technical discipline which applies to the organization of the community is that of *didactics*. It deserves to be dealt with in a broader sense and on a bigger scale, and carried through to a conclusion with constant reference to the particularity of a given people through all forms of communication.

§ 189 Considering the linguistic aspect, however, the technical discipline of *hermeneutics* arises from the fact that any speech is only valid as an objective depiction to the extent that it is taken from language and can be made sense of by language, but on the other hand only comes into being as the action of an individual, and as such, even if it is analytical with regard to content, nevertheless carries something of free synthesis within it, derived from its less essential elements. The balancing out of the two moments turns understanding and interpretation into art.

§ 190 The critical discipline in this domain is that of *grammar*. Even absolute grammar is critical because of the way in which expression is linked to thought. Even the best that has been achieved on this subject is merely an honorable beginning, primarily because of the obscurity which still surrounds the physiological aspect. For this very reason individual, descriptive grammar still wavers between the mechanical approach and that of arbitrary hypothesis. For the time being any approach to absolute grammar is only to be found in comparative studies, which need to be the more brilliant, the more one considers national character as a whole.

§ 191 Peoples are also mortal if considered as persons; there appears to be no intrinsic reason for this, since the physical side is always reproduced. A people may die, however, partly if its own structures become obsolete because it did not have the strength to transform them in accordance with changing circumstances and levels of formation. For then it will not have the strength to improve matters by radical, violent change either. Or else it may die if a level of formation comes about – either for the whole species or for the particular domain with which it enjoys a lively commerce – where, by virtue of its nature, it is out of place.[96]

General prefatory remarks,[97] concerning the ethical forms related to the particular side of both functions

§ 192 Since the community of states and of linguistic domains starts with a community of individuals, then even if this is only brought about through

[96] *Marginal addition 1816:* Thursday. 1. Addendum on personality of different peoples. The necessity of death. Political and literary [death] not simultaneous. Euthanasia. Continued existence of some peoples in others. (Community with posterity, which only becomes real at the end, belongs here.)
[97] *Marginal addition 1816:* Thursday 2. Comparison of individual forms with universal ones. The boundaries seem impossible to determine, except that if one takes a certain distance the very issue seems to be non-existent. If the church is dependent on the state, it is not yet properly separated; if sociability seeks to be quite general, it does not yet constitute content.
It is not easy to draw dividing lines between them, either. It cannot be done through formative and symbolizing activity. For the church also needs formative activity, and sociability also needs cognitive activity. The finest aspect of sociability is the display of symbolizing activities, wit etc. Levels of formation, as far as the church is concerned, are only external boundaries in the broadest sense, whereas for sociability they are internal ones and what is qualitative is the external boundary, whereas for the church it is only an internal one.

exchange transactions, we must presuppose, given the original division of languages, the existence of a way of making oneself understood, which is only to be found in gesture, as the direct expression of feeling. This leads us to presuppose the same sort of schematism extending beyond the nation.

§ 193 But just as often community proceeds directly from the interests of free internal sociability, without any significant interest in exchange, from the desire, that is, to perceive intuitively the particularity of others and allow the intuition of one's own. There is a corresponding and similar drive to depict and understand religion, although here, at any rate, we must presuppose an original identity of feeling as the basis of trust.

§ 194 It is clear, then, that both spheres strive to go beyond national unity; the unity of nature, however, through which they are bound together and which determines their scope, cannot generally be indicated, since it is not the unity of the human races.

§ 194b It is evident that they do have a boundary in the same way that there are peoples among whom there is no community of individuals, where, on the contrary, each individual is regarded as an enemy.

§ 195 One might take the view that actually both merely represent the original orientation of the individual against the totality of persons, and that they are externally checked rather than internally self-limiting.

On the church[98]

§ 196 Even if individual churches have an urge to spread [their message] indefinitely, it is nevertheless clear that they lose their own particular character in many respects and can only enjoy a productive and reproductive life if they remain within a certain mass; this mass, however, certainly cannot be determined by unity of race.

§ 197 If individual churches do not go beyond the limits of national unity, that is partly because they have not properly detached themselves from the state (the Jews, who made a naturalized citizen of everyone who professed their faith, represent an extreme here), partly because the force with which they spread their message was weak from the beginning.

One could say that the church is orientated towards intensive progress and its activity is, incidentally, symbolizing, while sociability is orientated towards extensive progress and its activity is, incidentally, formative.

[98] *Marginal note 1827:* N.B. In 1824 I placed free sociability before the church.

§ 198 The state of religion found in the horde, usually known as the patriarchal state, only ever passes over into the organized state, that of the church, once an opposition has been awakened, namely between clergy and laity, who stand partly in the same relationship as scholars to public, and partly as authorities to subjects.[99]

§ 199 When the religious institutions which grow up out of this opposition also appear to be dependent on the state, we should assess this in the same way as in § 170 and 171.

§ 200 As a unity of religion develops into a church, it also acquires an artistic system.

§ 201 It always proves impossible to transfer the character of an artistic system into the domain of another religion;[100] the most strenuous endeavors yield only lifeless results; whereas the poetry of a foreign people who nevertheless belong to the same religious unity can be appropriated quickly and easily.

§ 202 We must therefore posit, as something given by nature, several schematisms of feeling which are particular to great masses.

§ 203 The differences between them are rooted in the relationship between the four different relations of cognition, in such a way that any predominance of the mathematical and transcendental sides over each other denotes merely the degree to which feeling has been, or may be, ethicized and to which it can be corrupted if it is detached from reality; the question remains, however, whether the physical is placed under the power of the ethical or whether, conversely, this serves to distinguish between the two main classes of religious character.[101]

§ 204 Proceeding in another direction, we can make a distinction which rests on temperamental opposition; admittedly, since unity of religion even goes far beyond any national unity, such a formula must first be considerably intensified.

---

[99] *Marginal addition 1816:* In the patriarchal state what is definite is unconscious. Similar things exist alongside one another more than because of one another. The hierarchical state develops by means of *revelation* (analogy with state and knowledge), where what is definite first comes to consciousness. – Opposition, with its content, can develop simultaneously on a number of points, which appears to be the case in most mythological religions. – A revelation cannot be accepted unless it truly expresses the religious consciousness of a mass. Thus every revelation which has entered history is also true, if imperfect.

[100] *Corrected from:* nationality.

[101] *Marginal addition 1816:* Ethical and physical religion stand in the same relation as Fate and Providence. What is deficient in each is the lesser extent to which the other element has been raised to the power of the religious principle.

Note. Indian = phlegmatic; Greek = sanguine; Jewish = choleric; Christian = melancholic?

§ 205 Similarity of type is originally posited in the homogeneous mass, even if in an undeveloped form. People who are in spatial contact with one another are attracted to one another as homogeneous beings, and their community comes entirely under the [general] character and extent of the horde.

§ 206 It is just as possible for the genesis of the church to be analogous to the genesis of the state as for it to be straightforward democracy, but then it has a less powerful life force which is revealed partly by the incomplete way in which it breaks free of the state and partly by a greater readiness to merge with similar systems so that its own pure particularity is not disclosed.

§ 207 It is also partly analogous to the genesis of the state from an idea holding sway within an individual, which is actually the content of the concept of revelation, although this presupposes that the type is already present in the mass – since otherwise revelation would find no answering faith – and also, indeed, that the lineaments of the ecclesiastical opposition have also already been laid down and pre-formed.[102]

§ 208 This may also apply to the genesis of a new church in a region where there are obsolete churches in a state of decline.

§ 209 The essence of the church lies in organic unification of a mass of people of the same type for the purposes of subjective activity of the cognitive function under the opposition of clergy and laity.

§ 210 There is a negative view of the church, analogous to that of the state, which suggests that it is merely an institution devoted to the repression of the passions. In part, however, this can only be achieved to the extent that a person is in possession of the religious principle, and, in part, it is not then necessary to have the church for this purpose.

§ 211 There is also an excessively positive view which posits the church as the absolute ethical community and subordinates both state and knowledge to it. Such a view can only prove its worth historically in a period

---

[102] *Marginal addition 1816:* Perfect revelations are accepted at higher formative levels. This naturally calls forth an opposition.

It cannot be immoral in itself to defend the old ways, even if one is already obliged to resist the new principle which is struggling to emerge; on the contrary these are natural and necessary states. – In the same way early acceptance can be immoral. – The only thing which is downright immoral is to deal with the issue by invoking a principle which is foreign to it.

when the tendency to community of peoples, which also proceeds from religion, predominates strongly over the tendency to restriction on grounds
of nationality.

§ 212 Given that in the church each person experiences religious feeling
not merely as something personal but also as something held in common,
each endeavors to transmit the way he is affected to other people and
to share in depiction of the way they are affected in his turn. All the
gradations of the ecclesiastical opposition are merely various spheres and
forms in which this takes place.

§ 213 Just as all knowledge can be reduced to language, so all the actions
of subjective cognition can be reduced to art. The highest tendency of the
church is the formation of a collection of art treasures which enables each
person to form his own feeling and in which each can deposit his own
finest feelings and the free depictions of how he feels, just as it enables each
person whose depictive production does not keep pace with his feeling to
appropriate the depictions of others.

§ 214 It is not possible here even to strive towards totality unless both
forms of art are present: the one which generates permanent works of art
and the one which produces ephemeral ones.

§ 215 To the extent that the collection of art treasures forms a mass which
has real existence it is accessible to anyone at any time. Depiction which
takes ephemeral forms, however, requires the assembly of a group which
expresses and nurtures common life; it is for this reason that a particular
mode of public worship [*Cultus*] is added to [the life of] the church.

§ 216 By the same analogy, just as there is much that is in the church but
not in public worship, we may also judge there to be much that belongs
in the domain of art which is not in the religious style.

§ 217 Among the ancients it was not so much a matter of religious and
profane styles as public and private ones, and all public exhibitions were
more or less religious in character. Thus it was only at a late stage that
the two diverged.[103]

§ 218 There is a distinction in feeling that can be made in thought, though
the two cannot be divided in reality, because each is a measure of the other
and the two interact: a distinction, that is, between correctness of feeling

[103] *Marginal addition 1816:* In ethical religions there is greater divergence between extensive and
intensive progress, and for this reason a sharper division between church and free sociability also;
in physical religions both occur to a lesser extent.

on the one hand, inasmuch as the effect of a single sensory orientation can be correctly grasped in relation to the totality of the sensory person, and its morality on the other, the fact that the emotion experienced by the sensory person is itself related only to the moral person; in depiction, however, the two diverge to a much greater extent. Where there is greater emphasis in depiction on the moral aspect, that is religious, and where there is greater emphasis on correctness [of feeling], that is profane.

§ 219 The two are bound up together to such an extent, however, that any individually profane element may appear as material in religious depiction, and anything profane, to the extent that it is in fact irreligious, could not even belong in the domain of art.

§ 220 In high religious style the particularity of the person engaged in depiction diminishes in importance; in depicting he is merely the organ and representative of the church; for his depiction must be as objective as possible for the whole domain of the definite religious type.

§ 221 In private religious depictions, representing the church in the family, particularity comes to the fore somewhat more, since here the intention is for the ecclesiastical type to appear modified specifically by the character of the family.

§ 222 In the profane style personal particularity ought to come right to the fore while the part played by the ecclesiastical type is almost purely passive – that of a boundary which may not be exceeded.

§ 223 This is also the reason why in the great modern forms of religion, in the high ecclesiastical style, nationality hardly comes to the fore, if at all, compared with the profane style, where it is dominant.

§ 224 Since correctness of feeling rests on the equilibrium of the sense-functions and this is the very thing that brings forth beauty, whilst equilibrium is firmly, and solely, rooted in ethicization, it is evident that it is beauty alone, the objective of the profane style, which is also the objective of the religious one.

§ 225 Where there is a plurality of natural religions existing alongside one another in an originally peaceful relationship, they are positively likely to borrow from one another, for what is only individually different, that is, in terms of form, is readily viewed as materially different, that is, as containing real connections which are not present in the others; to a very great extent this is the reason for the monstrous form which most mythological religions acquire over time.

93

§ 226 The hostile relationship (intolerance) which is to be found both in the coexistence of natural religions and rational ones, and also where a plurality of rational religions coexist, is too widespread to be attributed to accidental causes; on the contrary, we must attempt to comprehend it as something occasioned by the very formation of these forms, something which has taken a wrong direction as a result of misunderstanding.

§ 227 In natural religions, self-consciousness stands predominantly under the power of necessity, whereas in rational religions it stands under the power of freedom. Thus here the opposition is offensive on the part of freedom but only defensive on the part of necessity, for the former must endeavor to free nature from the mere appearance of unification with reason, whereas the latter is able to subsume the appearance of freedom under the concept of necessity. The fact that external force emerges first on the defensive side arises from natural religion having never yet completely detached itself from the state.[104]

§ 228 Since history indicates that rational religions are to be regarded as a progression in religious formation, the hostile relationship ends with natural religion being absorbed into rational religion, depending on how far the latter is able to appropriate material belonging to the former, even whilst taking the route of convincing [its audience] by proselytizing.

§ 229 Since, in rational religions, the feeling of identity must predominate over any feeling of difference (since everything is trivial by comparison with the feeling of the unity of the absolute as agent in nature), individual difference is very easily misunderstood and considered to be a consequence of error;[105] hence there is a hostile relationship here which, however, can appear in the form of external force only where crudeness has become deeply ingrained.

§ 230 The great modern forms of rational religion observe a process which is exactly the opposite of natural religion in that over time they split into small, individual forms by reason of subordinate oppositions. Individual variations are very naturally misunderstood here, and are regarded as differences in the degree of perfection. Now since this split proceeds from an earlier state of unity, one party appears to the other to be clinging

---

[104] *Marginal addition 1816:* It is natural that those who want to disseminate a higher religion must also disseminate a higher level of development. It is for this reason that mission only genuinely flourishes where true colonization has taken place.

[105] Consequence of error. *Before this, crossed out:* varying degrees of perfection.

on to some antiquated imperfection or tearing one part away from the whole; positive hostility now lies with the second party.

§ 231 Comparative intuitive understanding of particular churches and the pinpointing of their individual differences is a matter for the critical discipline which we normally call the philosophy of religion, just as the technical discipline of practical theology will instruct us how best to deal with the ecclesiastical opposition in each individual church.

§ 232 Deduction of the cycle of the arts and depiction of the essence of the various art forms is a matter for the critical discipline which we now call aesthetics; in just the same way the techniques [which underpin] each kind of art teach us how best to deal with both the ideal aspect and the organic one for individual production.

On free sociability

§ 233 It is true that the community [created by] communication of what has been appropriated cannot be directly realized, not even in the relationship of the individual to the totality; its determining principle is, however, the most difficult to comprehend. For it goes well beyond nationality and the church, even if it becomes weaker with distance, and on the other hand it does not even need the family to maintain it, in that it also goes directly from individual to individual – in the former case in *hospitality*, and in the latter, in *friendship*.

§ 234 The external boundary of hospitality is set only where that urge towards the indefinite is checked by a general state of hostility.

§ 235[106] The plurality of the spheres can only become definite here by means of the plurality of formative levels; just as experience demonstrates that it is easier for someone to associate with someone who is at the same formative level but from a foreign nation than with someone from the same nation but at a different formative level.

§ 236 The fact that the formative levels are not sharply delineated but that one merges into the next is only one aspect of the matter, for seen from the other side they are separated in a subordinate sense in the same way as the various powers of organic life, each of which develops a new system, e.g. not yet of age and sexually mature, perceiving and constructing, natural in form and ethicizing, etc.

---

[106] *Marginal note 1827:* The general idea of formative levels has its basis in the ladder of development.

§ 237 The variety of the formative levels is the content of the moral concept of *class*, and identity within a class closes off the sphere of free sociability.

§ 238[107] Free sociability only appears as a separate organization by virtue of the fact that it is completely separate in this from the state. For the state can only establish [a notion of] class which relies on external distinguishing characteristics, which can very often be present in an individual who does not possess the necessary internal qualifications. Free sociability, on the other hand, dies away as soon as it attempts to organize itself according to external characteristics.

§ 239 Even if the relationship of the various formative levels in the ethical process is altogether that of a more and a less, each one is nevertheless of equal value as a sphere of free sociability in itself, and its perfection depends only on how much genuine intuition and pure communication develop from it.

§ 240 The identity of the type which runs through all the activities of the formative function and is defined by the character of a particular formative level or class, is *custom*. Every real, genuine custom is therefore as good as any other.[108]

§ 241 The intensity with which a custom emerges, i.e. with which each individual reveals his particularity only in this type and at the particular level that gives expression to its dignity, is the *tone* of that society.

§ 242 Good tone is therefore the greatest possible freedom of the individual under the power of the type, and the pure expression of a level that is neither lowered nor raised in an affected way; in all cases the opposite is bad tone.

§ 243 The object to be communicated is not only the totality of formed things but also the lively movement – whether gymnastic or dialectic – of the inborn organs.

§ 244 *Art* is either present in all formed things as their accident, or else they have their own system of artistic productions, whether their own or appropriated, which is to be found in the duplication of the religious and profane styles.

§ 245 Within this whole compass, therefore, free sociability is necessarily bound to the house, and the host is predominantly the one who gives; the

---

[107] *Marginal note 1827:* The more political it makes everything, the more it belies its own character.
[108] *Marginal note 1827:* Courtly custom, worldly custom, popular custom.
  1. Custom, 2. tone, 3. play, 4, art.

guests, placed outside the totality of their particular spheres, are those who receive and stand under his power.

§ 246 When free sociability dissociates itself from the house and becomes a kind of public life, then crudeness arises on the one hand, due to the absence of the existing artistic mass, and one-sidedness on the other, due to the loss of relations with the totality of a particular life; this can only be put right if a whole cycle of such connections develops, which gives rise, in appearance, to a greater style, although actually there is inner decay.

§ 247 Free sociability can only exist inasmuch as personal particularity stands out from the mass. On the whole this tendency is present, however, and so early on something analogous develops which stands in the same relation to it as the horde does to the state, where particularity held in common is depicted only in existence side by side.

§ 248 If the process which develops possession is well advanced while the process which develops property lags disproportionately behind, then besides common particularity the only thing to be exhibited is personal possession, so that the dominant element in free sociability is magnificence, which is a state of sickness.

§ 249 If the depiction of intellectual skills goes beyond formless speech, it must be brought [within the scope of] a particular form of mutual intrusion, which gives rise to the concept of *play*. The morality of play consists in the fact that it merely provides a cohesive form for a rich development of intellectual activities, the more varied, the better. The more the form becomes a mechanism and free activity can manifest itself only in what is trivial and random, such as cardplaying, the less moral play is.

§ 250 Since what is particular also features, in a subordinate capacity, in the actions of the opposing character, and the organs can be intuitively perceived in all activities, even those of the opposing functions, there is nothing that could not be material for free sociability; in this respect it provides us with a measure of the relationship in a given mass between the various orientations of the ethical process.

§ 251 The concept of *friendship*, set out above, does not encompass everything which we normally associate with that name. During periods of state- or church-formation common particularity is at first to be found in a very few individuals who then attract one another; a connection of this kind has rather the character of a community of organs and is directed towards the formation of state or church. These heroic friendships, which are more in the nature of alliances, may occur again later, with regard to subordinated individuality or factions in church and state.

§ 252 A qualitative distinction may be drawn between friendship and free sociability in that the aspect of rigidity becomes insignificant and the psychological aspect assumes greater importance; also because in the former the cognition of individuality ought to arise more out of observation, in the latter it is presupposed by feeling and ought to prove itself in the same way.

§ 253 Friendships between individuals ought to develop from the commerce to which free sociability gives rise, and friendships between individuals ought in their turn to form the basis of sociable connections. The more both of these things hold true, the more lively the function.

§ 254 Friendship naturally flourishes at that time when the family recedes in importance and the individual is in transition between family, church, and state; it subsequently recedes in importance by comparison with these two life forms but for the same reasons emerges more strongly once again in old age. The fact that it diminishes in importance proves nothing against its moral dignity.

§ 255 Just as community among a number of states and churches proceeds from free sociability, so the various spheres of the latter enter into community by being at one in the state and the church.

§ 256 In the church public worship must be absolutely popular, uniting all the classes, and then the more religious interest predominates, the more social connections are formed on this basis, proceeding outward from public worship without being too precise about class boundaries.

§ 257 Every state must have institutions with which to unite the [different] classes, and the same will be true of these according to the level of political interest.

§ 258 It is clear from this that in every sphere beyond those of state and church the bond of sociability can only be a loose one. The possibility of extending sociability thus far lies on the one hand in the specific inclination of certain individuals to deepen their acquaintance with what is unfamiliar by means of direct intuition, and on the other in the fact that anyone who throws open his house ought not to exclude anyone who is brought to him as a result of external circumstances and who faces him with the proper receptiveness.

Conclusion

§ 259 In general, the inclination of every great moral person is to enter into community with the past and the future; such an inclination can admittedly only be realized through works of (science and?) art, but nevertheless proceeds just as often from free sociability and the state as from the scholarly association and the church.

§ 260 Where the inclination to work directly for posterity through art goes beyond mere instinct, it rests on intuition of antiquity preserved in this way, and at times where formation has been perfected each is conditional upon the other.

§ 261 The more instinctual the inclination, the more its products lie in the mass, as Egyptian and oriental architecture may be regarded, so to speak, as the latest stratum of the earth [to be laid down]. The more they float, one-sided, in the air and the light, the product of painting and printing, the less the life which is attempting to communicate itself will be complete from the point of view of reality.

§ 262 Only in the sequence and coexistence of the various great ethical individuals – and to understand this cycle is the eternal task of history – is human nature revealed; however, for that very reason, we are only able to regard even this, in our innermost feeling, as one individual form of existence of the ideal within the real.

Ethics 1812/13: Doctrine of virtue and doctrine of duties

Doctrine of virtue

I Introduction[1]

1 [2] The object of the doctrine of virtue is not directly the totality of reason as against the totality of nature, but reason in the human individual.

2 On the one hand, then, [it is] everything that is posited in the highest good, because reason cannot be present in any other way; on the other hand, however, it excludes everything that is a product; that is, not only formed external nature, but also the organism as something that has been formed; for it features here only as agent.

3 In passing, then: what about the difference between virtue and talent? From the point of view of the highest good, we would say: so much virtue equals so much talent, and vice versa. Not from the point of view of the doctrine of virtue, however. For the virtue of the one has a share in the talent of the other, i.e. of the morally formed individual.

4 If there should be anything to say about virtue, it must be both one thing and many things, so that it is a nonsensical question to ask which of

---

[1] *Marginal note*: See general introduction X.–XIII.

[2] *Marginal addition 1827b, headed '1827' by Schleiermacher:* First hour. Reference to Introduction. Difference between highest good and duty. – Life force and intelligence in personality conditional upon the form of human nature as a sexual one. a) Does this also hold true for priests in higher orders? – We can only answer in the affirmative if we do not wish to become entangled in contradictions. b) with reference to successiveness. Second hour. Relationship of virtue to the various ages of man. Organic skill as such. § 3.

Third hour. Relationship to the highest good in other respects. § 9 and 10. A doctrine of virtue posits multiplicity and in relation to the highest good we can elucidate the concept. Genesis not according to the highest good, 5–8. After connection with nature can be thought [out] in two ways, division according to what is manifold in nature. 11. 12.

the two it is. The only question which remains is, in what sense it is one thing and in what sense many.

5 We might say that it is one thing to the extent that the highest good is one thing, and many things to the extent that the highest good consists of diverse spheres.

6 This cannot be the case, however, partly because these four spheres have a common root in the family, which also forms one sphere, so that in virtue, by means of which the human being exists within a family, the other virtues, by means of which he exists in every other sphere, would become a single entity again.

7 Partly also because there is no sphere without cognition, none without an external property, none without free sociability and none without devout disposition, and so virtue cannot be something separate in each one, as opposed to virtue in any of the others.

8 The relationship to the highest good must rather be expressed in these two formulae: each sphere of the highest good requires all the virtues, each virtue runs through all the spheres of the highest good.

9 (Like 3, no doubt a corollary to 2.) In passing, this is the way to make sense of the question as to whether virtue is sufficient to generate the highest good. The question needs no answer if we are talking about the two at the level of the whole, for the highest good can only be produced by virtue in everyone; it is nonsensical, however, if we are talking about the two at the level of the individual, because no individual can possess the highest good.

10 The following formula is therefore preferable: is virtue sufficient to generate happiness, where happiness is to be understood as the individual's share in the highest good? The answer is no, to the extent that each sphere can give the individual more or less, in empirical terms, than he is able to strive for, so that [we must conclude] partly that virtue makes people unhappy, and partly that people can be happy without virtue. The answer to the question is yes, to the extent that man's share in the highest good actually consists in his feeling that it is coming into being, and feeling himself in this. The two answers are united in the following formula, properly understood: virtue determines whether one is worthy of happiness.

11 We could say, furthermore, that virtue is one thing to the extent that reason is one thing, and many things to the extent that nature, in which reason is to be found, is many things.

12 However, we may not divide virtue up according to the individual functions of nature, because reason rules in all of them to the same extent, nor according to the diverse complexions of nature in the individual, because in that case one would quickly arrive at infinite multiplicity from a state of oneness.

13 We can regard the relationship of reason to sensibility in virtue as being one and the same [*Einerleiheit*], for virtue is only perfect inasmuch as no inclination can be distinguished from it. But for that very reason the way in which the inclinations can be divided, considered per se, cannot be the respect in which virtue can be divided.

14 We can regard the relationship as a conflict and all virtue as struggle, therefore, because only in struggle does virtue come into being and progress; but virtue cannot be divided as what is in conflict with reason can be divided.

15 It is wrong, therefore, to consider virtue to be an inclination: as the ancients do in Aristotelian theory, where every inclination is a virtue, provided that this is in due measure, and as the moderns do in the theory of harmony, where virtue consists in the relationship of each inclination to all the others. Yet it is not possible to be specific about such measure nor about the exponent of such a relationship.

16 [3] We find grounds for division if, as reason and sensibility become one, we consider what is posited in reason and not in sensibility, and conversely, what is posited in sensibility and not in reason. The former is the ideal content, the latter the temporal form.

17 Virtue understood as the pure ideal content of action is *disposition*. Virtue understood as reason set into temporal form is *skill*. The two can never be entirely separated. Disposition without skill can only be imagined in a hypothetical moment, for otherwise it would not be a force but only reason at rest, merely an idea. Skill without disposition would either be purely sensory, or else its morality would reside in the person possessing the appropriate disposition, for whom this first person would be merely an organ.

---

[3] *Marginal addition 1827b:* To the extent that virtue is both one and many, on the one hand each individually determined thing is related to the All, while on the other each individual thing is opposed to the many. The latter is only the case once one has entered into time and space and for this reason the former [is true] only when an action is stirring into being, the latter disposition, the former skill. In any action the disposition is only right if its object is equated with the totality of what is moral, while the execution is correct when treatment in the object is right.

18 [4] Further grounds for division are to be found in the original form of life, which as an individual thing consists only in the opposition of taking-things-into-oneself and taking-things-out-of-oneself-and-putting-them-down. With regard to taking-things-into-oneself, virtue *recognizes*, in the other case, it *depicts*.

19 The two can never be entirely divided. For, because all action is based on a type, as an idea, the action cannot have an ideal content if the idea does not. And since all taking-things-into-oneself is intent upon depiction, because it is also feeling, the depiction must have an ideal content if the taking-things-into-oneself does.

20 There is a crossover between the two oppositions, however; disposition in cognition is *wisdom*, disposition in depiction is *love*.[5] Cognition set into temporal form is *prudence*, depiction set into temporal form is *steadfastness*.

21 By virtue of this crossover of oppositions all the terms are bound up together, and from an internal point of view one can say that where one virtue is, there they all are; in empirical terms, on the other hand, the one may of course be highly repressed while the other may be intensified to a level of exclusive virtuosity. The same is also true of the subdivisions which we must assume to be present in each virtue.

22 Thus we can say, where there is wisdom, there is love also, and vice versa; but the wisdom of one man may be greater than his love, and the prudence of another greater than his steadfastness.

23 On the other hand we would be able to say that a man's steadfastness was the measure of his love, and his prudence the measure of his wisdom, if all the actions of life which bore the same name formed a single sequence. Since this is not the case, however, one man may show more love

---

[4] *Marginal addition 1827b, crossed out:* The other opposition is reason posited in the life of the individual and action which proceeds from the individual life, the two elements of all action which belong together, but in which the force varies, like expansion and contraction. This opposition is not a precise one, for disposition is also to be found in expansion and skill in contraction.

[5] *Marginal addition 1827a:* 1. a) is *wisdom*, 1. b) is *love*. In reality, we do not find one without the other. But one can, however, imagine wisdom without love and they can also be found together in unequal proportion.

In wisdom we may posit what has been determined above, and no more. No skill. Emerging into opposition is no longer the province of wisdom. But where the germ of an action has no ideal content and what is individually willed contradicts what is willed in the whole, there we find folly. 1. b) is love. It does not seem to be so at first because of self-love. But that is only moral to the extent that one thinks of reason and nature as not yet united.

in establishing new relationships than steadfastness in pursuing the old ones.

24 This classification provides absolutely no point of comparison with those depictions which attempt to construct a multitude of virtues empirically, without deducing any kind of cycle, but only with those which are intent on [discovering] such a cycle.

25 In the classification of antiquity, φρόνησις coincides with our wisdom per se, ἀνδρεία with our steadfastness, since the ancients themselves demand some relationship to an ideal in order to achieve it; σωφροσύνη coincides with our prudence, because it is not used of even a primitive comprehension of something new, but only of something that can be brought into definite connection with an earlier occurrence, hence a rightness which proves itself over time; finally διχαιοσύνη coincides with our love, because for them even the formation of what was ancient was also an element in διχαιοσύνη and all the other ethical forms stood under the power of the state, whereas we, given the greater autonomy of each form, need to find a term which does not remind us of one any more than it does of the other.

26 In modern Christian classification, charity is the equivalent of our love, and faith of our wisdom, given that the certainty of the conviction is the most important thing here, and faith also relates to what was originally there at the beginning. Since, however, from the religious point of view the issue is only one of principle and anything quantitative diminishes in importance, virtue-as-skill is not depicted at all in this triad, but only the general principle of becoming external, which is to be found in the fact that, even though the individual is not certain of his success, the idea will nevertheless certainly be realized; and that is hope.

[On virtue as disposition]

Wisdom

1 Wisdom is that quality by virtue of which all human action acquires an ideal content.

2 What strikes us immediately is the relative difference between feeling and knowledge. Neither can have an ideal content without the other, but

each is a different kind of activity, not only because there is difference at the level of the organic; on the contrary, the difference arises only when reason is united with the organism, since it is precisely in animal life that intuition and feeling do not really diverge.

3 The wisdom of feeling, therefore, consists in the fact that for the human being nothing is pleasure or unpleasure except by virtue of its relation to the ideal.

4 Since, however, there are and must necessarily be purely organic affects within the human being, this means only that what is animal can never constitute a whole action, but is only one element in it, i.e. no reaction proceeds from the purely animal but, on the contrary, what is animal must first be reduced to something intellectual.

5 Since, moreover, at every moment it is not just the animal side but also the intellectual one which is affected, while the state [experienced] at any moment is a single one, the pleasure or unpleasure which depicts this unity is also predominantly determined by the intellect.

6 Thus the dictum that the wise man is able to transcend pain cannot be understood to mean that inhibiting organic affects are not felt as unpleasure, the same being true of pleasure; for in itself true apathy would only be a negation in the organism and hence also in the ethical process; on the contrary, [what it means is] that neither of the two constitutes a complete state in itself.

7 The direct organic expression of feeling is only an annex of the same and cannot be regarded as an activity in its own right; that is why it is situated in the vicinity of what is involuntary.

8 The composite depiction of feeling as a combination, both in art and in life, constitutes an action in its own right, however, since the two are independent of each other in the moment, given that equally strong emotions may produce very different depictions (different also in degree) while similar depictions may be rooted in very different affects.

9 Thus the wisdom of feeling splits into *contemplative* wisdom, which is concerned with affects in the manner described above, and *imaginative* wisdom, which produces the types required for depictive combinations.[6]

---

[6] *Marginal addition 1827b:* Contemplation is reverence and serenity. Imagination is enthusiasm and comfortableness. The general expression for wisdom of feeling is devoutness. Its concentration or expansion are reverence and serenity. The two may be interrelated or apart from one another. The influence of the various relationships on the organization of the common life.

The transition into comprehension is devoutness (contemplation); the transition into depiction is enthusiasm (imagination).[7]

10 The one cannot exist without the other; for depiction can express no existence other than what is posited through the way one is affected, and the latter cannot stand to the power of the moral without also giving shape to a moral combination.[8]

11 The imaginative side thus consists in the fact that no type of depiction can be generated which does not have an ideal content. Here, too, it is a matter of correctly grasping the *unity* of the depiction, for elements of this sort clearly exist. Now, this unity will consist in relatedness to feeling, taken on its own terms, as action. To the extent that what is to be depicted is posited only as an element and is indirectly related to an ideal, even sensory elements can be imagined in a moral way.[9]

[*Inserted para. numbered 18.*] Everything jocular in life and art seems to be imagined more in a sensory way than an ideal one, and yet we consider it an exaggeration to reject it completely as something immoral. It is in fact immoral, however, when it is not imagined in full consciousness of the fact that it is only a subordinate element of something greater. That is why we cannot resist feelings of disdain when something whole in life is composed only of such elements.[10]

12 The wisdom of knowledge consists in the fact that nothing is thought except with an ideal content.

13 Here we may distinguish between the process which is predominantly analytical in character and the one which is predominantly synthetic. In the former synthesis is posited as something already complete and activity therefore turns away from it; its true object is what is individual, subsumed under the whole, and what is particular, subsumed under the universal.

---

[7] *Marginal addition 1827a:* On the side of feeling we find serenity and devoutness as comprehending [qualities], (the former extensive, the latter intensive); and comfortableness and enthusiasm as depictive [qualities].
Serenity is only right if it does no harm to devoutness and vice versa. Comfortableness and enthusiasm may either be purely receptive (when enthusiasm becomes reverence), or speculative; they may be found on the side of art or of life.

[8] *Marginal addition 1827b:* A general expression for wisdom of thought is reasonableness. Relationship of reasonableness to devoutness.

[9] *Marginal addition 1827b:* The transition to comprehension is profundity. The transition to depiction is (astuteness?), very important, as in every construction.

[10] *In the ms. this § has another section, marked with the number 18, but with the observation* ad 11.

In the latter synthesis is set as the task, and love and activity therefore turn away from the particular, which is actually used only as a point of departure, towards it.[11]

14[12] The former aspect, the *intuitive*, and the latter, the *speculative*, are different, since one is not a measure of the other, but inseparable, since each process rests on the other, in the sense that what is particular is only fixed by subsuming it, so that only to that extent can one use it as a starting-point, while every concept under which something can be subsumed is only produced by synthesis.

---

[11] *Marginal addition 1827a:* Wisdom in thought. There are double grounds for division: 1. Everything is an interrelation of unity and multiplicity. Thus in the process as well: production of unity from multiplicity, combination = profundity; generation of multiplicity from unity, analysis = astuteness; 2. Each is perfect if it contains a) the identity of the ideal and the real, = truth; b) if it contains the essence of reason depicted in concepts, = clarity.

[12] *Marginal addition 1827a, against §§ 13–17: Note.* This is the boundary between wisdom and prudence. In clarity there is something which can always be regarded as skill. However, this is also connected to the fact that every combination in fact goes back to an earlier one. But this is not just a matter of interpretation – whether profound or astute – but of what was there originally. Now and then we are aware of having some truth in us, which is not clear in itself. Human beings are unclear from the very beginning. For before the real utterances of reason χαὶ ἐξοχήν a system of concepts is already given. Only by means of this system can reason depict itself in consciousness (this is why we usually say that all higher thinking is merely figurative), and the greater or lesser degree to which reason seizes hold of this organ is relatively easy to separate from truth itself.

Profundity is the ideal post-construction of a given synthesis on the basis of the presuppositions or principles of that synthesis; a sense of what is lying in the depths and is now coming to the surface. But there is an early form of unconscious profundity, which brings definite manifoldness into what is chaotic.

Astuteness is clear per se. Only when we coordinate it with wit do we appear to pay more attention to the random and arbitrary elements, to what is not true.

Such ἀρεταί διανοητιχαί deserve to be ranked as virtues just as much as the sociable ones. They are just as much a matter of free will except where physiological disorder is concerned; but physiological defects exercise an influence over the other virtues, too.

The distinction between the general domain and a narrower one, here that of science, is to be found in all the others in just the same way.

Everything which plays a part in cognition is realized by means of all of them together. Profundity ensures that those things are thought which are without reason-content; astuteness leads from one thing to another across the whole surface and hence ensures completeness. Clarity is the guarantee of communication.

Error is unavoidable because clarity can never be perfect. It is always the case that imperfection is not merely lack of knowledge, but the mingling of insight with error. Error is not sinful when doubt accompanies conviction, for then internal truth is kept holy and the progress of cognition is not inhibited. It is sinful when the same conviction accompanies error, for then internal truth is profaned and progression is inhibited. It is also sinful when ideas which merely articulate what relates to sensory interest are regarded as objective ones which describe the essence of things.

15 Both these things, intuition and speculation, are not to be posited strictly and exclusively in the domain of science, [for] speculative elements, too, are to be found everywhere in life. It is only that anyone who produces in such a fragmentary way must know that what he produces cannot in itself have the same validity.

16 The intuitive stands in the same relation to the speculative as the contemplative to the imaginative, because of the spontaneity which predominates in these last terms. The intuitive also stands in the same relation to the imaginative as the contemplative does to the speculative; for one can only speculate as one has contemplated, and can only imagine what has been in one's intuition.

17 In every moral sphere man is only religious by virtue of the contemplative, otherwise for all his activity he is merely isolated, not a part of the whole; in each he only acts for himself by virtue of the imaginative, for otherwise he is merely the organ of the person in whom the type of the action was conceived; in each he is only sure by virtue of the intuitive, for without intuition we can only cast round at random; and in each he can only further progress by virtue of the speculative, because the self-cognition of every whole is only in the process of becoming and so synthesis is always given up.

18 [*Follows §11.*]

19 In the domain of the intuitive there is much that is subsumed not under genuinely objective forms of thinking, but under subjective ones. For example, all concepts relating to the properties of things, which only articulate impressions. This is not wrong, provided that it is posited not as cognition of the being of things, but as cognition of the subjective sphere and hence as the relation of things. Otherwise the transition from a state analogous to the animal one into one of genuine knowledge would have to be something immoral. What is immoral, however, is to consider this to be objective.

20 The speculative, as it emerges out of the contemplative, may indeed be in error, but the error is not an immoral one. If, however, instead of speculating outwards from the pure feeling of the state of a sphere, someone is directed by the feeling of their own position in that sphere or their relationship to other people in the same sphere, only then is the basis [of such speculation] egoistical and the error is a sinful one.

Love[13]

1 Love[14] is reason which wants to become soul, the entering of reason into the organic process, in the same way as the entering of matter into the organic process is a wanting to become body.

[13] *Marginal addition 1827b, against § 18, dated by Schleiermacher "1827":* Love firstly presupposes individuation; it is one individual coming out of himself and moving towards other individuals, and can be partly determined by the way intelligence is determined in the other, partly won by the relationship of their two natures. With regard to intelligence, we have only to distinguish the developmental process, so that love is either equal or unequal. With regard to nature, as long as we presuppose identity, what we have to distinguish is whether the two belong to the same [category of] close determination or not. The former is bound, the latter free.

[14] *Marginal material 1827a, pp. 11–13:*
Love.
Love may be imprudent and not steadfast, but it remains love nevertheless. – It cannot be unwise, however, without coming into conflict with its own nature. For it is only unwise when its object is loved more or less than is appropriate to its position within the totality. It follows from this that there can be nothing in love that is not posited in wisdom. Conversely, for this reason we also say that love underlies all the operations of wisdom. Wisdom is the activity of reason in nature, but more abstracted from nature's state of not-yet-being-unified, while love is more activity upon nature, but more abstracted from its already-having-been-unified.
Love is reason which wants to be soul: corresponding to this we find matter wanting to be love. This is why the physical and ethical views of love are so often confused and mixed up. Life is love and creation is love.
From the ethical point of view, then, reason must be the active, loving principle, nature the passive, loved one. This would appear to demolish the schema of "love for God," and yet the exposition of our concept ought to express the Christian basis of our philosophy. The solution is this: just as there is no exclusively fulfilling consciousness of God, neither is there any exclusively fulfilling urge towards God. Love for nature is only ethical if understood as love for God, love for God is only true if understood as love for nature.
Self-love gives rise to an awkward dilemma. If it is not a virtue, then no other kind of love is a virtue either, because they all follow on from self-love. (Parental love, sexual love, love of one's country.) If it is a virtue, then all the other kinds are only virtues inasmuch as they belong to it and everything that is most noble appears to be lost. This can only be resolved by superseding the dilemma. Self-love is only moral to the extent that it encompasses all the other kinds of love; every other kind is only true to the extent that it incorporates self-love.
If reason loves and nature is loved we could believe that there is no love that is directed upward. If nature loves (as appears to be the case, since much love is conditioned by a natural relation; Platonic formula states that what is neither good nor bad loves the good –) there could be no love that is directed downward. But what loves is always the element of reason already inherent in nature.
This leads us to the division between equal and unequal love, free and bound love. The one relates to the relationship of reason in those who are united in love, the other to the relationship of nature in them. It is therefore exhaustive.
The opposition is only a relative one, as is always the case. Equal love (civic) was originally unequal (despot[ism], usurpation), unequal love (parents and children) turns into an equal kind. The freest kind of love (friendship, sexual love) develops out of the bound kind (identity of peoples and of formation). Bound love (civic) develops out of the free inclination of a number of tribes, etc.
Bound, equal love is *justice*. Schema of all virtues to the ancients, because for them everything is absorbed into the state. To us it is not limited to the state but [extends to] all the concentric and intersecting spheres of common life. To a certain extent it is something different in each domain, but to a certain extent it is the same in all of them. It is only this last which makes it a true virtue,

for otherwise one love will destroy the other. Anyone who was entirely just within his own country, but loved that country itself either too little or at the expense of the church or intellectual freedom, would not in fact be a just person.

If we attempt to divide the concept, there are first of all two elements to consider. One is the general interest in the common life, the other the specific interest in the definite object of the communities. Both are found in everyone to a varying extent. Community people without a [specific] interest mostly concern themselves with form and mechanism. The latter, however, is not in itself a virtue but arises only from a feeling of the inadequacy of personal existence, making no distinction between moral and arbitrary association. This latter is not what is meant by our concept. This division of these elements leads us to grasp only the relative inequality in equality in terms of a greater or lesser degree of activity in common life. – Common linguistic usage makes a different division, making selfishness the underlying notion and comprehending love only in negative terms. Hence honesty, fairness, righteousness; two things make it clear that this is the case. Firstly, these qualities can only be present in circumstances where there is literally a law or where one can be assumed to exist, in that they refer only to the possible difference between spirit and letter. Secondly from the fact that there is no analogous term for the virtue of the regent or legislator (where justice signifies only impartiality and we usually speak only of wisdom and mercy), because there can be no conflict here between common and private interests. – This leads us, however, to a more accurate division. For in the one case what is dominant is interest in the individuals who together form the whole; in the other, interest in the development of the whole. Justice is a spirit of community and impartiality (the latter is, however, only a negative expression for the second moment). In every domain justice is the lively movement of the two towards each other.

Bound unequal love is *care* on the one hand and *awe* on the other hand. Man's relationship to God, eternally unequal, can be characterized in the same way. In human relationships care consists of two moments: *releasing*, which is concerned with increasing equality, and *directive*, concerned with present inequality. Releasing care limits inequality. The positing of an age of maturity comes not from the children – and this is always the case – but from the parents. Maturity is present in the same way in our relationship to God, if only we regard the spirit as something revealed, the external law entirely entrusted to man; also in civic terms when the individual shares in the making of the law. Physical care should not be regarded as something that can be separate, but should only take place in relation to the spiritual [dimension]. Any distorted relationship between these two elements is immoral, however. If it is unconscious it is lovelessness, if conscious, then a diminishing of the releasing [element] is arrogant unscrupulousness, while a diminishing of the directive element is lethargic unscrupulousness. – Awe is *obedience* and *timidity*. Obedience is willingness which stems from a feeling for the dominant power of reason; it is not external, then, but a disposition, however it is neither justice nor wisdom. Timidity is the reluctance to have something about oneself which is contrary to the will of the superordinate party, though not with reference to any command which has been given but as an intimation, that is, something constructed by oneself, which is, however, only something reproduced.

Thus the directive care found in one must be proportionate to the obedience of the other, and the timidity of that other ought to be proportionate to the releasing care found in the first.

[1827b] Exactly this duplication of bound unequal [love] is also to be found in the establishment of a civic association, if it is the work of a minority.

[1827b] Free love encompasses both what is closest (friendship and marriage) and what is furthest away (mission etc.). Nothing is achieved at either extreme which is irresistible. – What is close goes back to something bound. It is therefore only a specific emanation of the spirit of community which dominates here. No definite circle could continue to exist if personal friendships did not occur within it. Why exactly this should be the case is difficult to bring clearly to consciousness. We ought to be able to judge what is far away by the same analogy. What is bound there is merely the unity of human nature. What is revealed in it is the general activity of reason, directed towards the whole, and thus it is not the same at all times. And so free love is whatever depicts the entering in of reason to the greatest extent.

Experience shows that in this domain there is always a great deal which has missed the mark, much that is mere appearance. We must be careful to distinguish here. We could think, moreover,

2 The result of love can never be anything other than what is posited in the concept of wisdom, when one abstracts, that is, from the quantitative; but love is reason in its action upon nature, just as wisdom is reason in its action in nature.

3 For this reason we need primarily to look at the variety in the relationship of reason to nature. Two grounds for division present themselves here. If we confront reason in itself as a system of ideas with nature or the real in itself, then in part each occasion when that system passes over into a series of individual thoughts already constitutes, in itself, the union of reason with nature, a definite relationship to the way in which what is manifold in nature develops over time; in part a passing over of this kind presupposes an organic connection with nature, because reason cannot bring this about from within itself. This therefore gives rise to one duplication: love orientated towards the way in which nature draws things towards herself in the form of consciousness, and love orientated towards organic unification, i.e. love that forms nature into an organ of reason.

that a person might possess morality entire, but without free love, and that for this reason it would not constitute virtue. ad 1. Confusion is nothing if not everywhere, that is, when the internal is not given to the external. The only difference is that purity can only be recognized here from the absence of other motives. Examples of the two extremes: the urge to discovery and sexual love. ad 2. We can prove that free love can nowhere be entirely absent because it is the *conditio sine qua non* of bound love. For example: there can be no love of Christianity (spirit of community) without a relationship to individual people, and there will always be differences between them, from which preeminent points emerge in the form of friendships. Friendship as a genuine relation is perhaps not to be found, but virtue also consists only in endeavor. If someone is lacking in free love in every respect then bound love will not gain a foothold either.

From here [we move on] to *love for inanimate nature*. Also characterized by irresistibility and inexplicability. Thus all beauty, all art [arises] when nature, loved for its own sake, is made the object of formative power. Here, too, whatever is special among the talents rests on the enhanced singling out of one individual thing from the general relationship of reason to nature. It is the general activity of reason which, in possession of a specially formed organism, becomes a preeminently special activity.

From here we can best [move on] to the opposition between equality and inequality. (Equality exists with diversity in marriage and friendship, inequality with similarity.)

Equality requires 1. in each person in general an activity, *participation*, and a passivity, openness, *receptivity*. Then also 2. that the activity of each person is conditional upon the approval of the other; perfection in love consists in such agreement being present of its own accord without resistance and without delicacy of feeling.

Inequality is dominant, without caprice or mannerism. This last can best be shown through art. *[1827b]* Unequal free [love] is only to be found in the relationship between teacher and pupil, which runs through all spheres, however. Higher term: either direction through attraction or self-surrender as a result of affection. Lower term: enthusiasm. Dangers of the spirit of the school. Imitation etc.

On inequality of sex and race. Both to be refuted.

4 If we confront reason in itself with nature in itself, moreover, we can see no other way of entering in than in the form of personality. Here there is a different relationship, however, between the reason which inhabits that person and the nature which forms that person, to that which obtains between the same reason and every other kind of nature, and between every other kind of reason and the same nature; on the other hand, nature which is not encompassed by the personality stands in the same relationship to all forms of reason. This gives rise to the second duplication, namely love which is differentiated through personality and love which is not differentiated in this way.

5 The two divisions cut across one another, so that we find cognition and formation both differentiated and undifferentiated.

6 Note. There is no conflict between the dictum that love is a relationship of reason to nature and the fact that a relationship between individual human beings is only love to the extent that it is directed towards reason. For if love is in search of cognition, human nature, i.e. nature united with reason, wants also to be recognized in this relationship, and there can be no formation other than formation for reason.

7 Note 2. The same thing is evident from the fact that we do not love most the people who are most reasonable; on the contrary, we love many people who are less advanced, more. Hence also, the kind of love which is the same towards everyone stands in the same relation to the kind which is different towards some people as consideration of individuality to abstraction from individuality. If the two differ in this, they must be one and the same because of the higher aspect, namely that nature is the object of both.

8 Note ad 4. Differentiated and undifferentiated love are not separated by the mass of nature. For 1. it is only in relative terms that personal existence is something exceptional; personal nature can also be animated from without, and then certainly by a number of people to the same extent. Not all love for human nature is differentiated, then. 2. Individual modifications of the organic functions are related to something exceptional in nature, not only what is individual in the complex of nature, indeed, but also what is individual in each one separately. For this reason even love for non-human nature is differentiated to a certain extent.

9 All love which is orientated towards what is individual is differentiated, whether cognitive or formative.

10 The same principal divisions appear here, then, as we found when considering the highest good: cognitive and formative, individual and universal; this is natural and is the reason why love counts as the principal and primal virtue where the practical orientation dominates, just as wisdom does where the theoretical orientation dominates.

11 Every instance where a number of people come together to form an association of equality has as its basis the feeling that the nature which each person brings with him could just as well be animated by any other person in the association, for himself, and vice versa; it therefore rests on an undifferentiated love.

12 *Note.* This is true also of free sociability, regardless of the fact that, there, individuality is really the material. We only seek the company of those people of whom we assume that they can excite us as we excite ourselves, and that this is mutual.[15]

13 It is obvious that in reality cognitive and formative love do not occur in isolation, since formation presupposes the right ideas in order to be able to make some connection with the present state. The drive to form external nature can only rest on the consciousness that cognition informs human nature; for otherwise it would not be moral.

14 The object of cognitive love is not concrete things which are there to be recognized but rather the nature which is the subject of consciousness. In this, however, cognitive love strives for an equilibrium between the intellectual and organic sides. Now in every individual there is some divergence from the general which disturbs this equilibrium, however. And thus cognitive love must also generate formative love; for all formation is the superseding of such divergence.

15 Individual love cannot be present in a single consciousness without universal love; for what is individual is in itself non-transferable; the urge can only be justified by experience of the identity which underlies difference, and experience of this kind is only possible through some activity of universal love.

16 Moreover, something that is later preserved by universal love is originally [the product of] individual love, owing its genesis to an individual (this is often the case with state and church) or a small association of like-minded people, so that the two are bound up together in a gradual transition.

---

[15] *Marginal note:* No lecture on Thursday.

17 Universal love is not [to be regarded as] moral in a single conscious-ness without individual love; for this activity exists in reason united with nature, and this can only be posited as the result of an individual love.

18 In terms of intension [*Intension*], however, the difference [between the two] is posited in every experience and can go so far that the other term is present only as the merest suggestion.

19 *Note.* The many virtues which we generally subsume under love can only be understood from the point of view of the opposition within the personality, or else they articulate only certain sensory impulses which have been overcome; in neither case do they posit anything particularly moral.

20 *Note.* The absence from the common vocabulary of appropriate terms for the moments we have put forward stems principally from the fact that selfish relationships naturally took possession of language at an earlier stage.

---

21 The quantitative difference between wisdom and love, as well as be-tween the individual moments of each in a given individual, is not quan-titative in terms of time, but in terms of orientation and predisposition, and is posited inside a person before any definite action, as it were, at the same time as their moral disposition; it forms the particular morality of each person, or his character.

On virtue as skill

22 If disposition is that quality which allows the unification of nature and reason to be produced at all, then moral skill is that quality which allows such unification to exist in a human being to a definite degree and to continue to develop outward in all essential directions.

23 Since skill is something which grows over time but disposition, strictly speaking, is not – on the contrary, if we think of it as coming into being, it must be thought of as coming into being complete, in a single moment – a greater or lesser degree of skill does not denote a more or less in terms of disposition, but a later or earlier point in its effectiveness, allowing for individual advance or withdrawal in a particular direction.

24 Disposition is quite simply the producing of skill, therefore, and skill is merely the organic, temporal existence of disposition.

25 By its very nature skill is something which continues to grow to the point of completeness, though, empirically speaking, this can never be given.

26 The concept of completeness lies in the fact that there is no activity or complex of activities which is rooted in sensibility or its desire to exist in its own right; on the contrary, each activity has its roots in reason.

27 The magnitude of the skill can be measured by the sequence of similar moral actions which takes place within a certain period of time while remaining uninterrupted by actions which posit a lack of virtue, thus where everything depends on the ultimate purpose of the unity of action.

28 Unity of action is confined within the identity of the concept and the impulse [which mark] its beginning, and the realization of the concept and satisfaction of the impulse [which mark] its end.

29 It is possible to regard every action, however, as being composed of an infinite number of similar actions, in that the concept only becomes more closely determined and broader in scope as it progresses, and an impulse may then also arise which is directed towards something which was not previously its goal.

30 Also because the purpose is originally determined by the state of the subject, the object and what lies between them, whereas in the course of the action all the moments change to a greater or lesser degree, so that the concept of purpose and the impulse must also be modified.

31 Precisely because of what we said in 29, however, it is possible to regard every action as a component of a greater action, as determined in 30, and so on, until we come back to our original interpretation of moral life as concept and impulse, as a single action of which the others are [merely] parts.

32 On this basis, then, disposition and skill prove to be perfectly at one in terms of the matter itself; they are simply different ways of considering moral quality, now from the purely internal aspect of a force which is equal to itself and now according to the magnitude of the phenomenon.

33 All moral skill, as the organic side of virtue, will consist of two factors, a *combinatory* one, namely the ease and accuracy with which it creates a sequence out of those organic activities which proceed from reason, and a *disjunctive*, or critical one, namely the differentiation and suppression of those activities which proceed from nature.

34 From the very moment when the moral task is comprehended a double orientation is established; on the one hand, the personal character of every

action ought to disappear, to be replaced by a relationship to the totality of the moral spheres, which is the *universal* side of moral action; while on the other hand, this nature which is individual and distinct from all the others is everywhere to be permeated by reason, which is the *individual* side of moral action.

35 The way in which the two can differ in each individual is apparent from the fact that everyone can produce his own formula for moral development. If we imagine a constant attention to everything taking place within the person, together with a tendency to ethicize this, then the individual element will be dominant in moral formation. If we imagine attention directed towards the moral spheres and what the person can bring about there from their own position, then the universal element will be dominant.

36 We might gain a double false impression that the individual is subordinate to the universal and vice versa; however, as one refutes the other, they appear to be coordinated in every way.

37 Now, since this opposition occurs both on the side of consciousness and of the [unconscious] urges, the same grounds for division extend to both those virtues posited as skills.

Prudence[16]

38 If we regard comprehension of the moral task as the original act, and all those that follow merely as a further development of it, then prudence is the producing of all the acts of cognition in an empirical subject which posit a part of the moral exercise within him.

39 Considered in the form of prudence, every act of cognition can be regarded as the concept of purpose (in the broadest sense) of an action. For a concept of this kind also forms the basis of actual cognition, to the extent that it is a successive product, and in fact whatever is prudent in cognition relates to it.

40 The universal side of combinatory prudence is what, in a practical sense, we call *understanding*, and it relates both to the accurate assembling of the elements of an individual concept of purpose, and to the drawing up of a proper order for one's whole life, an order formed from the individual elements of the general concept of purpose.

---

[16] *Marginal note 1827b:* Prudence should be extended to cover the moment of feeling. Impossible to find common designations for the individual element in each.

41 The individual side of combinatory prudence is what we call *mind* [*Geist*] and relates both to the particular shape given to one's whole life and to the particular combinations within the individual.

42 The universal side of disjunctive prudence relates to the fact that at every moment activities of consciousness proceed from sensibility which have a purely personal significance.

43 If these mingle in a conscious way with those which proceed from reason this constitutes a deliberate immorality and the [person's] disposition must be thought of as suspended.

44 Disjunctive prudence is, however, the skill to discover what differentiates the two, and thus to prevent unconscious, unacknowledged intrusion, thus preserving the purity of the conceptional process.

45 Impulses which are directed against the individuality of the human person can only proceed from the person himself to the extent that an element of sensibility is posited within him, which brings his individual existence under the power of a stranger's.

46 This is posited in the urge to imitate, to the extent either that one's own individuality is repressed by the involuntary confusion of what is general and exemplary in another with what is particular to his own individuality, or that vanity deliberately goes in search of something foreign [to one's own nature] for the sake of applause.

47 Note to 44. It is principally the universal side of disjunctive prudence which causes virtue to be presented as a struggle.[17]

48 The universal side cannot exist without the individual one for the very reason that, when a man considers himself wholly in relation to the ethical spheres, he is commanded in those very spheres to be a particular individual. The individual one cannot exist without the universal one because the latter always forms the basis of the former.

49[18] For this reason, although it would appear that the individual constitutes the higher perfection, each is coordinated with the other, not subordinated to it.

---

[17] *Marginal note 1827a:* Individual prudence is presence of mind, universal prudence is understanding; combinatory prudence appropriates, disjunctive prudence fends off; combinatory and universal = cleverness, combinatory and individual = inventiveness, disjunctive and universal = caution; [*1827b: crossed out and replaced with the word* rigor;] disjunctive and individual = uprightness [*1827b: replaced with the word* tact].

[18] *Marginal additions 1827a and b (against §§ 38–44):* Opposition between moral and worldly cleverness. Moral cleverness rests on wisdom and love. The same is true of caution. Both must be moral because, if one extends prudence to be as far as possible on a par with wisdom, then without

50 The combinatory and disjunctive aspects can never be entirely separate: for the former, once perfected, encompasses the latter, because whereas something alien was generated, something that belongs might have been generated; and the latter, once perfected, also [encompasses] the former, because, if an urge for the moral is present at all, then when every alien element is kept away what belongs must have emerged completely; and so the two are merely different points of view.

51 The opposing terms in each are, however, relatively differentiated. For, whether one regards the ethical sphere predominantly as an organ of individual existence (which is predominance of the individual side), or whether one regards oneself predominantly as an organ of the ethical sphere (which is predominance of the universal one) constitutes two different forms of moral formation.

52 The same thing is true if one starts from the point of view of composition, that is, purely taken up with the task of reason and not expressly paying attention to the counter-effect of sensibility (this is predominance of the combinatory side), or whether one is taken up with this opposition and is not expressly paying attention to the individual in the task of reason (this is predominance of the disjunctive side).

---

cleverness and caution the moral task, i.e. objective moral consciousness, would be neither whole nor pure.

Universal prudence cannot stand alone because, during the imperfect process whereby the whole comes into being, the individual is not always offered everything necessary for his individual development as a matter of course. Individual prudence cannot, because the individual has often to intervene in the imperfect state of the whole.

The two principal moments of cleverness are presence of mind and attentiveness.

Caution is the ability to anticipate on the one hand what might arise out of any decision that has been made and on the other hand, what might oppose an intention from the outside.

[*1827b*]. In this domain, when considering the doctrine of moral appearance, it must be borne in mind that something is often considered an immorality that is only an as-yet-undeveloped morality.

Combinatory and disjunctive is also a positive opposition. –

On the terminology of constancy and cleverness.

Individual and combinatory = mind, it is inventiveness where concepts dominate and fantasy where images dominate.

On how the purpose of intelligence is only exhausted by the whole abundant range of combinations.

The combinatory principle in feeling is the opposition of universal and individual. In the receptive [mode] it is sentimentality in the good sense of the word.

Disjunctive feeling is conscience and taste.

Combinatory and universal is a consistent level of sensitivity – the opposing states are dullness and an unwholesome softness.

Combinatory and individual, interwoven [?] with fantasy, is liveliness of mood.

They stand in the same relation as epic and lyric.

53 The opposition which we assume in everyday life between enthusiasm and prudence is the opposition between predominance of the combinatory side and predominance of the disjunctive one. Since, however, the human being never attains the highest perfection in the one, in which the other is also posited, true morality consists only in the coexistence of the two, and strictly speaking the opposition is not a personal one but a functional one. This is true not only of human morality in general, but also of morality in each individual ethical domain.

54 To the extent that prudence is the manifestation of wisdom, it must be possible for all its moments to be traced in all the moments of wisdom, so that for example enthusiasm in the narrow sense of the word is individual, combinatory prudence in the imaginative domain, and in the broader sense [it is] scientific enthusiasm in the speculative domain.

Steadfastness[19]

55 Steadfastness does not contain something which is particularly posited within the concept itself, but in this respect only the mechanical aspect of implementing something as the dominance of reason in the organization.

---

[19] *Marginal addition 1827b:* Steadfastness, as the becoming and remaining temporal of the entire moral impulse, determines the completeness of moral life and thus also determines prudence; steadfastness as present in moral concept formation [proceeds] from the overall impulse.

Out of its relationship to love (temporality of the desire to be soul) and to prudence there also develops a relationship to wisdom. The original point of contact is that even comprehension contains an impulse towards outwardly directed activity.

All the virtues merely exist together but remain separate because each has its own measure.

To 58. The animal instinct is so confused, however, without any definite object, only definite about life itself, without either a definite striving towards it or a definite rejection of it. Habits do arise in the human individual, which are in a certain relative opposition to the direction taken by life in general; this does, however, limit his general capacity for life more completely the longer it persists. In the same way definite habituations and rejections develop from childhood onward in the interests of sensory self-consciousness.

The life which has already been limited by habit – an immovable mass – therefore resists the intelligent impulse beyond this circle, and overcoming this resistance is the combinatory aspect of steadfastness, because otherwise it is impossible to realize a sequence of moments. If the intelligent impulse is repeated in the same way, then this also gives rise to habit, begging the question as to whether what has come about in this way is moral.

If we posit it as immoral, then a significant part of education is immoral also, and if we posit it as moral there would appear to be no essential difference between a narrow rut and a broader one. Resolution. For those who have been educated the result is merely an improvement on nature which they themselves must turn to advantage. This is, however, a product of the virtue of the educators. On the whole, of course, if a nature which has been improved in this way continues to work unconsciously according to the dead letter either of the law or of custom, this does not constitute morality; moreover, the other virtues are also absent. We find steadfastness only where there are moral impulses.

56 It is also to be found, admittedly, in the domain of consciousness, in that steadfastness of cognition exists alongside a lack of that quality; but here too what it represents is not posited in the concept of purpose of the action; on the contrary, it is assumed that that concept of purpose is the product of prudence, while steadfastness provides only for it to be carried out with more or less success.

57 [Considered] as a manifestation of love it is only the quantitative aspect of the urge to reason, for the stronger that urge is, the more whatever is to be found in [an individual's] disposition by way of love will manifest itself over time. Viewed positively, therefore, it is by no means something mechanical, but rather the quantitative life of reason in the totality of the organism.

58 Here the opposition of combinatory and disjunctive rests on the fact that, since the organization does not contain the life of reason, it counteracts it in the form of mass, so that the force of the impulse towards reason gradually gets lost; one must work against this by continuously renewing

Disjunctive steadfastness presupposes organic activities which arise but are repressed. The desire to comprehend shapes sensory life into definite desires and reluctances; craving and abhorrence are associated with these and when such responses erupt into a sequence of moral movements they inhibit them and must be staved off. On this side, then, steadfastness is the power of intelligence over appetites and repulsions which have arisen by way of the senses. This raises the question as to whether it would be even better if they did not arise in the first place. That can only happen by virtue of combinatory steadfastness which, at its peak, renders disjunctive steadfastness superfluous.

Whether desire and reluctance should themselves be averted is the question posed by the Stoics. We should answer in the negative, because the indicative content of desire and reluctance is necessary to arrive at a consciousness of the whole state. If that state proceeds from the moral impulse, however, then the second element has not been morally posited. Organic progress can only be interrupted, however, by a moral impulse, i.e. by combinatory steadfastness, and until this has matured the two must carry on together. If one imagines morality beginning with struggle, however, then once this has become superfluous, there will no longer be any need for work and effort.

Leaving aside everything to do with prudence, the opposition of universal and individual does not appear to be applicable here if we imagine that the activity of the will on the organic functions proceeds only from intelligence in all its simplicity, and it is only a question of a more or less which would only be an unequal distribution of the force of intelligence. However, there is a difference of method in the counter-effect, and the exemplary effect of those who are more steadfast resides in the fact that they establish a particular type which others, who carry less particularity within themselves, will subsequently appropriate. The influence of the individual on the mass is always conditional upon this. No one who is incapable of implementing his own particularity will gain influence or found a school.

Disjunctive steadfastness is power in the organization which is reacting by translating desire and reluctance into craving and abhorrence. Reactions against desire and reluctance cannot give rise to a variety of virtues; but someone who cannot achieve one thing is helped by other sensory [forces] to achieve another. Courage and patience examples of this.

that impulse, which precisely constitutes the combinatory aspect; also on the fact that, since the organization is not a dead thing but possesses its own life, it endeavors to produce activities which must be suppressed and eliminated, which precisely constitutes the disjunctive aspect.

59 The universal and the individual also form an opposition here, in that a completely different relationship exists on the part of the combinatory, in which the organization, as a mass, counters the universal and the individual, whereas on the part of the disjunctive, something is posited here too in sensibility by means of which man is placed under the power of the general.

60 Steadfastness which is directed against lethargy, seeking only to implement the universal impulse towards reason, is what we call *diligence* or assiduity. Anything that has no individual character we posit as having been achieved through this virtue.[20]

61 Steadfastness which is directed against lethargy in the individual is *virtuosity*, the complete emergence of what is individual entirely overcoming the mass. If we take the domain of art as our starting-point the concept is always used in this sense.

62[21] The particular life of the organization opposes the rule of reason in general terms by means of sensory desire or reluctance. In general terms steadfastness which is directed against this is *constancy*, i.e. the refusal to allow oneself to give up other actions because of desire or reluctance, or to fail to carry out something which has been conceived and initiated. Directed against desire it is *faithfulness*, against reluctance *bravery*; indeed, steadfastness in the course of a single action, in the face of reluctance of various kinds is *courage*, while steadfastness in the face of a single reluctance in a succession of moral actions is *patience*.[22]

---

[20] *Marginal addition 1827a:* Virtuosity fits in with individual combinatory [steadfastness] directed against lethargy – correctness with individual disjunctive [steadfastness] directed against desire – autonomy with individual [steadfastness] directed against reluctance.

[21] *Marginal addition 1827a, crossed out 1827b:*
Steadfastness in the face of desire – in general terms – is integrity,
Universal integrity is firmness;
Individual integrity is correctness.
Steadfastness in the face of reluctance is constancy;
Universal constancy is bravery and can be divided into courage and patience,
Individual constancy is self-sufficiency and can be divided into pride = courage and faithfulness (?) = patience.

[22] *Marginal note 1827b:* Universal disjunctive [steadfastness] is bravery. Individual disjunctive steadfastness is self-assertion.

63 The individual cannot be opposed by sensibility in itself, since it is itself the source of what is individual, except to the extent that it contains some reason to bring the individual under the power of a stranger; here too this is mechanical imitation of something considered valid by other individuals or in wider circles.

64 Steadfastness directed against what is routine is *correctness*, ἀχρίβεια, exactitude. The concept is only needed where we apply something individual, such as linguistic character, to an action, using it as a standard by which to measure.

65 There can be difference at an individual level between diligence and virtuosity, great constancy and little exactitude and vice versa; between great diligence and little constancy, great virtuosity and little exactitude and vice versa.

66 In the same way we arrive at a different formation[23] starting from diligence and virtuosity, i.e. the combinatory side, than if we start from the disjunctive side.[24]

67 They are all essentially one thing, however; for taken individually, as soon as we imagine any of them completely separate from the others, even in terms of their endeavor, we can no longer imagine any of them to be a virtue, that is, something which proceeds from a pure impulse towards reason.

68 Every moment of steadfastness must be implemented by means of the different kinds of love, which would then give rise to yet more exact divisions of virtue.

Conclusion

69 If we think of the whole of virtue as a skill, present in everyone, then, since virtue as a disposition contains all the various spheres of moral life, the highest good must necessarily be realized, and will indeed always be realized where steadfastness and prudence are to be found.

---

[23] *Twesten reads Betonung, emphasis, here; Schweizer is correct in reading Bildung*, formation.

[24] *Marginal addition 1827a:* Opposition between steadfastness of mind and that of the senses. Most often encountered in the courage of rage and the patience of malice. When the human being becomes moral, these must come to nothing before they are transformed into true steadfastness. For only Nature's power to curb remains (just as after fear of punishment), the fresh strength of the moment is entirely opposed to it. In one individual self-importance is restricted to a single moment; in the other there is a broadening out into a general kind of love in which self-importance [is reduced to] a minimum and disappears.

Doctrine of duties

Introduction

§ 1 The doctrine of duty is the depiction of the ethical process as a movement, and is therefore the unity of moment and deed.[25]

§ 2 Since the highest good comes into being as a result of individual actions as well as through individual persons, closer examination must reveal how, if actions are always in accordance with duty, they must necessarily result in the highest good.

§ 3 The highest good can only be realized through individual actions to the extent that the whole idea of morality is present in them; for whatever is absent from individual actions will also be absent from the highest good.[26]

§ 4 The object of individual moral actions must be in a definite moral sphere, for the unity of an act can only be produced within a single sphere.[27]

§ 5 Now, since the idea of morality is not entire in any action, inasmuch as it relates only to a single sphere of the highest good, an opposition is

---

[25] *Marginal addition 1827a:* the moment is volition. Everything can therefore be traced back to a single [volition]. The moment of the effect becomes infinitely small. Everything therefore relative. Hence man's conversion. – Division proceeds from human weakness. Construction only by the purposes of the world-whole. The infinite whole is not a concept of purpose. In conversion, therefore, duties are posed. This then presupposes a division in direction.

The subject is the person, the individual, but as part of something greater. Everything therefore [related] to humanity; thus presupposing community and diversity.

[26] *Marginal addition 1827a:* In such a way, however, that the highest good need only be in a state of becoming; thus in each action, too, the whole idea of morality only in a state of becoming.

This is precisely why accordance with duty should quite definitely not be judged from the outside. Any formula must include the internal and should therefore only be applied to what is productive, insofar as this is possible.

[27] *Marginal addition 1827b:* With reference to my essay [*probably:* On the concept of the highest good, 17.v.1827]: Individual peoples are the first to be in the position of having a self-contained domain. A division of this kind is that more likely to take place internally, the more completely established the caste system.

Any division ought, however, to be a jointly performed deed and for this reason should have arisen in accordance with duty. Community does not feature in any active way in the doctrine of duties, however, but only the individual, because community only ever comes into being as a result of repeated activity on the part of the individual.

The four formulae: a) Enter into community as an appropriative [force]; b) Appropriate only when you enter into community; c) Act identically, but whilst reserving your individuality; d) Act with your whole particularity, but without damaging your identity – taken on their own, these are not formulae for duty, because they give rise to diverse action and yet each one can lay claim to every moment. They only become [formulae for duty] when placed within the general formula of the maximum.

created by the dicta "Actions which are in accordance with duty must contain the whole idea of morality" and "Every action which is in accordance with duty must relate to a single moral sphere," which it is necessary to resolve.

§ 6 Each individual already finds all the moral spheres within every moment, and his action can therefore only join on to what has already been given. Thus every action which is in accordance with duty is a kind of following on.

§ 7 Since the highest good can only come into being as a result of actions which are in accordance with duty, in that everything that is morally given constitutes ethicized material, then action which is in accordance with duty constitutes the earlier [event] and quite simply the original one.

§ 8 An opposition is therefore created by the dicta "Every action which is in accordance with duty is a kind of following on" and "Each one is an original [act of] production," which it is necessary to resolve.

§ 9 If the state of a moral sphere is given, then this, by comparison with the idea, necessarily leads us to posit what must take place in order to bring the phenomenon closer to the idea. Thus every action which is in accordance with duty is like that as a matter of necessity.

§ 10 We can only regard an action as being in accordance with duty if it develops out of the human being himself, from the moral urge within him; for otherwise it is either his own but sensory, or else moral but not his own. It follows, then, that every action in accordance with duty must be a free action.

§ 11 An opposition is created by the dicta "Every action in accordance with duty is a free action" and "Every action in accordance with duty is necessary."

§ 12 Since every moral sphere is always in the process of becoming, and every human being is a lively [presence] in each, then something can take place in every one at any moment. Now if the individual can only act in a single sphere at any moment, then the dispute between them all over that moment must have been settled, so that every action in accordance with duty is the resolution of a case of collision.

§ 13 The highest good is the totality of all actions in accordance with duty. If these were in conflict with one another, then individual components of the highest good would be in conflict with one another. Thus there can be no collision between duties.

§ 14 An opposition is created by the dicta "Every duty settles a case of collision" and "There is no collision between duties," which it is necessary to resolve.

§ 15 The resolution of the opposition is this: only an action which contains the resolution of a collision in its concept of purpose is a duty; however, concepts of purpose which are so constructed do not themselves come into collision with one another.

§ 16 This last is the *conditio* of the reality of moral endeavor, because the concept of every action that is in accordance with duty contains the whole idea of morality within itself.

§ 17 The collision which is resolved in the concept will always fall into those three oppositions which must be resolved before a construction of duty can even be considered, for outside these the only possibility is unity of relation.

§ 18 Both dicta are therefore true, but in a different relation; the collision which has been superseded is the one which heralds a new moral act.

§ 19 On the other hand, actions which necessarily follow from entering into a definite relationship in any of the moral spheres, including all those which are normally termed compulsory duties as well as other analogous ones, are not duties at all, because they do not constitute new actions but are only continuations of one which is already underway, which cannot be ignored or quashed in any way other than in the general terms in which it was posited.

§ 20 It is impossible to judge from the outside whether a collision has been correctly resolved or not, and thus whether an action is in accordance with duty or not; we can only judge when we know what was posited in the mind of the person acting.

§ 21 A resolution may be the wrong one, and yet there may have been no violation of duty in subjective terms if the accompanying feeling was one of having acted out of complete moral consciousness. Only the absence of such a feeling is complete violation of duty.

§ 22 Since the various spheres of the highest good are not absolutely separate, so that each has an interest in the other, it is possible that the interests of them all may be satisfied by an action which causes something to happen in only one of them.

§ 23 As far as the first opposition is concerned, then, action in accordance with duty will be an action which, while it causes something to happen in only one of the spheres, is at the same time posited in consciousness as one which will satisfy the interests of all of them; in this case the object of the action would be the individual sphere in the first sense, but the totality of all the spheres in the second sense.

§ 24 This resolution is satisfactory if the necessity to do something is posited in one of the spheres but not in the others. If a necessity is posited in several spheres at the same moment then an action is in accordance with duty if the person acting can say: Each of the other spheres must be satisfied with the fact that I did this particular thing at this moment.

§ 25 In general terms, then, the resolution is conditional upon the postulation of order in all the spheres such that time can be shared out between them; without order of this kind, the fulfillment of any duty would be impossible.

§ 26 The two other oppositions are not identical, although they might appear to be; might, to be precise, if we confuse following on with objective necessity and original action with free generation. For there can be a following on without objective necessity, as well as original action with it. The former opposition always refers to the priority of relationship over the individual, the latter only to the way in which being and thought are mutually conditional upon each other.

§ 27 Since all moral relationships consist only in actions, they would be destroyed immediately if a new action were not added to them at every moment; thus each action is to be regarded as something original in that the relationship is obviously created afresh by it.

§ 28 Since the ethical process does not have an absolute beginning anywhere, and each individual finds himself in a moral relationship which contains the germ of all the others, where, even when new relationships are established, they are preceded by an unconscious one, then even where an action is original it also always constitutes a following on [of some kind].

§ 29 If what matters here, then, is actually the opposition between establishing and continuing a moral relationship, it is only relative anyway, in that establishment nevertheless always follows on from something that has been naturally given, while following on nevertheless generates something afresh, so that both requirements are present in every action.

§ 30 Since every moral whole consists only of actions, they have no objective necessity other than the state of those acting and hence what is thought in them, and it is only present to the extent that there is free recognition of what must happen.

§ 31 Since the production of a concept of purpose is an act of reason which posits a unification with nature, every action which is genuinely freely thought must also possess objective necessity.

§ 32 Since here, then, it is only a matter of a difference in moment, action in accordance with duty here will always be such that internal stimulus and external demand coincide.

§ 33 In judging an action, these last two oppositions can only be taken into consideration when the opposition between the unity and totality of all the orientations which it contains has been resolved. Only there, moreover, is something material posited which provides us with a starting-point for division of the domain of duty.

§ 34 If we simply adopt the division within the domain of duty together with objective depiction of it, the doctrine of duties becomes an entirely contingent one; and we can never definitely ascertain the extent to which the highest good comes into being as a result of actions universally performed in accordance with duty, if we assume its basic outlines in advance.

§ 35 The particular divisions within the moral domain from the point of view of individual actions must come from intuitive perception of life as a multiplicity of actions.[28]

§ 36 Here, then, the first opposition is between formation of community and appropriation. It must be related solely, however, to the existence of reason in nature, that is, to the ethical process.

§ 37 The second is the relative opposition [to be found] in the individual's life itself between the general and the especial factor,[29] in that subordinating the former to the latter produces individual action while the converse produces universal action.

§ 38 Here the opposition between cognition and depiction, concerned as it is only with content, recedes into the background.

---

[28] *Marginal addition 1827a:* The active unity is the person (it does not matter which one; there are state duties etc. just as much as there are individual ones). Naturally, he is in relationship on the one hand with those acting alongside him, which gives rise to duties which would not exist without a plurality of persons; and on the other hand with the material which is to be acted upon, which gives rise to duties which would not be there if it were not for things. His relationship to those acting alongside him is one of either identity or difference. In the case of the former, the action is a common one, in the case of the latter an appropriative one. Does his relationship to the material thus produce universal and individual action? How can this be so? All universal action rests on putting one thing on a par with another, all individual action rests on setting one thing against another.

[29] *Crossed out:* universal and individual.

§ 39 Since the two oppositions are independent of each another, so that every action belongs in one term of each, fourfold action is the result, and hence four different domains of duty.

§ 40 Universal formation of community is the domain of the *duty of right*, universal appropriation the *duty of profession*, individual formation of community is the *duty of love*, and individual appropriation the *duty of conscience*.

§ 41 Every action within these domains will only be in accordance with duty to the extent that it unites in itself the oppositions put forward above.

§ 42 Each of these domains has a province in cognition and one in depiction, which are, however, subject to the same formulae.

Duty of right

§ 1 The object of this duty is all action performed upon nature by reason in the form of identity, beginning with personal nature and going through to external nature. Its essence is the surrender of this action to reason in general.

§ 2 The first formula is the one by virtue of which the other term of the determining opposition is also present in the action: *Enter into every community in such a way that your entering is also an appropriation*; posited in this formula is indifference [of the distinction between] universal or individual character in appropriation.

§ 3 Applied to the formative province, then, we find here the positing of a general state of contractuality as identical with the positing of possession or the acquisition of rights in the community as a whole.

§ 4 Since the opposition between entering into community and appropriation is also only a relative one, in that entering into community is already present in the identity of the schematism of the organs with others, and appropriation is already present in activity for others, inasmuch, that is, as this cannot exist without forming a result in the organs, we find here the whole sequence of gradations from the predominance of one view over the other, namely the person as a maximum of community and minimum of possession in the family, and as a minimum of community and maximum of possession in external commerce; and things, conversely, as a minimum of possession and a maximum of community in external traffic, and a minimum of community and a maximum of possession in the family.

§ 5 Applied to the cognitive province it tells us that the establishing of cognition in a system which is universally valid is identical with holding it firm in individual consciousness. Thus producing cognition without having it in one's memory ready for use is contrary to duty.

§ 6 The second formula is the one by virtue of which the other opposition is also present in the action: *Enter into every community reserving your whole individuality*; posited in this formula is the indifference in individuality [of the distinction between] entering into community and appropriation.[30]

§ 7 Since the opposition between universal and individual is only a relative one, and in reality the one is never completely separate from the other, we find posited here all those concentric circles where, as each gets smaller, it contains the individuality reserved in the larger one, while this very individuality becomes community in its turn, and so on to the smallest circle of all.

§ 8 This occurs both in the formative province and in the cognitive one, starting with language in the broadest sense, and the broadest community of feeling, and going right down to the philosophical school and the most intimate friendship, inasmuch as one can still posit a universal element in such things.

§ 9 Anyone who enters a universal community without bringing his whole individuality with him does not actually enter himself, so that entering into [community] and existence within it are only possible [when accompanied by] love. Anything which is dead from this point of view is contrary to duty. Community can only be a way of being of individuality.

§ 10 The third [formula] refers to the identity of beginning and following on and actually falls into two parts: *Enter into community in such a way that you are already reconciled to it*, and: *Be reconciled to it in such a way that you enter into it*.

---

[30] *Marginal addition 1827b: ad § 6 f.* The individuality of a community only comes to consciousness through contact with others. Personal particularity develops long after the ego and to an unequal extent. As long as it is only poorly developed, states will persist almost everywhere in which the individual is almost mechanically determined by custom; these persist in good conscience and are then generated all over again in accordance with duty. – Reform can be distinguished from revolution only by the way in which the transitions have been effected either in accordance with duty or contrary to duty. Yet even in reform, common feeling, however conscientious, can decide against the good conscience of the individual, the snubbing of misalliances, etc. – Expressions of individuality are also given up in accordance with duty, e.g. idioms, once a common language has developed, but only if they are limitations which inhibit further development. Hence in this case the attempt to turn idioms into something literary is essentially a complementary activity. In the transitional phases of giving something up we also encounter ways of acting which express opposition carried out in good conscience.

§ 11 Thus the entering of an individual into the state and into language ought not to be something arbitrary; he can only enter into something if he feels at home in it by nature.

§ 12 Any exception to this rule – which can only ever be rooted in an immoral state – must be reconciled to it once again, if it is to constitute a moral action on the part of an individual; that individual must already have found himself outside the natural connection and, moreover, must only enter into connection with something alien to the extent that he feels at home in it, i.e. is thrown into it.

§ 13 The same holds true for (b); feeling at home with something is only moral to the extent that it is also an entering-into, and the result of a confirmatory choice, which consists precisely in recognizing that a community provides a well-rooted scope for individuality, and is the form of appropriation which is most right for the individual, whether this occurs with a greater or lesser degree of consciousness.

§ 14 Until these two propositions coincide, being in community is not a moral action at all but merely a natural process.

§ 15 The question as to whether, for example, an individual who did not feel at home in the state ought nevertheless to enter into it, is thus a nonsensical one, since his feeling at home in it can only become moral by dint of his entering it freely, while on the other hand he cannot enter any state if he does not feel at home in it.

§ 16 If, according to the formula put forward in § 7, coming into community could be something fluid, then by virtue of that same formula it is now bound up with natural points such as the human being, his race, people, tribe, etc.

§ 17 The final formula is that of the identity of objective necessity and internal self-determination as invention, and concerns itself more with the actual manner of community. Following § 32 of the Introduction it runs: *In every community, act in such a way that internal stimulus and external demand coincide.*

§ 18 Since this must be a matter of individual action, to the extent that it cannot be encompassed by an earlier, more general one, because otherwise there would be no necessity for any particular internal stimulus, yet the opposition between these two kinds of action is only a relative one – for if my entering into the state, for example, has been its complete absorption into my consciousness, then from the point of view of its internal stimulus, every subsequent action which relates to the state is already posited in this deed – then a whole series of different solutions appear, where at one moment stimulus is the maximum and demand the minimum, and conversely, at another moment, demand the maximum and stimulus the minimum. Fundamentally, however, the two are always in equilibrium, only the same demand is not as great for one person as it is for another.

§ 19 Whatever is separated from objective necessity would be something hazardous. It would always be hollow and could never further the moral condition of a community; on the contrary, it fades out into empty exertion.

§ 20 Whatever is separated from internal self-determination would be mechanical and could never document the morality of the person acting.

Duty of profession

§ 1 The object of this duty is all action performed by reason upon nature, to the extent that it is a formation, with the character of identity, of these for and within personality, hence both the formation of the cognitive capacity and every other capacity that is in fact formative, as well as the inculcation of external nature itself.

§ 2 First formula: *Always appropriate in such a way that your appropriating is also an entering into community*. Posited here, in the entering into community, is indifference [of the distinction between] identical and particular character.

§ 3 Applied to the formative capacities this means, therefore: in possessing, you concede other claims, whether of a general or an individual nature.

§ 4 Given that the person is the minimum of community in external commerce (Duty of right, § 4) it follows that a minimum of community is to be found even in things, if all formation follows the analogy with the person, i.e. single and complete in itself, which is the state in which there is no division of transactions.

§ 5 With reference to persons, universal appropriation must therefore take place according to the principle of unity, and with reference to things, according to the principle of difference; this latter arises from talents and situation.[31]

---

[31] *Marginal addition:* Every gradation, from holding things close to the person and function, to the loosest of existences, is to be found here.

§ 6 Applied to the province of cognition, it contains firstly the identity of thinking and speaking, for community is in speech; and also (since everything is appropriated under the schema of what is especial, but community exists by means of the general) the identity of the general and the especial.

§ 7 The second formula, combining the other opposition, [is]: *Undertake all universal appropriation whilst reserving your own individuality*; posited in individuality here is indifference [of the distinction between] entering into community and appropriation.

§ 8 If we consider the formation of community, then the duty of profession and the duty of love are meshed together here, and this means that all property must serve [the needs of] individual sociability and cannot be a limiting principle upon it; in this way external class prejudices as such are posited as being contrary to duty.[32]

§ 9 If we consider appropriation, then the duty of profession and the duty of conscience are meshed together; individual appropriation is to occur within universal appropriation. Thus externally there is an element of art in all formation, containing every gradation by which the individuality maintains itself in forming the domains – which are in relative opposition – of the duties of conscience.[33]

§ 10 With regard to the province of cognition, we find appropriation posited both as a concept and a common feeling here; if we balance this against individual entering into community, we have posited that the concentric circles of communication by means of depiction are at the same time the fulfilling of consciousness.

§ 11 If we think of individual appropriation, it follows that free combination should exist at the same time within all general positing and that the acknowledgment of schematism is only moral to the extent that it allows scope for this.

§ 12 Third formula: *Appropriate in such a way that you find what you have appropriated already present as part of you, and find everything that is present as part of you in such a way that you appropriate it*; this formula expresses the identity of the ethical and the physical as being what everything must follow on from.

---

[32] *Marginal addition:* With every gradation of [the extent to which] external property enters individual sociability.

[33] *Marginal addition 1827b:* Absolute uniformalization is the most powerful apparent opposition.

§ 13 Also direct appropriation: skill only develops to the extent that one finds it already present as a force of nature; hence the successive aspect of the ethical process is dependent upon the successive development of nature.

§ 14 Also indirect appropriation: things are only taken into possession inasmuch as they are already directly connected with nature, and hence only to the extent that such a connection is gradually revealed in clear consciousness or instinct – where in broad terms the laws which determine progression are therefore to be found.

§ 15 To the extent that it is a question here of the relationship of the individual, special laws are posited determining development by means of the situation of the individual within the whole, in that man's existence in the ethical sphere appears here to be a natural relationship.

§ 16 Fourth formula: *In all appropriation, act in such a way that internal stimulus and external demand coincide.*

§ 17 The internal demand is inclination; the external one is need and opportunity; duty is to be found only where the two coincide.

§ 18 Internal demand is permanent, but also manifold, and for this reason cannot determine action on its own.[34]

---

[34] *Material added in 1832 [at end of ms.], pp. 38–40:* 1832. With regard to the individual aspect, preliminary remarks on the position it has occupied up to now in the doctrine of morals, together with a critique of the concept of what is permissible.

Then I began with appropriation as I did in the other notebook, having previously discussed the fact that this is necessary because of the impossibility of transference and thus going back to the transcendent fact, which I used as a linking-point, that intelligence, entering into the opposition and then, [functioning] as an agent within nature, individualizing itself everywhere at the same time as nature does, so that its becoming human reason in human nature already rests on the appropriation of the latter, as individual, whereas here community is merely the partial superseding of what is otherwise an absolute [process of] isolating.

To create a better basis, what would otherwise be the two last formulae are now placed at the beginning of [the section on] duty of conscience, [namely] following on as finding and the coincidence of stimulus and demand.

1. Finding oneself goes back to the transcendent fact that nature is capable of being individualized. This gives rise to the casuistical question, with regard to descent from a higher unity to a smaller one, as to whether, when the horde has found itself as an individual unity, this then becomes lost to the higher order when it makes the transition into a state? In that case either our formula must contain a further collision or else the larger state would only be able to come into being in an immoral way. The solution lies in the fact that earlier the horde had not yet discovered the greater unity, but had also only developed its particularity within those circles of which it continues to consist; to take [that particularity] over into the higher [unity] is affectation and is not a task that is posed. The Ionic and the Doric would not have had to cease to exist even if the Greeks had managed to form a confederation of states. If there then comes a time when the smaller unity is submerged in the larger one, this is then its euthanasia, and entirely comparable to the death of the individual.*

[* *Marginal addition:* If the greater unity exerts the more powerful stimulus, then ultimately the smaller one can only remain an impulse towards appropriation in those that are only passively receptive towards the greater ones.]

2. But even this can never be something deliberate, but only something that comes about, and then only in the form whereby stimulus and demand must have ceased, just as the demand will cease to an ever-greater extent to avail oneself of the Alemannic or Saxon [dialect]. – Now, just as all individual appropriation in the domains of both functions proceeds from self-consciousness that has become impulse, so individual appropriation is always found to have been present here earlier.

3. The coincidence of internal stimulus and external demand can be explained by the fact that this very impulse is the stimulus. Great variation, depending on how far the exponent of particular development is within a people and within an individual. Demand here is not to be found within nature in general nor in the influence of other people, but in the domain of universal appropriation, for which we have already reserved individual appropriation. Here, then, demand is contained in assets, both in the domain of knowledge and of formation. If there is great demand for the domain of property in the narrow sense but [only] slight stimulus, then what we find is tasteless ostentation and hollow luxury. If there is great stimulus for the domain of knowledge but small demand, then what we find is empty versifying instead of poetry. With these same proportions what we find in each domain is deception, in an attempt to satisfy the stimulus. If the proportions are inverted then in the symbolizing domain what we find is mindless collecting.

4. Appropriation ought also, then, to be community.

Introduction, final version (probably 1816/17)
A new beginning for ethics

This would have to be printed[1] in advance, as a sample, but then the rest should follow in its entirety.[2]

---

[1] *Corrected from:* sent out.

[2] *A piece of folded paper, half-folio sized, was found together with the 1816 manuscript; the observations it contains were probably written at around the same time:*

On the Ethics.

First hour. Before § 1.

One can also attempt to comprehend science historically.

There are very many diverse and contradictory phenomena here, so that it is difficult to discover what determines the limits for each one. [*Question mark in margin.*]

This is generally difficult, because the beginning comes out of nothing and the infinitely small is indeterminate. [*Question mark in margin.*]

In our cultural sequence the gnomic poetry of the Greeks forms the starting-point. There are ethical elements in it but they are not in scientific form. [*Marginal addition:* In § 58 there should be more discussion as to why the two cannot be combined to form a whole.]

This is first found in the Socratic school. But here we already find all the conflicting systems [*corrected from:* principles] of subsequent times. How are we to know, then, which is the right one? [*Question mark in margin.*]

The Hedonist systems are opposed to the others. It is possible to sympathize with the polemics against Epicurianism, but not to claim that all Hedonists were unworthy [of respect].

Relationship to the individual is opposed to relationship to the greater whole.

What all of them have in common is the relation to a feeling which approves or condemns. If this is not the same in all of them, however, how do we know which is the right one?

There were originally as many different doctrines of ethics as there are feelings shared in common, depending on race and level of formation.

Every one of these abstracts on the basis of personal differences.

A general doctrine of ethics cannot be the most powerful abstraction from all especial, diverse peoples and ages.

Their richness is then entirely lost to us. There is nothing left because what is particular is not specially located anywhere. [*Question mark in margin.*]

Nothing is gained in terms of intension. For since a doctrine of ethics does not help us to be good, it can only help us to understand. But feeling, such as is given in each one of us, cannot be understood on the basis of [a general doctrine] of this kind.

I Conditions for the depiction of a particular science

1 If any one especial science is to be perfectly depicted, it cannot begin purely on its own but must be related to a higher knowledge, and
finally to the highest knowledge, from which all individual knowledge
must proceed.

For any especial science there are necessarily others which are coordinated with it. If each
is the development of a particular intuition, then either they belong together as parts of a
greater way of thinking which alone allows us to understand the way in which they belong
together, and so on as far as a highest intuition which encompasses everything and which
would then be the object of the highest science; or else they belong apart from one another,
but even then each is only a perfect science when there is an accompanying knowledge of
this relationship, cognition of which would then be the highest form of knowledge.

If each especial science is a whole[3] composed of logical deductions following from a
particular point, then either that point is a subordinate one, itself found by a process of

We cannot say that right resides in each especial thing that argues from the generality, nor that
whatever does not is wrong.
Second hour. Before § 1.
For the basis even of things which find their place in a general doctrine of ethics is no different
from the basis of things which do not, and taken together with what brought them into being they
constitute one and the same truth.
No true science can be derived from feeling. The more or less conscious development of this insight
is the turning-point [which ushers in] a new period in [the history of] ethics.
However, if feeling cannot provide a foundation for the whole, what can?
We have feelings, and ideas which are dependent on feelings. A general doctrine of ethics must also
consist of ideas and concepts, and they must also be in accord with feeling. However, if they are not
to be rooted in feeling, then either they themselves must form the basis of feeling or else both must
be rooted in the very same thing.
We cannot assume the former to be the case, for feeling is also to be found where concepts are not,
and concepts do not produce virtue, which is always based on feeling.
What do feelings and concepts have in common, such that they could be based on the very same
thing?
They are both movement. Thus the steadfast mobility which underlies them both would have to be
that very same thing. [*Question mark in margin.*] If, then, concepts are its movements just as feelings
are, but the former carry within them necessity and singularity just as much as the latter do difference,
then the two can be related to each other, and there can be a general doctrine of ethics.
However, this would not explain ethical phenomena to us. We must also look at the concepts themselves
and what they are based on in order to find the reason for the multiplicity and diversity which is
present in feeling.
We ought therefore to go into our innermost being and see how ethical movements become on the
one hand concepts, and on the other hand feelings.
But here we are halted once again. For even if we go beyond feeling, we still have no right to posit
what is ethical as an object existing in its own right and so we do not know why there ought to be an
especial science of ethics either.
On this point, then, we must deliver ourselves into the hands of Fate. [*Question mark in margin.*] If
ethics is an especial science, then as such it must have its basis in the organization of all knowledge.
We must seek this first of all, and then we can seek the doctrine of ethics within it.
[3] *Corrected from:* system.

deduction, up as far as a highest point which is both necessarily and originally posited, together with the way of arriving at it, by the highest knowledge, without which even that science is imperfect; or else the starting-points for all the especial sciences are originally posited, each one separately, and then they are all only perfect sciences if the relationship between their beginnings is known to each one of them, so that this would then be the highest form of knowledge.

2 Even when it is derived from the highest knowledge, a subordinate science can only be perfectly understood when it is taken together with those which are coordinated with it and those which are opposed to it.

If each differs from the others only in terms of its object, removing a particular domain from a more general intuition can only be understood if what is not included here is also explicitly understood in its relation to the higher intuition; and a particular series of conclusions drawn from a particular point can only be understood if those remaining are understood in just the same way as having their origin in the same point.

If each differs from the others by virtue of its method, the particular method in each one can nevertheless only be perfectly recognized when what exists alongside it is also recognized as such.

3 Unless we regard them as being derived from the highest knowledge, all especial [branches of] science are simply the product of opinion.

If there is no recognition of the law which governs the way in which a mass of knowledge is selected from the whole, nor of the distinction between what is included and what is not included, then the fact that one opposes some knowledge to some other knowledge and forms it into a whole which is separate from the rest, and the way in which this is done, is purely arbitrary. Arbitrary acts of thought are, however, [the expression of] opinion.

4 To the extent, say, that the highest knowledge itself were something manifold, a science, the above (2 and 3) would also be true of what is individually contained within it.

For these individual [strands] would be coordinated with one another or opposed to one another just as necessarily, either because of their extraction from a highest beginning or else outright, and they can only be perfectly understood if that relationship is understood.

5 The highest knowledge, however, is also only perfectly understood if what is especial[4] and subordinate to it is perfectly understood.

For if the two do not form an opposition, then even the highest knowledge is not the highest; if the two are opposed to each other, then each can also only be understood together with what is in opposition to it.

6 Thus all knowledge can only be both complete and perfect if it can be taken as a whole.[5]

---

[4] What is especial. *Corrected from:* the way in which it is distinguished from it.

[5] *Later marginal addition (1827? 1832?):* This enables us 1. To declare that all interest in knowledge is a delusion and to relate all revision of ideas simply to the emotional state; 2. To give up science but nevertheless to strive for the refining of opinions and the eradication of error; 3. To regard

Follows from 1, 2, 4, and 5, since all knowledge is either altogether simple and hence the highest, or else composed of derived elements which are thus in opposition and then belong in a particular domain of knowledge, that is, a science.

7 Thus far there is no reason why knowledge should not be in a process of becoming on all points simultaneously.

Since, in perfection, both lower and higher, as well as what is coordinated and what is opposed, are equally very much conditional upon one another and each is an equally necessary part of the whole, then every point can just as well become a starting-point in its orientation towards knowledge as a whole, and every beginning is equally imperfect.

8 Depiction of an individual science can begin imperfectly either in that it is not related to any [form of the] highest knowledge but is simply put down independently, or else it is derived from [a form of the] highest knowledge which is, however, itself never perfectly present nor depicted as such.

In the first case it will seek to perfect itself as far as possible within its own limits, but will create a connection once the highest knowledge, which has been coming into being at the same time, is complete. In the second, it will seek to come into being itself in correlation with the highest knowledge, which is coming into being at the same time, and reserves the right to perfect itself [6] on all sides as everything is perfected.

9 With the first kind of beginning, determination of the object of the science is arbitrary, and the whole depiction sinks back into the domain of opinion.

For we are unable to recognize the necessity for the object, as the object of knowledge, to be something especial and whole in itself. (Following 3.) This does not, however, prevent all the parts of the depiction from being perfectly true.

10 The delimitation of the science must therefore have been determined by an interest which is alien to knowledge.

For there must be a reason for it. This severance of any connection with the totality of knowledge cannot proceed from any orientation towards knowledge. This method is at best based on an interest in the object for its own sake. Any other way in which it comes about is even more a matter of chance and creates an expectation of even less truth in the depiction.

11 Diverse depictions of the same science can come about in this way even if the highest knowledge remains at exactly the same level.

That is, because arbitrary determination of the object is manifold, as is the interest which determines it.

science in the highest sense as what is internally complete but at the same time to recognize that in reality science, and the depiction of the highest knowledge, can only ever be a reflection, caught up in approximation[.]

[6] *Corrected from:* to be perfected.

12 Since the object and its treatment are not necessarily determined by one another here, the starting-points and results of these depictions can stand in highly diverse relation to each other.

Not only will perhaps more, perhaps less be included and excluded, but also from the same beginnings a diversity of results will be achieved, while opposite beginnings may provide the same result.

One might compare, for example, the diverse doctrines of eudaemonism, or compare many of these with many moral law doctrines.

13 The other kind of beginning will also permit of diverse depictions of each especial science, starting from diverse beginnings.

That is, as long as the highest knowledge is not perfect it will be present in a number of forms, just as everything imperfect is multiform, and each individual science will be derived differently from each of these.

14 Here the determination and demarcation of an individual science does not proceed from an interest which is alien to knowledge, but from the agreement felt by the person depicting with one of the diverse shapes taken by the highest knowledge as it is still in a process of becoming.

Thus it is interest in knowledge itself which prevails here, while object and treatment are conditional upon one another, so that what we noticed with the other kind (see § 12) does not take place here.

15 A depiction of this kind has a qualified scientific quality, because it retains a connection with the whole of knowledge and expresses the state of that knowledge; but its truth is entirely dependent on the truth of the shape which it assumes that the highest knowledge has taken.

That is, because it is derived from it, so that at the same time it posits a certain shape taken by all the other individual [branches of] knowledge; but all these things which have been determined and placed in opposition only hold true if, and as long as, that higher [knowledge] holds true.

16 Every depiction of a science which is of the first type will be entirely valid for everyone who comprehends its object in the same way, out of the same interest, if they can agree as to scientific method. The same will be true for every depiction of the second type, for everyone who is inclined to give the same shape to the highest knowledge and to appropriate it, insofar, that is, as they are driven to the point where the domain of this especial science becomes discrete from the others.

This means that, on the one hand, almost every particular individual who enjoys perfect intellectual freedom will have his own way of depicting a science, while on the other hand all depictions of all sciences can nevertheless be brought back to certain subdivisions.[7]

---

[7] *Question mark in margin.*

17 Both kinds of method will renew themselves side by side in diverse products until the highest knowledge and all the especial sciences are perfected simultaneously.

This perfection is a goal, it is true, which can never be achieved outright, but an approximation to it should be seen in the fact that in each science, even in terms of content, the two kinds of method will coincide more and more closely; moreover the diverse shapes taken by each science as a result of one or the other will come closer together.

18 The multiplicity of these imperfect depictions generates a critical method which accompanies each science in its process of becoming and seeks, as it brings these shapes into a necessary relation to one another, to discover the perfection of that science even as it comes into being.

Namely historically, as the limiting influences of alien interests cancel one another out, so that the science is truly present in the freedom of its own particularity, and [also] as the one-sided attempts at derivation supplement one another, so that, both as cognition of the object and also as a term within the whole of knowledge, the science is present in truly complete form.

19 This historical recognition brought about by the critical method is, however, never given as perfect but is only ever in a process of becoming.

For the one-sided attempts would all have to be present in order for their composite effect to replace the perfection of science, or else those which are lacking would have to be able to be found by scientific means. But the latter would only be possible, and the former would only be known, if the perfect concept of science had already been given from elsewhere; moreover, their necessary relationship to one another could only be recognized from this concept.

20 For this reason science cannot achieve perfection originally and solely by means of the critical method.

For everyone, however, the best safeguard is not to remain caught up in one's own particular one-sidedness. And thus it increases the speed with which the goal is approached from all sides.

Without this talent, even the greatest scientific force can achieve little which contributes to true historical furthering [of this end], but can only provide yet more material which is difficult to work through.

21 The present depiction of ethics is not intended to put that science forward as if it were independent of anything else, but to derive it from a highest knowledge which is assumed.

It therefore does not start out from a so-called moral principle either, such as is established in that other form; all these prove to be one-sided and vague when treated critically.

II Derivation of the concept of ethics

22 Before the highest science has been completed, nothing that is communicated of it for the purpose of establishing the derivation of a subordinate science can be regarded as having universal validity.

Not even if we are building on a depiction which is already familiar; for even this is only one of many and is not universally valid. Certainly not if individual features are picked out, as they are here. Conviction can only arise when these features coincide with what everyone can find in his own consciousness.

23 We only encounter knowledge and being in relation to one another. Being is what is known, and knowledge knows of what exists.[8]

No one will say that he knows what does not exist; and if we assume a being to which our knowledge simply does not relate, then at the same time we are obliged to imagine a different knowledge which does relate to it. We can only ask that everyone should be conscious of this dictum. For anyone who wished to deny its necessity, there would be no truth in the following derivation; indeed it is altogether true that that person is at a point where for him there is no truth but only a provisional denial of all truth, the point of general doubt.[9]

24 At the very earliest moment of coming to consciousness we find that what is knowledge in us and being for us is a plurality.

We simply conclude from the differentiation which emerges more and more clearly the existence of a confused earlier state in which plurality was not differentiated but was not in fact a true unity; and from the ever more clearly developed tendency to make connections the existence of a later, perfected state in which everything is combined to form a unity which is nevertheless not the end of plurality.

25 To the extent that knowledge corresponds to being at all, or individual knowledge corresponds to individual being, it is the expression of that being; and to the extent that being corresponds to knowledge at all, or an individual being corresponds to an individual knowledge, being is the depiction of knowledge.

These names are chosen from many others as denoting the necessity which informs the relationship of being and knowledge, or what in each corresponds to the other, the one with the originality of being and the particularity of knowledge, the other with the originality of knowledge and the particularity of being.

26 Knowledge and being are each the measure of the other, so that knowledge is knowledge because of the definiteness of being, and a being is a

---

[8] *Later marginal note:* Simple expression of this: *That is so.*
[9] *Later marginal addition:* If we believe that there is no knowledge of what is individual, we do not actually consider it to have any existence.

being because of the definiteness of the knowledge to which it corresponds; and a being is perfect because of the exactness with which it corresponds to knowledge and a [piece of] knowledge is perfect because of the exactness with which it corresponds to being.

If we call something an imperfect example of its kind, that is because it does not correspond to the concept, and vice versa.

The unity of appearance of a [single] moment only separates into multiplicity in a particular way through relationship to various concepts. And as far as a concept in itself is concerned, there is no reason not to split it into the plurality of its subspecies, nor to hide it among the higher [species]; [such a reason] is only to be found in the definiteness of the being to which it is related.

27 Every especial [kind of] knowledge, and hence also the being of which it is the expression, consists only in oppositions and continues to exist through them; and every [kind of] knowledge that consists in oppositions is necessarily something especial, which must have other things alongside it.

1. For it is only something especial to the extent that something is not posited or negated in it. If, however, this [particular thing] were not posited elsewhere, nothing would be negated in that [particular thing] either.
2. If one [kind of] knowledge has several things alongside it, it must be different from them, so that something which is posited in this [other] one is not posited here.

28 Every [kind of] knowledge, and hence also the being of which it is the expression, is determined by more oppositions the smaller it is in scope, and by fewer the larger it is in scope. Conversely every [kind of] knowledge, and hence also the being which is its depiction, is encompassed by more manifold oppositions the smaller it is, i.e. the more it is something especial, and by fewer, the larger it is, i.e. the more it is something general.

For every individual [kind of] knowledge which is combined together with several others under the same general [heading] has more to which it is opposed, namely everything which is coordinated with it. And every more general [kind of] knowledge has fewer, for everything that is subordinate to it and mutually opposed is not. From which all else follows.

29 The highest knowledge which we seek is not determined by oppositions at all, but is purely the simple expression of the highest being, which is its equal; just as the highest being is merely the simple depiction of the highest knowledge, which is its equal.

If the oppositions become fewer the higher one goes, one can only have reached the highest point once they have disappeared altogether.

Every [kind of] knowledge which is determined by an opposition has another one (27) alongside it and is therefore not the highest.

30 The highest knowledge is, however, not at all the denoting of a definite scope either, but the indivisible and unmultipliable expression of the complete and absolutely highest being which is its equal, just as the highest being is the indivisible and unmultipliable depiction of the complete and absolutely highest knowledge which is its equal.

If one could attain the highest knowledge by ascending from the especial to the general it would have a scope that could be determined by the relationship of the lower to the higher. But just as there is no continuous transition from the lowest especial thing to the infinitely small, the absolutely individual, so there is none from the most general of all to the absolutely highest.

The world, as the epitome of everything real except for what is merely possible, and God as the supreme power from which everything can proceed except for what is impossible, are examples of this; for an outer limit is set by virtue of their form, and for this reason they are insufficient expressions of the highest being, always becoming entangled in contradictions. All scope [*Umfang*] is determined only by opposition, and what is in opposition can only express that opposition within something higher.

31 Hence the highest knowledge is not present within us in the form of a linkage, i.e. as a sentence, or as a unity of subject and predicate, which in a definite way excludes other things from what is posited and circumscribed; neither is it within us in the form of a designation, i.e. as a concept or as a unity of the general and the especial, encompassing what is manifold and hence opposed.

Concept and sentence are the two fundamental shapes in which all particular knowledge appears in us. The above does not deny that within the schema of subject or predicate the highest knowledge could not express absolute being, only that it cannot be the unity of any other subject and predicate. It also does not deny that the highest being could be expressed within the schema of the most general or the most especial, only that it cannot be something definite between the most general and the most especial.

32 Hence the highest being is not present to us either, neither as a thing nor as an activity.

1. Thing corresponds to concept, activity corresponds to sentence; for in the same way as the sentence presupposes concepts and the concept only arises out of a series of sentences, so activity, as the way in which things are related, presupposes things, and every thing is posited only as something which has sprung from activities.
2. As activity alone it would have to exist within something else and would be numbered with it; it would not be the highest, therefore. As a thing it would be the same, existing alongside other things, and would have to suffer at their hands.

33 Thus the highest knowledge does not reveal itself directly in our consciousness, but exists within it only as the inner ground and source of all other knowledge, just as the highest being is not directly available to our consciousness, but is the inner ground and source of all other being.

For the highest knowledge within us must be this at least, if especial knowledge is to be derived from it. And for the same reason the highest being must be this to us as well. We must accept this or give up our demand. Whether the highest being and highest knowledge is anything else in addition, within us and for us, is a question we must leave to one side, like the question as to what they might be in themselves and how the two stand in relation to one another otherwise.

34 A knowledge which contains only one term of an opposition within it cannot be posited as a [kind of] knowledge in its own right, corresponding to a [kind of] being, but only as existing within something else, which also encompasses the other term of the opposition.

For, if all individual knowledge is differentiated from the highest knowledge by the fact that it consists in oppositions, then each could for this reason contain parts of oppositions or whole oppositions. The former, however, cannot constitute a whole knowledge in its own right. It cannot be the subject of a sentence; for it cannot have a predicate. If the predicate is not the subject itelf, then the opposite of the predicate could just as easily be combined with the subject, and it then contains an entire opposition, contrary to our presuppositions. Something of this kind cannot be an independent concept either, for it would have to be a general one which is broad in scope (28) and as such encompass many lower ones, and hence also contain these opposing concepts entirely bound up together within it, contrary to our presuppositions.

35 Only that knowledge which contains oppositions entirely bound up together within it is knowledge that can be posited in its own right; accordingly, as far as we are concerned, only a being of this kind constitutes a [kind of] being.

A third possibility is inconceivable for any knowledge outside and below the highest knowledge; knowledge is, however, the measure of being.

36 A knowledge which contains oppositions bound up together within it is to this extent the image of the highest knowledge, whose place is above all oppositions, and thus also the being of being.

For to the extent that, whilst containing an opposition within it it is nevertheless a single thing, according to our presuppositions, the opposition as such has disappeared within it, and it resembles what is placed above all opposition altogether. It generates those oppositions out of itself, however, as they break free, resembling that which generates all definite knowledge out of itself.

The highest knowledge within us thus directly generates a lively knowledge which is similar to itself. Any knowledge, however, which articulates only one side of an opposition is dead, considered on its own terms, for it does not allow the development of knowledge to go any further. In the same way the highest being directly generates a similar lively being.

37 Perfect, steadfast equilibrium between the two terms of an opposition cannot fall to the lot of definite being and knowledge.

For then it would be something self-contained, at rest. As surely as definite knowledge and being is not this, but is also partly defined by what is posited alongside it and is dependent on that, so its equilibrium is also disturbed.

All definite being and knowledge, moreover, is repetitive, given in plurality. There would be no distinctions to be made within this repetition, however, and plurality would be merely an illusion, if the essence of each were an unwavering equilibrium.

38 To the extent that it is given in a definite being and knowledge, then, each opposition must be given in the twofoldness whereby one of its terms predominates here, and the other there.

For the one has the same right as the other to exist as the predominant one, and only in this twofoldness is the opposition perfect.

39 That definite being and knowledge which, posited as a single thing for itself, unites both ways of binding together what is opposed, just like every species which consists in the twofoldness of the sexes, is higher and more perfect than one which is posited in its own right only as a single way of binding together the oppositions.

For the latter resembles more that essentially dead [form of] being which contains only one side of the opposition within it, since the two ways of binding together are also in opposition; the former – for this very reason – resembles more the highest [form of] being which stands above all oppositions.

Hence it is natural and necessary for us to seek out that twofoldness in all definite being and knowledge, and to regard whatever it is found in as the more perfect thing.

40 A definite being or knowledge which is posited only as something especial or only as something general does not exist to that extent in its own right but has simply been taken arbitrarily out of something else.

For what is quite simply general ought not to have anything similar alongside it, since otherwise it would constitute something especial and would have to be opposed both to it and to something higher. Thus it would have to develop everything else out of itself and be quite simply the highest thing, contrary to our presuppositions.

And what is quite simply especial, as the smallest in terms of scope, would not be permitted to develop anything else out of itself and would thus not constitute an element in the development.

Both things, then – what is infinitely big according to the concept and what is infinitely small according to the concept – are separate, and, taken in their own right, are only boundary-points and hence in reality nothing.

41 What is finite and definite, however, as knowledge within us and as being for us, cannot be a pure simultaneity of the general and the especial, but only predominantly something general, which can nevertheless turn into something especial, or else something especial, which can nevertheless turn into something general.

Otherwise one of them or each of them would have to be the focal point of the whole system, which does not exist for us anywhere, however, because the ends do not exist anywhere.

We cannot posit predominance here, however, in anything other than the fact that the one appears from the other's point of view and appears to be dependent upon it.

42 That definite being and knowledge is the higher one which, posited as a single thing in its own right, unites both species of this imperfect simultaneity of the general and the especial, like the genus which consists in the plurality of its species and the species which adopts a shape derived from the genus. Anything, however, which as something general is indeed also something especial, but does not take on the appearance of the species, anything which as something especial is indeed also something general, but does not produce a genus – that is the lower one.

For the latter resembles more that in which one of the two really disappears, that which is one-sided, dead; the former more that in which the two entirely permeate each other. For this reason we too seek always to produce a genus and take on the appearance of a species, and to order being and knowledge accordingly.

43 Knowledge which is thus in opposition to the highest knowledge and stands below it, and thus also the being which corresponds to it, forms only one totality, in which we can find the knowledge that we seek and its particular place, to the extent that all the oppositions in which knowledge consists stand in a definite relation to one another.

See § 1. For the starting-points are then the higher oppositions from which the others develop.

44 This relationship, however, can itself only be determined by oppositions; for this reason we must seek a highest opposition.

In seeking to establish a highest opposition, we necessarily enter the domain of those manifold depictions of the highest knowledge which are, all of them, imperfect. This is where arbitrariness begins, and the conviction which accompanies the process on which we are engaged can only be made firm by success, that is, when a coherent view of knowledge can be expressed in a clear and definite way.

45 We must also be able to find the highest opposition within our own being, and since this is [what is] given to us most directly, we must seek it here first of all.

For as something individual and exceedingly small in scope, our being is determined by all the oppositions. For this very reason, however, we lack any indication as to which one is the highest; and it is easy for dispositions to diverge and decide that it is first one and then another. In this way the shape assumed by the highest knowledge inevitably becomes a matter of one's cast of mind[10] and the direction taken by the will.

[10] *Corrected from:* character.

46 The highest opposition, in which it is dimly apparent to us that all the others are encompassed, is the opposition of material and spiritual being.

Being is material in terms of what is known, spiritual in terms of knowing, both of these taken in the broadest possible sense, of course.

We have only to look at ourselves for this opposition naturally to become the highest, at least here, by virtue of the purpose we are engaged on within the activity of knowledge. It is, however, inherent in all the activities of knowledge as its most general condition.

Each term of this opposition taken in its own right, separately, is nothing in being and knowledge, but remains merely a dead letter.

47 The interrelation of all the oppositions encompassed by this highest opposition, seen in material terms, or the interrelation of all material and spiritual being regarded as something material, that is, as something known, is *nature*. And the interrelation of everything material and spiritual regarded as something spiritual, that is, as something knowing, is *reason*.

Initially, then, we are talking about a single nature and a single reason. But every unity of material and spiritual being, taken from its material side, and even knowledge regarded as something known, i.e. in material terms, becomes nature. And in the same way, anything which has the tiniest share of the spiritual is, in this sense, a [kind of] reason.

It is evident that reason must immediately be thought of again as nature, if it is to be an object and thus known, and likewise nature as reason, when it is thought of as ideas, conveying and bodying forth purposes; this simply proves the subordinate and imperfect nature of any division.

Of course the use of such expressions will not be familiar to everyone. This would equally have been the case, however, if we had employed any others, given our state of linguistic confusion, which is as ludicrous as it is salutary.

48 The highest image of the highest being, however, and thus also the most perfect conception of the totality of all definite being, is the complete permeation and unity of nature and reason.

Indeed, one could say that, even though nature posited on its own terms and reason posited on its own terms contain a wealth of oppositions all bound up together, we are nevertheless already abandoning lively intuition of them when we divide one from the other, and must at the very least hold fast to the fact that, as an image of what is highest, they cannot exist apart from each other and without each other.

49 In the individual, who can however in a higher sense be posited as existing in his own right, the interrelation of the material and spiritual is expressed in the coexistence and opposition of soul and body.

Only if the two are taken together are they one. Each of the two expressions, however, signifies the subordinate unity and totality of everything which is one of the two, [either] the knowing or the known. But what we call the body is as such already always an interrelation of the material and the spiritual, and the same is true of what we call the soul. For this reason it is also only the subordinate view of our existence that regards soul and body as a mutuality, each mediated by the other and conditional upon the other. The same is true of nature and reason in general.

50 The work which is the activity of the spiritual within nature is always shape; the work of the material in reason is always consciousness.

Body is always body because of shape; without it, if it were merely raw material, it would be a material thing without anything spiritual to it. Material is thus the element of the bodily which suffers, shape is what it suffers. And soul is always soul because of consciousness, for without it, if it were merely the nameless counterpart of what is material, the location of concepts, it would be a spiritual thing without anything material to it.

The body and soul of the human being constitutes the opposition under the most extreme tension, a twofold interrelation of the material and the spiritual. We see that opposition diminish in the animal and plant worlds, but we never see it disappear except where what can be posited in its own right also disappears, so that we are driven back towards something higher. Where there is shape there is a corresponding consciousness, and vice versa.

This opposition, which appeared to be derived from our being and calculated only with that in mind, thus runs through everything which is real in our eyes.

51 The greatest diversity of scope in real being, in which it is dimly apparent[11] to us that all the others are encompassed, is that between force and manifestation.

If we call the relationship between the material and the spiritual an opposition, and the relationship between the general and the especial a diversity, that is because the former is, so to speak, more rigid, the latter more fluid. But distinction itself is fluid; opposition is only diversity which has become rigid, diversity only a fluid opposition.

Each one of the two, taken on its own terms, is also nothing, if completely separated from the other (see § 40). The highest being cannot be posited as a force, because every force is measured by the totality of its manifestations and thus necessarily has a definite scope; and again, a manifestation which were not itself a force would not constitute the lowest form of being either, for nothing would be manifest in it and it would be a mere pretence.

52 The simultaneity of force and manifestation, posited as a force, or in a general way, is essence; the same thing, posited as something especial, is existence.

What was stated above (§ 47) about use of language is true here too. The terms should be understood in this sense with regard to each and every domain of being, insofar as it can be closed off from the others and exist solely in its own right.

53 The purest image of the highest being in relation to this diversity is the organism.

For within it, force is conditional upon manifestation just as much as manifestation upon force, and the opposition between the two is superseded in simple intuition. Indeed, if

---

[11] *Corrected from:* appears.

we say that being is dynamic, to the extent that it is posited predominantly as something general, and mechanical to the extent that it is posited predominantly as something individual, we must acknowledge that if both are posited outside what is organic, neither can exist on its own. Only inasmuch as we are able to pursue the sphere of the organic can we assume that something continues to exist in its own right.

54 [12] The complete unity of finite being as the interrelation of nature and reason within an all-encompassing organism is the world.

What is merely dynamic and merely mechanical can only be imagined before the world [came into existence], while what is purely material or purely spiritual can only be imagined outside the world, which is as much as to say, nowhere. Anyone who talks of a plurality of worlds does so only in a subordinate sense, by presupposing a total world uniting this plurality of partial worlds.

55 If the totality of knowledge relating to a domain of being which is defined by oppositions constitutes a science, there are necessarily only two main branches of science, one concerned with nature and the other with reason, and these must encompass all the other definite, self-contained [branches of] science in the form of subordinate disciplines.

Each one of the two necessarily presupposes the other, however, and so each is imperfect if separated from the other. Other [branches of] science, however, cannot be directed towards true being, according to § 35 and 46.

56 Like being, the knowledge which is its expression must also be a simultaneity of the general and the especial, of thinking and imagining. But a pure equilibrium between the two will never be found in any real, definite knowledge.

In reality there is no purely especial knowledge which might express one [kind of] being, any more than there is a purely general kind. The more the two are interrelated, however, the more perfect each one is. Thinking denotes a simultaneity of the general and the especial to the extent that it is posited as something general, but no true thought is without pictoriality, i.e. without any expression of the individual. The reverse is true of imagining; but no true imagining is ever without schematism, i.e. without any expression of the general.

57 With regard, then, to the twofoldness of being as force and manifestation, there is also twofold knowledge, a contemplative kind which is the expression of essence and an observing kind which is the expression of existence.

In contemplative knowledge the same being is expressed in archetypal images as is expressed in observing knowledge by reproduced images. If, however, thought predominates in the one and imagining in the other, what was stated above is true of both. See § 56.

---

[12] *§ 54 and its gloss were entered later in the margin.*

58 The two main sciences thus also fall into two aspects, in that both nature and reason can be known both in a contemplative way and an experiential one.

This is only decreasingly true of their possible subdivisions, however, in that the contemplative aspect, posited in its own right, must diminish in importance the more the object is posited simply as a manifestation. The opposition can never disappear entirely, however. Even the highest being can be known experientially, because every force is at the same time a manifestation; and even the lowest can be known by contemplation, because every manifestation is at the same time a force.

59 The contemplative expression of finite being, inasmuch as it is nature, or the recognition of the essence of nature, is physics or natural science; the observing expression of the same being, or the recognition[13] of the existence of nature, is knowledge of nature.

The fact that "science" tends to denote the contemplative element, while "knowledge" tends to denote the experiential aspect probably corresponds to the use of the terms in everyday life.

Since, incidentally, taken purely on its own terms the general cannot form any real knowledge simply by thinking, without imagining, natural science cannot be purely contemplative either. Hence there are various stages in the handling of such knowledge. The strands of what we have called knowledge of nature include not only what we customarily call natural history or natural description but also what we customarily call natural philosophy, and there must be an element of thinking in both; hence various stages arise in the handling of this knowledge, too.

60 The experiential expression of finite being, inasmuch as it is reason, or the recognition of the existence of reason, is the study of history; the contemplative expression of the same being, or the recognition of the essence of reason, is [the discipline of] ethics, or the doctrine of morals [*Sittenlehre*].

The reason that the customary term does not purely describe the situation here is because we use the term "nature" when speaking of both manifestations and forces. We cannot use the word "history" to describe the force, however, and say "science of history," for example, instead of "doctrine of morals"; similarly we cannot use the word "reason" to describe manifestations and say "knowledge of reason." The expressions "science of reason" and "doctrine of reason" have already been anticipated by something else, however. The relationship is nevertheless the same. Just as natural science contains within it the beginnings of nature, in which, as in their living generality, all natural manifestations are rooted, as the especial things which belong in it, so the doctrine of morals contains the beginnings of reason, in which, in just the same way, the manifestations of reason are

---

[13] The contemplative . . . the recognition: *Added in the margin, but subsequently crossed out:* The highest unity of all knowledge which expresses both domains of finite and definite existence in their interrelationship, as the permeating of the ethical and the physical and as a simultaneity of . . .

rooted, the whole course of which goes to form history in the widest scope of the term. Mores in the higher sense, like ἦθος, are simply a definite force of reason, spread over a certain area, which produces definite manifestations. Given that the name necessarily also expresses something especial, it very properly expresses the fact that no true knowledge of an object occurs without also positing some especial element.

61 The highest unity of knowledge, expressing both domains of being in their interrelatedness, as the perfect [mutual] permeation of the ethical and physical and the perfect simultaneity of the contemplative and the experiential, is the idea of "world-wisdom" [*Weltweisheit*; usually translated: philosophy].

This is the perfect reproduction of the totality of being, just as that is the direct image of the highest being. It can never be complete, however, as long as ethics and physics continue to exist as separate sciences. In both, however, [philosophy] is the endeavor to achieve [mutual] permeation; it is only as a result of this that both are really sciences. The Hellenic name φιλοσοφία signifies more the fact that this is present only as an endeavor, and encompassed both physical and ethical efforts; the German name, world-wisdom, indicates more the fact that it is only by means of such [mutual] permeation that all knowledge is an expression of the world. And all ethical knowledge is only truly philosophical inasmuch as it is physical at the same time, all physical knowledge only inasmuch as it is ethical at the same time. In the same way, everything empirical is unphilosophical if it is not speculative at the same time, and everything speculative is unphilosophical if it is not empirical at the same time.

Something which is not the [mutual] permeation of both ethical and physical, contemplative and empirical, however, but in fact none of these, is dialectics, the reproduction without content of the highest knowledge, which only possesses truth inasmuch as it is present in the two others. Opposed to it is mathematics, which is only concerned with the form and condition of the especial as such.

III   Exposition of the doctrine of morals [*Sittenlehre*]

62 The doctrine of morals, then, as a contemplative science, is on the one hand equal to natural science and coordinated with it; on the other hand, as an expression of reason, it is equal to the study of history and coordinated with it.

A natural diversity of treatment is thus already present, depending on whether an inclination towards history or an inclination towards physics predominates. The endeavor to bind the two together greatly and equally is the truly philosophical impulse.

63 Since the doctrine of morals only stands in opposition to natural science by virtue of the content of the being which is expressed in it, there is no reason for any essential diversity between the two in terms of form.

It is already clear from this alone that what is peculiar to ethical knowledge, by contrast with physical knowledge, cannot be that only the latter expresses what is, while the former expresses what ought to be; this distinction arises only if natural science is treated more experientially, whilst ethics is treated more contemplatively. For what is individual diverges from the uniformly general concept just as much on the side of nature as on the side of reason. Now if what is general is regarded in the same way in both cases as producing what is especial, then ethical knowledge is also just as much the expression of what is, as physical knowledge is the expression of what ought to be.

64 Just as in the being of the world, seen as the complete interrelation of nature and reason in everything which can be posited in its own right, the one can be measured against the other, so also as world-wisdom comes into being, the doctrine of morals and natural science are measurable by one another and conditional upon one another.

Whenever more is posited in nature than reason, or vice versa, then no true whole has been posited which can be regarded as [constituting] a world in its own right.

In the same way, whenever more is posited in physics than in ethics, either no scientific whole has been posited, but only a part of one, which is completed by the other [part], or else world-wisdom is not yet in a process of becoming but consists only of scattered elements.

65 Just as in the world, regarded as the mutual confusion of the general and the especial, force and manifestation are absorbed by each other, so also as world-wisdom comes into being, the doctrine of morals and the study of history are absorbed by each other everywhere and are thus conditional upon each other and measurable by each other.

If force and manifestation do not exhaust each other in some way or other, then in some way or other they do not belong together: either something is posited in the manifestation which actually emanates from another force, or else something is posited in the force whose manifestation occurs elsewhere. In the same way, where something occurs in the study of history which cannot be understood by means of the doctrine of morals, or vice versa, then either no scientific whole has been posited, or else the science does not encompass its object.

66 Those elements that permeate each other entirely in complete world-wisdom and therefore no longer exist in opposition are conditional upon each other in especial knowledge.

Only by being conditional in this way can permeation of knowledge which is otherwise one-sided – and false in its one-sidedness – come about; and the uniform development of knowledge is only given through being conditional in this way. The two together bring world-wisdom into a state of becoming.

67 The doctrine of morals is conditional upon natural science in terms of content, because the material element in reason can only be recognized in and with the totality of what is material, that is, in and with nature.

For reason is the material and the spiritual all bound up together; but the material takes second place and can therefore only be recognized if it is thought of as being one with the more prominent brightening in nature.

68 The doctrine of morals is conditional upon natural science in terms of shape because, as a contemplative science, it only has a firm foundation inasmuch as the contemplative orientation is posited in general terms within the cognitive agent, and is thus also directed towards nature.

Only if physics progresses at a uniform rate will ethics become a science; for otherwise it manages to exist only because of interest in its object, that is, by chance. Where one part of world-wisdom is superseded, there is no life in science, and the part that has been posited and cultivated must also perish.

69 For this reason the doctrine of morals is never better than natural science, and there is consistent uniformity between the two.

The same vicissitudes and the same deviations in terms of the shape they assume must feature in both. That is, on a large scale, considered according to peoples and stages of development; but on a small scale, too, it is just as natural that fluctuations should take place. It is self-evident, however, that this is mutual and that physics is conditional upon ethics in just the same way.

70 The doctrine of morals is conditional upon the study of history in terms of its shape; for in its existence as something separate from natural science it only has a firm foundation if the affinity with the object – and thus also the inclination towards the study of history – is posited in the recognizing agent in its entirety.

Where participation in history has not yet emerged in scientific shape we do not find any continuous separation in the business of contemplation either; either there is quite simply no ethical element in knowledge or else it is mixed up with the physical and gets lost within it. This does not constitute the interrelatedness of the two in world-wisdom, however.

71 The doctrine of morals is conditional upon the study of history in terms of content; for the general cannot be recognized as producing the especial if there is no knowledge of the especial itself.

The doctrine of morals is only ever guaranteed inasmuch as it has the study of history alongside it. The more sketchy the latter, the more sketchy and one-sided the former also, or else, if inclination predominates, the more arbitrary.

72 For this reason the doctrine of morals is never better than the study of history, and there is consistent uniformity between the two.

Which must be lively and mutual. What we can comprehend historically will only truly become the study of history depending on how far the doctrine of morals has developed and progressed.

73 If, then, we add to the various ways of finding a scientific basis for the doctrine of morals (§ 8) its dependence on natural science and history, themselves still imperfect and arbitrary in their formation, these two things will cause us to understand all the imperfections of the doctrine of morals and all the deviations in the way it is treated.

Alternation, and existence alongside one another, of one-sided [approaches] which stand in connection to relationships.

74 Since, therefore, all [aspects of] real knowledge come into being with and through one another, the growing perfection of the doctrine of morals takes place within its growing separation from natural science and the study of history and its lively exchange with both.[14]

Taking this formula as a starting-point it is easy to understand retrospectively how the state of the doctrine of morals initially had its roots in the confusion of its elements with those of natural science and history.

75 Since all emergence from generality into especial being is an action on the part of generality, and thus all contemplative[15] knowledge is the expression of an action, it follows that ethics is the expression of the action of reason.

Action, activity belong together with force. All action is only recognized contemplatively, and in the empirical sphere it is always the side which is turned towards the contemplative.

76 Being, considered as something especial, becomes manifold[16] not least because of the temporal and spatial diversity in which it is posited, that is, when determined mathematically; considered as something general it becomes manifold only because of the diversity of the oppositions bound up together within it, that is, when determined dialectically.

For since there is a plurality of what is especial within the same generality, which is the same to that extent in the latter respect, it can only be diverse in the former respect. And since the same force, as a single entity, produces a plurality of manifestations, which are varied in the former respect, so that it is itself multiple in the former respect, it can only diverge from the others in the latter respect.

77 The action of reason is thus expressed in ethics as something manifold which, leaving aside spatial and temporal determination, is divided according to definition.

It must be something manifold, for otherwise ethics would not be a science. Thus it can only be this. To the extent that the especial aspect which emerges from it is also expressed here, however, it must be expressed spatially and temporally.

---

[14] *Later (1832?) marginal note:* This § is an ending. – What follows is concerned with the depiction of content, but it would be best to start with § 80, which picks up the concept of history. § 76 and 77 ought probably to be held back until later.

[15] *Corrected from:* speculative.   [16] *Corrected from:* diversity.

78 None of these individual expressions can contain an original entering of reason into nature, however, much less an entering of the spiritual into the material.

Not all of them [together], nor a single one; for they would not be real knowledge and would consider reason outside the world.

79 It is just as impossible, however, for the doctrine of morals, regarded as something separate from natural science, to express a perfect oneness of reason and nature.

For in such a state perfect equilibrium would result in complete superseding of that opposition. And because it could be regarded equally as the action of reason and the action of nature, knowledge of it would not be ethical knowledge.

80 The action of reason, however, produces unity of reason and nature, which would not exist without that action; and since this corresponds to sufferance on the part of nature it is therefore the action of reason upon nature.

1. That is, of reason which has always been united with nature in some way.
2. Since, however, unity of reason and nature is produced outside [nature], we must posit a becoming of nature without any action on its part, that is, a sufferance. Whatever suffers when another acts, however, is acted upon.

81 All ethical knowledge is thus the expression of reason becoming nature, a process which has always already begun but is never complete.

For since everything which has been brought forth is in its turn such a unity of reason and nature, in which reason is acting, but in which it could not act apart from this, it becomes more at one with nature each time as a result of what is produced; this can therefore also be expressed in this way.

82 There is thus a oneness of reason and nature which is never expressed in ethics but always exists as an assumption; and another which is never expressed but to which ethics always points.

Exists as an assumption: just as every expression of finite being already assumes a binding together of oppositions; to which ethics points: just as all being and knowledge ruled by opposition points towards the superseding of opposition.

83 Since, however, all ethical knowledge is dependent upon this assumption of unity, it must also be intuited in all ethical knowledge as the existence of reason in nature as a force which is given before any action on the part of reason.

That is, without the possibility of its being comprehended ethically; it must therefore be posited as a real knowledge with its roots in the material side of knowledge.

84 This is the existence of nature within the human organism, and knowledge of it is thus intuition of human nature as such, given before ethics,

so that every real oneness of nature which suffers and reason which acts can be traced back to this original [fact].

Everyone must accept that this is true. For in the partial world in which our being and knowledge are enclosed, no other action of reason is given to us except what proceeds from its existence as a force within human nature.

85 Since human nature as such is at the same time necessarily something especial, the doctrine of morals must at least leave the question open as to whether contemplative natural science can bring forth an intuition of this kind, in the way that it needs to.

For it would have to have physical knowledge before it, complete, and pass judgment on it, which it is not able to do because at the same time it is necessarily in a process of becoming, and because it is self-contained.

86 Thus since it cannot appeal to the knowledge of nature any more than to the science in which this intuition ought already to be given experientially, it can only demand the individual elements as and when it requires them.

That is, it expects everyone who is unlikely to possess ethical knowledge to know this unity because of the action of reason or nature within himself, and leaves it up to the material sciences somewhere and somehow to raise this knowledge to a scientific level.

87 Since contemplative natural science finds itself in the same situation because of its complete uniformity [with ethics], and must also work from the assumption of a reason that has become natural, there has been a tendency, either separately or together, to use the demands made on both sides to establish an independent doctrine which will close the circle between the two, so to speak.

Anthropology in general terms, or separately, physical and psychical. We ought not to regard this assemblage as a science, however, since the individual parts are never completely established in the whole to which they actually belong, and its usefulness is purely didactic; no reference will be made to it here.

88 That oneness of reason and nature, which is indicated everywhere, is where there is no longer any necessity for reason to act nor nature to suffer; it therefore assumes that the action of reason is complete, but for that very reason it is also rooted in every real action.

It is thus something which is not produced by any real action on the part of reason as expressed in ethical knowledge, and is therefore not to be recognized in ethics, neither in each separate point nor in one final end-point.

89 Pure reason and a blissful life never feature directly in the doctrine of morals, therefore, only natural reason and earthly, resistant life.

For pure reason would only be reason that has not yet been united with nature, which cannot be contemplated at all in true knowledge, not even in action. A blissful life is thought of only as one, however, in which no suffering is posited. Pure reason is posited, admittedly, in all ethical knowledge, but not in its own right; a blissful life is also posited, but not *in* being as expressed, only *through* it. [*Translator's emphasis.*]

90 All ethical knowledge, however, necessarily expresses a relative disappearance of the nature which is posited as being outside reason, and thus also of the suffering of nature at the action of reason.

For a gradual uniting is posited, which would not exist if it were not for the action of reason, and in which reason is again active; thus in every descent there is less separateness between the two.

91 The opposition of good and evil means simply the setting against one another in each individual ethical domain of what is posited within it as the interrelatedness of reason and nature and what is posited as the separateness of the two.

All definite being is good, inasmuch as it is a world in itself, the reproduction, quite simply, of being, where oppositions are absorbed by each other. – Given that good is posited through the action of reason, however, it is not possible either for nature itself to be evil, for it, too, is posited in what is good, nor for there to be a counter-reason which, if it were at one with nature, would be evil. For if this were so there could be no presupposition of the [ultimate] unity of reason and nature. Good as opposed to evil has only a moral significance, however, for we normally posit good and bad in opposition to one another everywhere. A moral domain is a definite, limited [instance of] being which may be posited as moral in itself. Only within such a domain do we posit evil together with good and so it can only express what is described above.

92 Given that the doctrine of morals interprets the action of reason as something manifold, it is the ever-renewed positing and superseding of the opposition of good and evil.

The opposition is posited, in that definite moral domains are posited; and superseded, in that an interrelation of nature and reason is posited which did not exist apart from the action thus expressed.

As a formula, then, it can no doubt be established in advance; but its content cannot be predetermined, namely what kind of being is good and what kind is evil, with what is thus determined forming the basis of the doctrine of morals; on the contrary, it comes into being alongside the doctrine of morals, and the development of the one is the development of the other. – One can only say in advance that it is possible; that is, [the problem is] posed by the fact that originally reason is not nature and nature is not reason.

93 If ethical knowledge assumes the shape of a law or moral imperative it expresses neither the interrelation of reason and nature nor the disappearance of their separateness as the action of reason; it does not express true being but only a definite separateness, that is, a non-being.

A doctrine of morals which consists of categorical imperatives expresses only the negating aspect of the action of reason, and posits everything which is reason's true being as non-being as far as the doctrine of morals is concerned. For we only find a moral imperative where there is non-being, and to the extent that this is so. Thus in a doctrine of morals of this kind reason is not even posited as a force at all.

94 If ethical knowledge assumes the shape of[17] good counsel which may be followed, but may equally not be followed, the successful [implementation] of which is however the interrelation of reason and nature, it expresses neither the relative separateness of the two, nor the way in which that interrelation has come about by the excluding action of reason: not reason's true being, then, but only what is always pointed to; and its true being is non-being as far as this [approach] is concerned.

A consultative doctrine of morals essentially supersedes the opposition between good and evil, as we readily discover. – What it has in mind is a being which can just as easily be comprehended in terms of the action of nature and related to this, as it can to the action of reason. What we are in search of as a moral doctrine, namely what stands in the same relation to the study of history in the broadest sense as contemplative natural science does to the knowledge of nature in the broadest sense, is something which can never come about in forms such as these.

95 The propositions of any doctrine of morals ought not, therefore, to be commandments, whether conditional or unconditional, but inasmuch as they are laws they must express the true action of reason upon nature.

The desire to discover conformity to the law in the course of history is a contradiction which is destructive to knowledge, if one does not seek the law in active reason but surrenders reason to what is arbitrary, that is, to chance.

96 To the extent that reason acts upon nature, its work in nature is that of shaping, and nature stands in the same relation to it as mass does to force.

For reason stands in the same relation to nature as the spiritual to the material, and in all its behavior it stands in the same relation to what nature produces as does the unity of the general to the multiplicity of the especial. What is material and especial, however, considered as the manifold and leaving shape entirely out of consideration, is mass. – Nature which is the object of the action of reason has indeed assumed shape in its own right, but relative to the shape which it is to receive from reason, it is [nevertheless] mass.

97 To the extent that reason has only acted when nature has been united with it, and the nature which has become one with active reason must also be active and productive alongside it, the action of reason upon nature is the formation of an organism from the mass.

For nature in the action of reason thus becomes the mutual dependence of force and manifestation (53).

98 Given, however, that in all individual knowledge the doctrine of morals expresses an organic interrelationship between nature and reason as the

---

[17] *Corrected from:* is expressed as.

action of reason, it is not possible for any such knowledge to express an original entering of reason, regarded as a quickening force, into nature, regarded as a dead mass.

Neither one [piece of knowledge] nor all of them [together]; for if one of them constituted a starting-point it would not be the same as the rest and could not form a single whole together with them. Neither would all of them together be the expression of true being, because they would posit something general in its own right and also something especial in its own right.[18]

99 There is thus a unity of reason-force and nature-mass which is expressed nowhere in the doctrine of morals, an assumption which is always made of nature being organized for reason; that is human nature as a species.

For all the ways in which shape is conferred upon nature for the purposes of reason proceed from human beings; but only to the extent that human nature is a species can reason always have been present within it.

100 Similarly, there is no kind of ethical knowledge that can express a state of having been organized for the purposes of reason in nature so perfect that in the nature that is acted upon nothing is [mere] mass any more but everything is already united with acting reason.

Even if we were to posit the possibility of finite being carrying the seeds of such perfection within it, the doctrine of morals would not be the expression of this. As certain as its refusal to posit a perfect unity between reason and nature, is its positing of nature which has not been united [with reason] as a mass capable of being organized, one which has thus not yet become force.

101 There is thus a unity of reason-force and nature-mass which is not expressed in the doctrine of morals but which it merely points to.

This is the making moral of the whole of earthly nature in time and space, which is never given as the work of human reason.

102 However, all ethical knowledge necessarily expresses a relative disappearance of nature as mere mass, so that the action of reason never ends in the especial as such; on the contrary, what is also posited is that each manifestation becomes force.

If reason ended in the individual, it would always end in death. Everything which has become moral must become a component of what is morally productive in its turn, and thus return to its source.

103 Thus the doctrine of morals must also demand a knowledge of nature-as-mass which is given elsewhere, without being able to wait until this has been acquired by a perfect scientific route.

---

[18] *Question mark in margin.*

Just as [we saw] knowledge of humanity as nature above, so here we find knowledge of humanity as a species, that is, knowledge of the steadfastness of individuals, inasmuch as every manifestation becomes life again in them, and knowledge of the connectedness of individuals, for that is the condition on which any mass becomes force.

104 The opposition between freedom and necessity means simply the setting against one another in each individual ethical domain of what is posited within it as the interrelation[19] of force and mass and what is posited as the separateness of the two.

This opposition is enacted entirely in the moral domain, for in every other the opposition is between necessity and chance. Freedom is where manifestation and force are posited within a single entity, however; necessity where they are posited in a diversity, and to the extent that this is so. If one regards everything moral as a singularity, the opposition does not exist; it only arises as a result of individuation, inasmuch as this is only relatively [the case for] each individual thing, posited in its own right. Now inasmuch as each one is posited in its own right, it also has the productive [capacity] of its manifestations within it, and these are free; inasmuch as this is not the case, they are necessities.

105 Thus, in that the doctrine of morals interprets the productive action of reason as something manifold, it alternately posits and supersedes the opposition between freedom and necessity.[20]

It is posited every time a larger moral domain is fragmented into several small ones; for these are posited less in their own right, more as conditional upon one another. It is superseded when smaller moral domains are brought together to form a larger one; for then reference is to a single entity where before it was to a diversity.

106 Since at every point moral being contains force which is conditional upon mass, inasmuch as an original interrelation of force and mass always forms the basis of it, a pure moral doctrine, so-called, is a thought without substance.

For this always attempts to start from [the idea that] reason as a force precedes all man-ifestation and is not conditional upon it in any way, and thus goes far beyond reality. A doctrine of this kind can only ever consist of empty formulae, as can readily be seen, in which there is no expression of actual being, so that nothing is gained by it.

107 Since it is only in relative terms that each individual moral domain can be posited in its own right, and is never entirely self-contained and comprehensible on its own terms, an applied doctrine of morals, so-called, is a thought without substance.

---

[19] *Here the words that followed were crossed out:* of mass which has become force and mass which has not become force.

[20] *Marginal addition 1832:* It is superseded in the construction referring to the end-point; and posited in the construction for judgment of the individual.

For this attempts to regard active reason as if it were a conditional state, necessarily including immoral elements which must be superseded. But it has no starting-point from which to recognize the laws governing such superseding, and knowledge of this kind, since it is ethical, cannot be posited in its own right.

In the opposition between pure and applied science, then, the doctrine of morals does not emerge as a real science. Indeed, this opposition is no more relevant to the doctrine of morals than to natural science.

108 However far the doctrine of morals may extend into individual matters, it will never become the study of history; on the contrary, the two will always remain separate, and neither will ever become simply the opposite pole of the other.

Given that the assumption is made everywhere in the doctrine of morals that mass has become force, [some kind of] existence has admittedly already been presupposed, but it is precisely not one which is comprehended ethically. The more [moral doctrine] goes into individual detail, the more existence must be presupposed, and so, for it to become the study of history, what has been comprehended ethically must have come to nought. For this reason there is no continuous transition from the doctrine of morals to the study of history. In the same way, the latter cannot give lively expression to individual matters without encompassing the general, but not in an historical context. The more it generalizes from a particular manifestation, the more it has to presuppose essence; but before it could reach the point where it could express the essential context, what has been expressed historically would have had to come to nought. – An applied doctrine of morals and the contemplative study of history are matching misconceptions; a pure doctrine of morals and the pure study of history are matching nullities. The doctrine of morals and the study of history will always remain divided entities, existing in their own right; taken together, the study of history provides the illustrations to the doctrine of morals, while the doctrine of morals provides the formulae for the study of history.

109 Quite separate from the doctrine of morals and from the study of history, there is both a critical and a technical method according to which the contemplative and the experiential may be related to each another.

The critical, or examining, method relates the contemplative and the experiential according to world-wisdom. It lies outside [the domain of] real science and it lacks real science's universal validity and its firm shape; for as the bodying forth of a real knowledge it is always to a very great extent the work of what is most particular to man. This moral critique of history ought to be kept separate from both the study of history and from the doctrine of morals, because, as an added element it can easily ruin both. Its main concern is to prove the significance of individual portions of history in relation to the activity of reason as a whole, attempting to dissolve those moral elements which are given by experience into what is contemplatively known, and then to arrive at philosophical comprehension; this must, however, be preceded by something else, which is able to distinguish, within what has been given, between what has come about in a moral way and – mingled with this – the action of nature on its own behalf.

The technical, or regulatory, method relates the contemplative and the experiential to each other in practical terms and lies outside the scope of science altogether on the side of art. Its object is each individual, morally determined uniting of reason and nature, and the way it develops in the natural domain which belongs to it in the conflict between reason, and the nature which is already united with reason, and the nature which still resists it; and it investigates, by means of comparative observation concerning active entry into such a domain, the circumstances and conditions under which it is easiest or most difficult to raise resistance and reason can most easily and most completely take possession of nature. Examples: the art of education, statesmanship, etc. These are not so much sciences as instructions, conditional upon and held together merely by interest in the object itself, and the most appropriate form for them is that of regulations, which in some connections might be more categorical in character, in others more hypothetical.

If the doctrine of morals depicted in this form is also intended to be instruction of this kind, it ought at least to be the epitome of all the others, but even so it would presuppose another science in its turn, which cannot in itself have this form, which would provide the ultimate purposes for all these instructions.

Belonging to this endeavor to create philosophical elements from ethical ones, there is another method apart from that critical one which is easier to connect with it directly; at its main points it leads us across from ethical to physical consideration, but to all intents and purposes has not been worked on at all.

IV   The shape given to the doctrine of morals

110 [21] The oneness of reason and nature which is to be developed in the doctrine of morals as something manifold can be separated out in the first instance into multiplicity of goods, to the extent that both reason and nature contain oppositions within themselves, so that there are many kinds posited in their own right, belonging together but separated from one another, which are preserved in the interaction of force and manifestation, and which are in part at one.

The fact that this oneness of definite aspects of reason and nature is called a "good" is entirely in accordance with the meaning of the word in the opposition of good and evil. For in any concept of this kind we are only positing the interrelationship of reason and nature; and this is posited independently to the extent that it is preserved organically in a similar way to the whole. But also only in this way, for otherwise the renewed separation of the two would also be posited alongside it, and then it would not be a good. It is as certain, however, that there must be a multiplicity of goods as that reason and nature form a higher opposition and are at one with each other.

[21] *Later marginal note (1832?):* Good. Reason as manifold functions, each of them in relative unity with nature.

111 [22] Then [into] multiplicity of virtues, to the extent that there can be diverse ways in which reason can inhabit nature as a force.

Here, too, this is exactly what the the word signifies in common linguistic usage. A basis can be found for individuation of this kind partly in the manifold ways in which nature performs, partly in the manifold ways in which reason inhabits. It is as certain that there is a plurality of virtues as that this is true.

112 [23] Then [into] multiplicity of duties, to the extent that there are various procedures according to which the activity of reason can be both something definite, directed towards the especial, and at the same time something general, directed towards the whole.[24]

Common linguistic usage is confused here, and often uses the words "virtue" and "duty" to describe the same thing. The manifestations produced by any given activity of reason occur sometime and somewhere, but they are only moral inasmuch as they also give expression, in this especial instance, to the orientation of reason towards its oneness with nature as a whole. And to the extent that both these things are incorporated into the concept of an activity of reason, that activity is posited as a duty. Common linguistic usage can also be traced back to this, if it desires to be even-handed.

113 If the doctrine of morals attains its most complete state of development as the doctrine of goods or the doctrine of the highest good, it is also the complete expression of the unity of reason and nature as a whole.

The highest good is not something individual, of the same kind as the others, but towering over them, the best, in any comparison; on the contrary, it is the organic coherence of all the goods, that is, the whole of moral being expressed under the concept of the good.

If we unfold the subordinate oppositions contained within the higher one, they too can only be contemplated as unified and in necessary connection with each other. And so they are the same as what is posited in simple intuition.

114 In the same way, a complete doctrine of virtues is also in itself the whole of the doctrine of morals.

1. If, in general moral intuition reason is posited as producing all interrelation of nature and reason, then all the various ways in which it can be productive in nature are contained within it. The doctrine of virtues is thus simply the unfolding of this general intuition.

2. Since every force is measured by what is epitomized in its manifestations, the totality of manifestations is posited alongside the totality of the forces of reason in nature. They are also posited, however, in the totality of goods; thus the same being is expressed

---

[22] *Later marginal note (1832?):* Virtue. Reason as multiplicity and reason in nature. a) Duplication of the connection, as a belonging together, and as understanding. b) Connection with receptivity and with independent action.

[23] *Later marginal note:* Duty. Movement outward from individual points in the identity of the general orientation and the partial one.

[24] *Later marginal note:* The fact that there cannot be any forms other than these 3.

in the doctrine of virtues as in the doctrine of the highest good. In a different way, however, for neither goods nor duties feature in the doctrine of virtues.

115 If the formulae of duty are set out in their entirety, then here too every interrelation of reason and nature is expressed, and the doctrine of duty is the whole of the doctrine of morals.

If the interrelation of reason and nature disintegrates into a multiplicity of goods, each of them exists as something per se, it is true, but conditional upon the totality of the others. Thus all of them come into being and persist in coherent being only by means of such activities, which are directed towards the especial, as it is posited in the general, and not in any other way – i.e. activities which are taken up in the formulae of duty. If these are all posited, then the first thing is posited too. But in a different way; for the goods as such do not feature in the doctrine of duty.

116 Since these three developments, each of which contains the whole, are also to be found in natural science, they must be rooted in the essence of contemplative knowledge.

Organic natural science, whether dynamic or mechanical, is, properly understood, simply the development of the idea of nature, each separating out individual elements in a different way. In the first, in the system of living forms which reproduce themselves; for if these are contemplated in their own right and their necessary coherence, then nature is contemplated in a similar way to reason within the form of the highest good. In the second, in the system of forces. These are combined in every living form in a particular way and in particular relationship. Thus, if all these forces are contemplated, then the whole of nature is contemplated in a way similar to the development of the doctrine of morals as a doctrine of virtues. In the third, recognized in a contemplative way in the epitome of all interlocking movements. All forces are absorbed, however, within this epitome, as is the existence of all living forms. Thus the system of movements is also the whole of natural science, just as the system of duties is the whole of the doctrine of morals.

Apparent superfluity in one science justifies the same thing in the other. It is exactly the same relationship; for it is merely a misunderstanding if these three approaches within natural science are regarded as being in conflict, canceling one another out.

117 If all the goods are given, then all the virtues and all the duties must be posited at the same time; if all the virtues, then all the goods and all the duties too; if all the duties, then all the virtues and all the goods too.

For since in every interrelation of reason and nature reason is active, and only acts once it has been united with nature, the totality of goods only exists and comes into existence through the totality of virtues, and these are posited in and with the former. Since in every good there is a confusion of force and manifestation, but all goods are conditional upon one another, the totality of goods only exists and comes into existence through the totality of the activities of reason, to the extent that individual manifestations are posited through them, manifestations which are conditional upon all the others.

Since every virtue is already the force of reason within that nature which is morally united with it, and all virtues are conditional upon one another, they all have their place in the totality of the unification which has come into being between reason and nature, and all of them exist only through the activity of reason, which is general and especial at the same time.

Since all duties have as their object that nature which has already been united with reason, when we posit them in their totality we also posit the totality of goods; and since they only exist within that reason which already contains and inhabits nature, then when we posit them in their totality, we also posit the totality of all virtues.

In the doctrine of goods, however, the concepts of virtues and duties never specifically appear; and neither do those of goods and duties in the doctrine of virtues, nor those of goods and virtues in the doctrine of duties.

118 The doctrine of goods is concerned with the pure interrelation of reason and nature, while the doctrines of virtue and of duties are concerned with the relative opposition between the general and the especial contained therein, the one regarded as generating it and the other as being generated by it. None of them, then, are the result of chance and none can be dispensed with.

None of them are the result of chance, because they all have their basis in the way the opposition is bound up, and no other can have the same basis; none can be dispensed with, because each one places emphasis on something which in the other remains in the background, so that only when each is seen in relation to the others is our consideration complete.

It is obvious that in the pure consideration of organic forms the opposition of force and activity is superseded, while in the other two it is posited by placing definite emphasis on one of the terms.

119 In the doctrine of the highest good the doctrine of morals turns its attention above all to world-wisdom, in the doctrine of virtues to natural science, and in the doctrine of duties to history; but in the former the perfection of particularity goes less into individual details than it does in the other two; and in the latter there is less of an overview over the whole domain than there is in the former.

For both the opposition between reason and nature and diversity in the form of knowledge are superseded most in the first of these. However, given that the interrelation of reason and nature is considered as a whole throughout, but nature is already something especial in that original unification, then the more the subordinate oppositions are developed, the more this especialness must come to the fore, and as a result the proportion of what may be presupposed must mount up and knowledge be perfected which is not in the domain of that definite science.

Virtue in the individual human being is thought of as being almost unavoidably primitive, and so at the same time we think that greater or lesser success, depending on a greater or lesser degree of coincidence between individuals, cannot be understood simply as the result of what is ethically posited here, namely virtue. Its comprehensibility, and hence the interrelation and mutual absorption of the doctrine of morals and history, is thought of least of all, and so the doctrine of virtues turns away from history. And given that every virtue points towards that original unification, that is, to the way in which nature was intended for reason, posited before any action, it turns its attention to natural science, not as if there were more nature posited here than in the doctrine of the highest good; but the opposition is more strongly emphasized here.

The doctrine of duties expresses possible ways of acting in the relationship of the individual to the whole; thus its object is what is most individual, and contemplative consideration could not descend any lower; hence it turns its attention most of all to history. But it points back least of all to nature in its opposition to reason, and for this reason turns away from natural science.

120 [25] The doctrine of the highest good considers [its object] in the most self-contained way, at rest within itself, while the doctrine of virtues stimulates critical methods most and the doctrine of duties technical ones.

Given that reason, which is united with reason [*erroneous for* nature] in action, is not perfectly united with it, it is apparent everywhere that being deviates from concept, and this stimulates the provisional critical method which draws the other after it. And given that in any action upon nature success rarely corresponds to the exact concept of construction, this stimulates the technical method, in order to overcome the resistance of reason [*erroneous for* nature] which has not yet been united. The doctrine of the highest good offers no point of comparison, however, with respect to what occurs in experience or to the individual caught up in action.

121 All three forms are of course always simultaneous; but in differing proportions it was the highest good and the doctrine of virtues which predominated in antiquity, and the doctrine of virtues and the doctrine of duties which predominate in modern times.

The more one form represses the other, the more deficient science will be with regard to one side or the other. The finest shape was sketched out when the doctrine of the highest good and the doctrine of virtues began to develop at a virtually uniform rate. The more the idea of the highest good was misunderstood, the more deficient the whole of the doctrine of morals became from the time of Aristotle onward. The doctrine of duties could not properly emerge in antiquity, because domestic matters and all other relationships were absorbed far more into the state, and no object of action was posited at all other than the state. In modern times, on the other hand, the more diverse the ends, thought of as separate from one another, the more the doctrine of duties necessarily emerged. Transition to a less autonomous form is not to be regarded as a backward step, however, because it made it possible to catch up with something that was indispensable, and even what is perfect had only imperfectly been put in place. Only when things that have been one-sided up to now are absorbed into one another can a better state of scientific knowledge arise.

---

[25] *This paragraph and its gloss are absent in Schweizer's edition, but included in Twesten's.*

122 The doctrine of the highest good, as being closest to the highest knowledge and most similar to it whilst remaining autonomous, must precede the others.[26]

[26] *On pp. 3 and 4 of the outside cover are notes which probably date from a later period:* Finite being, considered in physical terms, can also be depicted in an analogous way as the totality of forms which reproduce themselves, as a system of living forces and as the sum of mutually limiting movements.

Each form contains the whole of ethics; but since the doctrine of virtues and the doctrine of duties refer only to subordinate relations, they are also subordinate as forms.

Ethics, as a real sc[ience], should depict the existence of reason in nature in the form of an opposition, that is as the totality of everything which exists in ethical terms for its own sake.

Everything which exists in ethical terms for its own sake depicts a unification of the same on the basis of a unification of reason, already posited, which has already come about, and at the same time, a general existence of reason, which brings forth what is especial.

Everything [existing] for its own sake – which is at one and the same time, with reference to its whole sphere, something which generates and is generated – is something organized, which has become ethical; it is a good. Thus the totality of what exists in ethical terms for its own sake is the system of goods and the organism of reason, so that ethics is the doctrine of the highest good.

To the extent that the unity of reason and nature, considered in ethical terms, is an action of reason upon nature, the object of ethics is the action of reason within human nature; considered in ethical terms, however, reason exists in [human nature] as a force, and what that force disseminates in the form of opposition, so that every force of reason, posited in its own right, is virtue, and so ethics is the doctrine of virtues, and the doctrine of virtues is the whole of ethics.

The totality of being as action is the totality of movements. To the extent that ethics depicts this as something already perfected, it has to depict the totality of formulae for those [movements], i.e. ethics is the doctrine of duties.

[*p. 4*] Every good exists only to the extent that reason inhabits it as a virtue and to the extent that time and place are filled with actions that are in accordance with duty. Thus the system of virtues and duties is also posited in the doctrine of the highest good.

Every action in accordance with duty is moral only to the extent that it is an element in the coming into being of all goods, and to the extent that all the virtues are at work in its genesis; thus in the doctrine of duties [we find] the expression also of the highest good and the system of virtues.

Every virtue exists as such only to the extent that no good can be produced without it, and to the extent that it is at work at every moment to help bring forth what is in accordance with duty. Thus in the doctrine of virtues [we find] the expression also of the highest good and the doctrine of duties.

The highest good corresponds to physics as the expression of the system of forms, the doctrine of virtues as the expression of the system of living forces, and the doctrine of duties as the expression of the system of movements.

In the doctrine of the highest good, ethics moves most of all towards the absolute alone, in that it attempts to express it in its own particular way, and to express the difference between the absolute and itself.

In the doctrine of virtues, as a perfect science, it moves towards physics, in that it attempts to express it in terms of the difference between them as a definite science.

In the doctrine of duties, as a special science, it moves towards history, in that it attempts to express the historical in terms of the difference between them.

Doctrine of goods, final version (probably 1816/17)

1 Introduction

1 Since the interrelation of reason and nature which we have taken as our premise in the domain of the doctrine of morals is the reasonableness of human nature, taken independently of all action, and yet this[1] interrelation, which must be conceived in moral terms, encompasses all those aspects of nature which come into lively contact with human nature, then the totality of everything that can be posited as having an independent moral existence is the totality of our conception of the effects[2] of human reason in the whole of earthly nature.

Human nature posited as nature [itself], inasmuch as it is a species, is conditional upon and sets conditions for the whole of earthly nature. It rests upon all other [aspects of nature] as the highest development of the spiritual in the material, but all the rest, even as life and organism, can only be understood as a striving towards it. To this extent the doctrine of morals presupposes the whole of earthly nature.[3] But for this very reason nature in this sense can only achieve perfection where human nature achieves perfection. The activity of reason is thus all directed towards it too, and the totality [of that activity] is the absorption of the whole of nature into that interrelation with reason which was originally presupposed in human nature and which is realized in action in and through human nature.

2 Inasmuch as all being, as expressed in the doctrine of morals, is the expression of the action of reason and nature together upon nature, the

---

[1] *Marginal note 1824:* which is to be striven for however, which is absolute etc.: thus
[2] *Marginal note 1824:* of moral being which can be posited as existing in its own right – totality of effects.
[3] *Marginal addition 1824:* The identity of material and spiritual which is posited in all that exists does not however prevent the action of human reason on what has already been imbued with mind.

interrelation of nature and reason is to be thought of as nature organized for reason, and the activity of reason as an organizing principle.[4]

For the moral domain is formed to this extent by[5] reason already acting in unity with nature; the nature which is acted upon is to this extent assumed to be outside the moral domain and to exist merely as raw material.[6] In such action, however, reason alone is posited as originally active, i.e. the inner part of the action or its principle, and nature what is acted through, i.e. the outer part of the action or its organ.

When reason has acted, however, upon that nature which we assume to this extent to be outside the moral domain, then to this extent nature too has become one with it, and since reason is only [ever] active, it becomes one with such activity, i.e. it has also become the organ[7] of reason. Or, generally speaking, since all genuine at-oneness of nature and reason should be comprehended in moral terms, any instance of nature functioning as an organ must be comprehended in terms of the action of reason, so that we must necessarily assume that the latter is organizing [in nature].[8]

3 Now, since there is an interrelation of reason and nature which is not expressed through the doctrine of morals but which it only points to, reason as a force in nature is always an organizing activity.[9]

If the doctrine of morals is to be found in the relative opposition of reason and nature, then everywhere in real, definite being reason and nature still exist apart from each other and thus, since reason can only be active, [we see] the action of reason on nature, which (following 1) is organizing in nature.

If we do not posit such a state in which each exists apart from the other, we cannot posit any organizing activity either, for the whole of nature has then become an organ. But to that extent we cannot posit reason as producing anything that is conceptually diverse either, but only the purely especial, which is merely repetition. In this way any action of reason which was not an organizing one would have to be posited as existing outside the moral domain. – Mythic representations, in which such interrelatedness of reason and nature appears.[10]

---

[4] *Marginal note 1824:* Derived from the actual meaning of "organon" as tool.

[5] The moral . . . by. *Corrected from:* unity only takes place between.

[6] *Marginal addition 1832:* The more the organizing is conditioned by the material, the more it is necessary to apply physical moments.

[7] *Marginal addition 1824:* Organic oneness is thus organism, as soon as it can be thought of as existing in some self-contained [state of] perfection.

[8] *Marginal addition 1827:* NB. It must be postulated that being organized is always something which has come about through an ethical process, for otherwise we lose the demarcation of this [branch of] science, together with the certainty of direct moral consciousness, thus excluding the possibility a) that there is no state of being organized which proceeds from the activity of nature and b) that there is none which proceeds from a demarcation of reason which is directed towards something else. This is the special presupposition for the form of the doctrine of morals as the highest good. It must also be possible to find analogues for the other two [forms]. 1827.

[9] *Marginal addition 1824:* All moral being, as an image of the original presupposition, is being organized. NB. Newborn shape is a symbol, not originally [present].

[10] *Marginal addition 1824:* From the point of view of absolute perfection, organizing is only possible while progress is still taking place, and thus the absolute has not yet been attained.

To the extent that human nature, as soul, is that which contains within itself all the roots of the interrelatedness of reason and nature in the moral domain, it is drive which is organized for reason first of all, and the interrelatedness of reason and drive is will. Everything, however, is the organ of reason, its tool, to the extent that its interrelatedness with reason is continuing action upon nature.

4 To the extent that we posit reason as active in the moral interrelatedness of reason and nature, but nowhere else, reason must be recognizably present in that interrelation, and to that extent it is nature being symbolized for reason, so that the action of reason is a symbolizing one.[11]

For each is a symbol of the other to the extent that in the one we recognize the other, each in a different way. Reason is not, however, the interaction of reason and nature, but both of them in different ways. We therefore posit in that interaction a capacity to be recognized which would not otherwise be posited, and it is the only one, since reason which has not been united with nature does not exist in our eyes. Now, to the extent that it is rooted in the action of reason, it is not reason that has become something in which it is possible to recognize reason, but nature. The action of reason, however, is what produces this capacity to be recognized; it is symbolizing action.[12]

5 All symbolization of nature is rooted in the action of reason; and when reason exists as a force in nature it is symbolizing.[13]

1. For what was originally [there], that which cannot be conceived [as proceeding] from the action of reason, is nowhere given to us. It is simply presupposed, to the extent that nowhere are we given any original entering of reason into nature. Thus everything that is definitely thought, everything individual that can be posited as existing in its own right, is to be posited as something moral.
2. Given that each especial way in which reason exists as a force in nature is to be posited as an interrelatedness of reason and nature which is conceptually distinct from every other, then each of these is also an especial symbolization of nature. If we do not posit a relative separateness of reason and nature, so that the whole of nature is symbolized, it is no longer[14] possible to think of reason as acting on nature, and thus all action in this domain is concluded.

It is sense which is most immediately symbolized for reason, and the interrelatedness of reason and sense is understanding. Everything is symbolized, however, which, as a result of the action of reason bears the stamp of understanding, i.e. everything, to the extent that the action of reason upon it has gone through the understanding, so that the

---

[11] *Marginal addition 1824:* All moral being, as an image of the asymptotic point, is symbolized being.
[12] *We therefore posit ... symbolizing activity. Marginal addition, crossed out:* Given that everything which is posited as a moral entity is an interrelatedness which is conceptually distinct from every other, each one is also a definite symbolizing of nature. And all such are to be conceived in moral terms, that is, as proceeding from the action of reason, for what is original, and cannot be conceived in moral terms, is also not given anywhere but merely underlies everything else.
[13] *Marginal note 1832:* The effect of reason.
[14] It is no longer ... on nature. *Corrected from:* and symbolizing action is merely repetitive.

interaction of reason and nature is mediated through the understanding. Of course sense and understanding, on the one hand, and drive and will, on the other, are taken here in their broadest sense.

6 Since reason acts through all nature which has been united with it, every symbol of it is also its organ. And since it can only act through nature which has been united with it, every organ of reason is also its symbol.[15]

The two activities do not create domains which are distinct in accordance with their object, as each encompasses everything within it, and everything which results from the one can also be related to the other. Starting with the most direct and the most internal, understanding is firstly and in itself a symbol, but also an organ, while drive is firstly an organ, but then also a symbol. For in drive we can recognize the action of reason, and sense acts with cognition upon nature. The same is therefore also true of all those things that belong in the system of understanding and those that belong in the system of will.

Each activity is therefore conditional upon the other; neither can be posited or begun without the same being true to the same extent for the other, and neither can be completed or resolved without the same being true to the same extent for the other.

7 [We can define] symbol as every interaction of reason with nature, inasmuch as we can posit that here nature has been acted upon, and [we can define] organ as every interaction of reason with nature, inasmuch as we can posit that here nature will be acted upon; each is thus both, but in unequal measure.[16]

1. For organ is nature as a channel for the action of reason, symbol is nature resting with and in reason.
2. For there is nowhere a point of equilibrium in the relative interaction and separate action of reason and nature. Every definite interaction thus relates predominantly either to the one or to the other.

8 Everything which can be posited as having an independent moral existence must at the same time be conceptually distinct as an individual [entity] from all other individual [entities], just as individual people are originally conceptually distinct from each other, i.e. each must be a particularity.

Conceptually, i.e. not merely because they are different in time and place, but in such a way that there is a distinctive unity underlying the development of what is posited in space and time. Originally, i.e. in such a way that this diversity does not merely develop from coexistence with what is diverse, but is internally posited.

All individual beings belonging to a particular species are all the more internally diverse according to whether the species itself has a firm identity; the more imperfectly defined

---

[15] *Marginal addition 1824:* Being separate is only posited at the two extremes.
[16] *Marginal addition 1824:* or insofar as we can exclude becoming action and vice versa. Inequality follows from the general theory of the formation of the opposition.

it is, the more we attribute diversity merely to external influences. It is thus true to say of humankind, regarded purely as natural beings, that the concept of each one, insofar as it can be perfected by the individual, is different.

All moral existence is posited by the action of the individual, however, and must therefore participate in it, and if what expresses a single interrelatedness of reason and nature in fact appears as a plurality, then each one must also take various forms, because it is posited by the action of various individuals.

9 Everything, therefore, which can be posited as having an independent moral existence, and every especial action[17] of reason, is posited as having a twofold character; it is something which is always and everywhere the same, inasmuch as it always stands in the same relation to reason, which is everywhere one and the same; and it is something which always varies, because reason is always already posited in something that is varied.

Reason, in its unifying action upon nature through nature, must, like nature itself, be differentiated, not in itself, but in its interaction with nature, because only as a differentiated entity can nature be its symbol and its organ, and thus actions which are performed through nature must also be [differentiated].

But inasmuch as reason is originally and exclusively the active principle, everything which is posited in the same way, that is, under the same moral concept, must be the same.

10 Although these two ways are in opposition to each other, they do not create separate domains, neither is one subordinate to the other.

1. For the interaction of nature and reason is conditional upon both in the same way. Because they are always interrelated, the totality of what is moral can be accommodated in each. Precisely for this reason, however, they are the same; it is one-sided to regard only the κοινὸς λόγος as moral, while the opposite view would be equally one-sided.

2. Precisely because each encompasses the whole, and everything which is various has always incorporated everything which has independent moral existence in a context which always remains the same, and because that same reason which is always like itself is always in the process of producing what is various, which then forms that whole context, neither of these two ways is at all separate or distinct.

3. The distinction is, however, that – given that each is one thing in one respect, and the other in the other, as is natural, since their whole twofoldness rests on the fluctuating opposition of the general and the particular – the ranking of relations in various contexts emerges as something various.

11 This distinction modifies the opposition referred to above, and moral existence is therefore the organization of reason with both constant and differentiating characteristics; the same goes for the symbolization of reason.

Only with difficulty and confusion could one reverse this and say that there is an unchanging interrelatedness of organizing and symbolizing content, and in the same way

---

[17] *Corrected from:* activity.

[an interrelatedness] which is characterized by variety. For the former opposition intrudes more upon the content. Admittedly the result must ultimately be the same.

12 The whole moral domain may be comprehended from each of these individual points of view; but each of these views is one-sided and not everything emerges uniformly.

One can say for example that all interrelationship of reason and nature is the acquisition of nature, whose character is always the same. For since everything which is a sign must also be a tool, the totality of what is signified must also appear to be a tool, but only in a subordinate fashion and in such a way that its internal coherence as what is signified does not stand out. And since moreover the diverse[18] is part of our presuppositions in that it is present in the originally unified [state] of nature, so everything which is characterized by variety is also posited, since all activity of reason upon variety and with variety is after all the same as itself in reason. But in this way the coherence of what is uniformly various does not emerge.

We must reach the same conclusion regardless of our starting-point.

13 Now since each of these orientations may be taken as an expression of the whole of moral being, and within the whole all are uniformly [at] one, there is also only one individual thing that can be posited as having independent moral existence, i.e. one good, in which all are unified.

Every individual term in these oppositions is only one element, it has no independent existence and can only be isolated [from the others] for the purposes of examination. True being lies only in the twofold interaction of the general and the especial, and this is never to be found in just one of these terms on its own.

Only in such an admittedly uneven unification of all [being] can individuated being exist as a reflection of the whole.

14 A diversity of goods is therefore only to be sought in the diversity of ways in which these oppositions are combined, and in the diversity of the activities of reason in itself and of nature in itself, which are so combined.

Provided that the same sort of things can be distinguished in both of these activities, so that both, reason and nature, are in a certain sense something especial in moral being.

In the determination of goods material and formal diversity must keep pace; otherwise those things become confused which should be coordinated or subordinate, when functions are isolated here but left together there, when what is identical and what is diverse are separated in one domain, but not in another.

15 Every *good* which varies conceptually from the others is, however, given as a genus only in a plurality of individuals separated from one another in space and time.[19]

---

[18] *Corrected from:* particularity.

[19] *Marginal addition 1824:* Nature cannot lose its essential way of being even when at one with reason. *Marginal addition 1832:* For every speculative interpretation there must also be an empirical one, for every essence an existence.

This is founded equally in reason and nature and anything else is unthinkable. It is unthinkable that every interaction between nature and reason, posited in essence as one [and the same] thing, should also form one whole coherent mass in existence.

16 Thus since every action of reason of a definite kind is only real, inasmuch as it is posited in a definite space, it would not be a moral action inasmuch as it is confined within that space.

The former, because otherwise it would only be a generality, which has no reality. The latter, because it did not strive for the interrelatedness of reason and nature as a single entity and, serving only the individual aspects of a phenomenon, could also only be grasped in those terms, and not by contemplation.

17 With respect to individuation, the existence of reason as a force in nature is posited in two moments:[20] in the production of what is individual, and in the emergence from what is individual.[21]

If the former were absent in any activity, nothing would be posited. The mass of nature on which reason works is the single magnitude against which reason, as a force of definite proportions, as it must be in every real action, can be measured.

If the latter were absent in any activity, only what is individual would be constituted, without any relation to the whole, i.e. the activity would only exist in outward appearance. The emergence from what is individual is, however, simply the superseding in the community of the individuation of all that is homogeneous and thus [both] related and divided. However, the partial positing and superseding of what is individual is separate only in time, i.e. two things which are separate but which only together form the morally formative moment.

18 Since the various goods similarly have no other way to be, but form the highest good, not in their separate existences but in their combined existence, so moral being, interpreted in the multiplicity of goods, can only be conceived as this same twofoldness of being posited and superseded.

That is, none is completely isolated, either, even by its essence, but only when it joins in community with the others is reason contained therein. At the same time, however, the one life of reason in nature is the positing of these diverse goods, and only as such is it real.

19 We have no especial knowledge of the highest good as the unity of the being of reason in nature except this knowledge of the interaction and confusion of all the individual goods.

---

[20] Posited in two moments. *Corrected from:* is twofold in character.

[21] *Marginal addition 1832:* We can only acknowledge here what is individual and postulate a generality for it and at most look for classifications of what is individual from the standpoint of reason. As soon as we are obliged to approach the domain of division from the standpoint of differentiated nature, however, we leave the ethical domain and move into technical processes, e.g. the theory of how to treat individual languages and states.

We can only express it, moreover, in a general formula which is empty of content and does not constitute real knowledge. Intuition is only complete, however, when we comprehend the way in which this community of all the goods can be formed from every moral starting-point.

20 Separate consideration of each good must be preceded by an exposition of the individual oppositions in terms of their various functions.

We must be familiar with the individual elements before we can understand the various ways in which it is possible to combine them. Only when each term of an opposition is familiar as regards scope and content can we recognize its contribution even where it is subordinate to the others.

21 In this act of sifting consideration it would be easy for engaged intuition to get lost if it did not first make visible, in an incomplete way, the basic outlines of the shape taken by the moral world in the interrelatedness of what is to be in opposition.

It is not possible to dispense with this rectification of the process of abstraction; the only choice is whether to divide it up in different places or to keep it together as a single mass. The latter alternative seems less distracting and therefore more congenial to the depiction of what is unfamiliar.

22 The doctrine of the highest good thus falls into three divisions: depiction of the basic outline; exposition of the oppositions, or the elementary part; and the noting of the distinctive features of the different goods themselves and the way in which they are connected, or the constructive part.

Section One

Basic outline

23 As inculcating activity and signifying activity are always interrelated in ethical being, overall the former points back mainly to everything which is always presupposed for the moral domain, the other towards everything which is not achieved within it.

Whatever interrelation of reason and nature we relate to signifying activity, we posit within it nature which has been acted upon [and] become one with reason; whatever we relate to inculcating activity, we posit within it nature which is to be the means of action, which has become one [with reason]; the latter therefore more for the sake of an action, before it has taken place, the former more by virtue of an action, therefore after it has taken place. Or, when we think of something that has become one in being we think of a symbol; when we think of something that ought to become one, we think of an organ.

If we imagine that the opposition between reason and nature has been entirely superseded by gradual progression, the last term is this: that the last thing to be separate from reason has become a symbol; for to what purpose should it have become an organ? If we imagine the superseding of the opposition at the very beginning of the moral path, then what was first to become one must have become an organ, so that reason could enter actively into nature in the first place. The humanly structured figure is the most fundamental symbol of reason to each one of us, but only insofar as we posit in it some sort of activity of reason right from the beginning and something in it which can channel that activity.

But this is admittedly only relative. For we cannot imagine that the activity of reason on nature began at one point rather than at another, except inasmuch as one point belonged more than the others to reason before any activity took place, and thus was also able to recognize it. Even if [this is] only true in relative terms, it is nevertheless sufficient to justify the beginning of inculcating activity.

24 Inasmuch as a first entering of reason into nature is nowhere to be found, then what is organized must already be in existence, always and everywhere; inasmuch as the action of nature is to be found everywhere, however, what is organized must have come into being through the action of reason.

The one exists therefore only to the extent that the other does, and so there is in everything something which has come about morally and something which was already in existence prior to moral activity.

25 Wherever nature has been organized for the sake of reason, *what has been inherited* contains within itself what was already in existence prior to moral activity, whereas *what has been acquired by practice* brings together that which has come about morally.

There is no straightforward opposition and division between the two, or else what has been inherited could not exist within the moral sphere. Rather, just as every individual human being was born with certain organs, those organs already contain what has come out of the practice of previous generations, both in the larger things and in the individual things. And if one compares individual functions in terms of what has been acquired by practice, the difference between them is rooted equally in what has been inherited.

Things are as we have claimed predominantly because practice can only be posited where reason is active, while inheritance is also to be found where no reason is posited. For we would deny that animals [are capable of] practice if left to themselves. The development of their organic skills is embedded in the developmental period of their nature, thus the mere continuance of procreation, and belongs only to the domain of inheritance; in human beings these skills continue to increase long after nature has come to a halt, still holding on when nature is in the process of decaying once more, thus [they continue] obviously through the activity of one's higher spiritual side.

The expression [we have used] includes influence, uniformly and consciously repeated, thus, by means of practice, a gradual prevailing over what has been inherited. Hence, in appearance also, the more perfected the moral element, the more apparent what has been acquired by practice and what can be attributed to practice even in that which has been inherited. If we imagine the opposition between reason and nature to have been entirely superseded, each element must have been permeated by the other so that they have become the same.

26 Considered within the limits of moral being, organizing activity is the growing tension and the gradual superseding of the relative opposition between nature originally united with reason and nature that never quite becomes one with reason.

The tension increases the more powerfully at one with reason [nature] has become, as a result of practice on the part of what has been organized, and the more, therefore, nature which is not yet at one keeps itself distinct in resistance. The less organization starts from a point of reason, the more weak and confused is the distinction between I and Not-I, which we therefore posit as quite chaotic in animal consciousness.

The [possibility] of superseding increases, the more widespread the unification from every point. Since, however, if the opposition were entirely superseded there would be no more tension, [tension] decreases from one side the more [the possibility of] superseding increases, as resistance decreases in the same measure. And the opposition of I and Not-I could ultimately only be maintained through the consciousness of a nature posited outside organizing activity.

Yet we can never posit superseding as having been completed in terms of its extent, because it is never complete in terms of its exactitude, in that unorganized and less organized elements remain even in the human body.

27 The same is true of the organized nature of the human body, which has always been a given, and the never completely to-be-organized nature of the earthly bodies.

Neither of them exactly, in fact. For apart from the human body other organized entities are always [taken as] given; air and light are just as much organs before all moral activity as eyes and lungs. And there also remain non-organized parts of the human body, even if we cannot deny the influence of the activity of reason, even on the most willful of them.

In the same way, it is true, we can imagine that reason might have an influence on everything belonging to the earthly body by means of the human frame, one that would be continuous, indeed. But on the one hand we must also always include in such activity the forces and influences of other celestial bodies, since the earthly body is only given as coexisting with them, and all life [on earth] expresses that coexistence. And on the other, inasmuch as human nature is itself a product of the earthly body, it cannot have an effect on it. The internal unity [of the earthly body], which is the common root of all its products, cannot therefore be drawn into inculcating activity.

28 Inculcating activity is outwardly limited by signifying activity.

Their movements are connected to the internal unity of life [which encompasses] the earth and the other celestial bodies. In recognition of their mutual relationship, as they are taken into consciousness, they are symbolized for reason, and are organs of reason to the extent that they have become a measure for all movement. Organizing activity thus ends in something which is only an organ to the extent that it is a symbol, and which only comes into the realm of moral activity by virtue of its recognizability, whilst remaining quite outside it in terms of its essential nature.

29 Inasmuch as there is nowhere an original entering of reason into nature, that which has become symbol must already have been present everywhere, and been presupposed. Inasmuch as all symbolization is to be found within moral activity, everything which has been symbolized, even what we mentioned first, must have come about through the activity of reason.

That is, the one is only the other to that extent, and in every symbol both must be present; that, by means of which something else emerges from it, and that by means of which it rests on something else.

30 In all symbolizing activity *stimulation* represents the way in which [activity] rests on an earlier activity, and what is arbitrary represents the means by which something else rests on it.

Reason depicted in nature is unthinkable without stimulation and the arbitrary. The immediate symbol of reason is consciousness; everything else is only a symbol of reason insofar as it is an image and depiction of consciousness. Every form of consciousness, as something moral, must have arisen out of stimulation and the arbitrary. Where the opposition of these two entities – which may be understood as the opposition of independent activity and receptivity – does not definitely emerge, we are in the presence of an animal confusion of consciousness, not human clarity.

But both terms are also bound up together everywhere. Definite consciousness never comes into being without stimulation – that is, the action of nature which has not yet been unified on nature which has been unified – even when it is most free and when it most proceeds from what is internal; otherwise this symbolizing activity would be an original entering of reason into nature. But if that same nature is caused to influence different people, they develop very different [states of] consciousness, and this we attribute to what is arbitrary. Every human affect, considered as stimulation, is just as vague and confused in the first moment as that of an animal, but we do not posit this state as a completed action, but await a second moment. In it, as a result of what is arbitrary, the affect will become for one person one kind of definite consciousness, encompassing the whole of existence, and for another a different kind. All definite forms of consciousness, once perfected, thus appear to be the work of what is arbitrary; yet we do not posit this moment as a complete action either, for in that case it would not be human doing but an inspiriting [*Eingeistung*], and what is absolutely arbitrary would become in its turn the greatest absence of independence; instead we return to an earlier moment and seek out or presuppose the causal stimulus in that inpenetrable obscurity.

The two things are only in opposition in the way I have described as long as they are considered in [the context of] one single act. For elsewhere sensitivity to stimulus is everywhere determined by preceding arbitrary acts, and repeated arbitrary acts exclude more and more those stimuli which are in opposition to them.

Just as the opposition of stimulation and the arbitrary does not emerge any lower than the moral domain, we must imagine it to have been superseded, as it would be if the opposition between reason and nature had been superseded, and stimulation and the arbitrary were one and the same thing. The nearer to this state of perfection they approach, however, the more they must permeate each other and for this very reason leave each other free.

Note. From the above, compared with what is said in [para.] 25, it must be evident that it is not a matter of indifference or chance to relate stimulation and the arbitrary to symbolizing activity, and inheritance and practice, on the other hand, to organizing activity.

31[22] Considered within the limits of ethical existence, symbolizing activity is the growing tension and the gradually superseded opposition between nature originally signified by reason and nature which can never be entirely signified by reason.

As consciousness develops, something comprehensible is removed from the mass of the unconscious, in which the comprehensible and the incomprehensible are mingled, to become something comprehended. The opposition between comprehensible and incomprehensible thus only arises as a result of this action, before there is only its absence. Since, however, the development of consciousness [does not take place] outright, each state of consciousness is merely transitional, from what is less conscious to what is more conscious, an intensification, therefore, of this opposition. If we imagine symbolizing activity to be quite simply complete, however, the incomprehensible has disappeared and the opposition has hence been engulfed, so that even within its moral bounds such activity is the superseding of that opposition.

Within such activity, then, we find everywhere the intensification of this opposition combined with an extensive reduction of it. But for that very reason neither is ever complete, because the other is not. If anything in nature were ever completely permeated [with consciousness], everything would have become a conscious thing, for everything is only completely permeated when its coexistence with everything else has come to consciousness. And vice versa, if everything had become conscious, everything would also be permeated, because all conditions for such permeation would have been met.

If there were a strict distinction between comprehensible and incomprehensible existence in our eyes, we could posit [the possibility of] perfection, even if only in infinite time; but what we have necessarily been given is an interrelation of the comprehensible and the incomprehensible at every point. For this reason there is only a twofold progression, that is, to subordinate the extensive factor to the intensive one, and vice versa.

32 In the context of the whole, then, nature which has always been comprehended is external, earthly; nature which will never be entirely comprehended is internal, human nature.[23]

---

[22] *The following note from 1827 is to be found on a slip of paper inserted in the text:* Ethics, Basic Outline. § 31 ff. Consciousness and shaping thus no doubt intended for each other. The shaping which proceeds from this. Art and science, language, image.
The more something is determined as an individual entity, the more powerful the tension between what is inmost and the expressive functions. The more the symbolizing system becomes one, the more the opposition is resolved. Maximum: intellectual unity of life completely expressed.

[23] *Marginal paragraph and gloss, deleted in the text itself:* 32. Signifying activity is substantially limited in an inward direction by formative activity.

Neither of these exactly either, in fact. For in part, the nature that is comprehended goes beyond earthly nature, because extraterrestrial influences on the earthly must also have penetrated consciousness and are indeed already present in any beginning of consciousness, and uncomprehended fragments remain, moreover, in the most external of earthly phenomena, the purely sensory. In part, too, what is most inwardly human is always included, in that whatever is conscious is only comprehended in terms of opposition, and every lower [order of] opposition is a mere shadow of the highest opposition posited in man; however, just as what is most inwardly human is not comprehended, neither is what is most inward in all other forms of existence, for the same reason.

33 Signifying activity is inwardly limited in essence by formative activity.

What is completely inward in humankind, even in the interaction of reason and nature (not merely simple abstracted reason, for instance), is – precisely because it is in no way external, but only possesses an external aspect – never a symbol itself, but can only seek out or produce symbols. Only to the extent that it is divided can the part be a symbol of the whole. The innermost unity of life as such is not an object of consciousness, either for the whole, as humanity or for the individual, as self. Both can only be presupposed in themselves and everything else related to them.

What is posited as a part of this inner unity, as far as speculative contemplation is concerned, is individual energy, function. The individual functions of life are, however, already to be regarded as organs, and only as such, in their activity, are they comprehensible. Thus what is to the greatest extent still symbol, taken inwardly, is symbolic only to the extent that it is not – and because it is not – itself the innermost aspect of life but its organ.

34 Now, since both activities are conditional upon one another at their extremes as greatest and least, all moral existence is in every point a more or less of both at once.

The same thing that we saw in § 6 appears here in another guise. If the extremes of organizing activity are to be found where something is an organ simply because it is a symbol, then at this point the maximum is symbol, the minimum organ. In the same way, at the extremes of symbolizing activity the maximum is organ and the minimum symbol. It follows from this that where less than the maximum is organ, more than the minimum is symbol, and where less than the maximum is symbol, more than the minimum is organ; but nowhere is one separate from the other. The circle is thus closed, and neither activity can relinquish its hold on the other.

Now if everything moral is simultaneously organ and symbol, however, this is the case only if there is a simultaneity of inheritance and stimulation on the one hand, and practice and the arbitrary on the other.

Its outward limitation is a matter of chance, because the comprehensible and incomprehensible are not strictly distinguished here. The more smaller, close objects are permeated by consciousness, the more something comprehensible can be apprehended in what is larger and more distant.

35 Given that human nature is split into a plurality of individual beings, the existence of reason in human nature is only complete[24] if there is moral community amongst those individual beings.

Human nature is only real in the existence of individual beings alongside one another and following on from one another, so that reason, too, is only active in human nature when it is active in them. As an individual [instance of] interaction between reason and nature, posited in its own right, each individual being is himself only an organ and a symbol, however, and is therefore only moral to the extent that nature in general is organized and symbolized in him and starting with him on behalf of reason in general. If, however, reason acts only in individual beings, and if its action in each one is separate from its action in all the others, then all the others are excluded from whatever unification takes place in separate individuals, be it symbolic or organic. Thus unification on behalf of reason does not take place anywhere, and the unity of reason in its action upon nature, that is, the completeness of moral existence, is entirely superseded by the way in which nature is split into a plurality of individual beings.

Given this arrangement within nature, moral existence is only possible to the extent that this division is superseded by the positing of community; i.e. if the individual points of reason are thrown together and exist for one another. We can only imagine this taking place as follows, however: if, when the activity of reason is applied to one individual being and connects up to the system of his original organs and symbols, the same action is also related to the other individual beings and finds its place in the system of their organs and symbols; and if, in the same way, their action were also related to that individual being and found its place in his system of organs and symbols.

Thus, as a component of the whole of moral existence, each moral [action] is also only posited as existing in its own right to the extent that it is conditional upon this community of individual beings and the community of individual beings conditional upon it. For everything that is moral exists through the action of individual beings, and must therefore exist through community. And community exists only in and through whatever is, morally speaking, an organ and a symbol.

36 Given that same split [in human nature], the existence of reason in human nature is only complete to the extent that each individual and his domain is separated from the others and their domains.

1. Spatial [division ?] also encompasses the broader organic cycle, of course. Individual intelligence can only act upon nature on behalf of reason with its whole organic sphere.
2. For if individuals must vary, not only according to space and time but also as a unity of the general and the especial, i.e. conceptually, in the same way as everything that has an independent moral existence, then the action of reason which proceeds from each individual, if each one is entirely active, that is [acting from] his own peculiarity,

[24] *Corrected from:* possible.

must necessarily vary too. What has been organized is organized for just this diversity, and what has been symbolized also leaves the imprint of this same diversity. Every taking of moral action is thus entirely bound up in such diversity, and what it can be is only complete in relation to it. For anyone else it would only exist in an imperfect and subordinate way, for it cannot stand in the same relation to any individual being whose peculiarity is something quite other as it does to its author.

As surely, then, as the action of reason encompasses the whole of the nature that has been given to it through [the agency of] individual beings, so too does splitting spread out from those individual beings and the nature which is within them – originally unified with reason – over the whole of that nature which has yet to be acted upon; and the perfection of moral existence is at the same time the completeness of that division. For this reason everything moral is only something whole and single, posited in its own right, to the extent that it is conditional upon this division of the domain of individual beings, and this division in its turn is conditional upon it.

37 Now, since community and division are mutually exclusive, yet both ought to be posited by everything moral, each can only stand in relative opposition to the other, so that something can only be a perfectly moral thing, posited in its own right, if it posits community, which in another respect is division, or division, which in another respect is community.

According to the above, this obviously sets a condition for the completeness of moral [action]. Anything in which only the unity of reason is posited, and not the especial determination of the individual agent, is incomplete; the same is true of anything in which only this last is posited, and not the singleness of reason in all individuals. Anything of this kind would either be not something moral, or else not something posited in its own right, but [could only be regarded] as part of something else, in which the other thing was also to be found.

The possibility of a merely relative opposition of this kind is posited only in the proposition, however, that individual beings are not separated absolutely and in every way; this is the condition of the moral which we have to demonstrate here.

38 The inculcation of nature can be the same in everyone and for everyone, insofar as they have the same nature before them to be formed, and the same formative nature within them.

Assuming, that is, that there is the same original singleness of reason in everyone, thought of [long] before any personal unification with nature. For insofar as their formative action proceeds from the same nature, they will also form things in the same way, because [it is all done] for the same nature, and, at the same time, insofar as formative action is applied to the same nature, they will no doubt also form the same things.

Under these conditions, conceptual variety is thus superseded in the way nature is organized; so that the particular relation to a single individual above all others is only the mathematical one. In this way, then, we can posit community provided that we also posit temporal and spatial mobility of what is formative or what has been formed, i.e. in ethical terms it is really posited.

In fact, these two conditions are one [and the same]. For formative nature, thought of as something that has itself not already been morally formed – this taking place originally – is nature thought of before any unification with reason, i.e. human nature in its purely natural aspect, forming a single whole together with the rest of the nature we have been given, posited externally. To this extent, however, the same measure and grounds for singleness must also be present in formative nature and in the nature which is to be formed.

39 Thus, inasmuch as the same original organization is given in a number of individuals and the same system of shaping nature is given for a number of individuals, there is given for a number of individuals one single formative moral domain as a whole self-contained area of common usage or *commerce*.

Since external nature is raised to a higher level of the spiritual through organic unification with reason, that aspect of it which is acted upon in organizing activity is also originally its spiritual aspect, shape, and not its material aspect, matter. In true being, in any case, the two stand only in relative opposition. The singleness which is the point at issue here is thus that of natural shaping. In everything that has been morally organized, then, to the extent that it is something to be held in common, we must posit a relation to a definite singleness of the natural shaping which surrounds it.

The same is true of the singleness of formative nature, which is the point at issue here; it, too, is the singleness of shaping. For only to the extent that it organizes, i.e. is posited predominantly under the power of shaping, can reason act by means of it through other things which have been organized as well.

Therefore, to the extent that we posit these two things, we also posit conceptually that an inculcating activity begun by one individual being can be continued by another as entirely the same thing; and that in entirely the same sense whatever has been the property of one individual being can also become the property of another; which is precisely what is expressed in the term *commerce*.

40 For the human species as a single entity, the largest formative domain that is given, as a single entity, is the earth, and hence a moral commerce which extends throughout this whole domain.

For the unity of the earth is the basis for a singleness of natural shaping proceeding from it, and in the same way a singleness of relationship between all that is human and everything else which is posited as having an independent existence on earth. In this sense, then, there must be an organizing which is the same in everything and for everyone.

Regarded as one single thing, however, this would not be anything moral if there were not other things alongside it from which it is separate. This, however, is not a given for us, so that on the one hand, within these parameters moral and natural contemplation are on a par with each other, while on the other hand we are set [the task] of positing something moral outside the earth as well and attributing to every celestial body a moral being and life that are unknown to us, from which our own is completely separate.

The same thing, regarded as a multiplicity, to the extent that it proceeds from many points and is related to many, leads to the conclusion that, insofar as these are to be posited as existing in their own right, they must be just as much separated from one another as in community with one another, in both cases relatively speaking.

41 The inculcation of nature will be different in each individual and for each individual, to the extent that each has a different formative nature within him and a different nature to be formed in front of him.

If we take the first premise in 38 as our starting-point, the way in which one and the same organized natural whole remains attached to one and the same organizing point is determined only by spatial and temporal circumstances, and in ethical terms is thus purely a matter of chance; any assumption that a division of this kind is ethical would be merely to supersede community without positing something else which is ethical [in its place], that is, to destroy what is ethically necessary. Taking these premises as our starting-point, however, what is posited is a division of what is organized according to the organizing points, without any consideration of spatial and temporal relationships, and hence ethically.

Here too, however, the two premises are one and the same. For if we do not regard it once again as being itself morally formed, formative nature is merely a part of the whole of nature that surrounds us, and the principle of differentiation posited in it must be derived from that whole and run through it. Even if we wished to say that for a number [of people] nature which has yet to be formed could vary in two ways, in that in reality a different one is given to each, or the same thing given is comprehended differently by each one, this too comes down to the same thing, for diversity of interpretation can only be rooted in the diversity of that nature which was originally united with reason, which must correspond in turn to an ultimate diversity of natural shaping. Thus this, too, is essentially one and the same, and both forms of expression will always be valid, though to a varying extent.

42 Thus, to the extent that a number of individual formative beings undertake their formative activity, each with an organization which differs from the others from the very beginning, and each standing in a different relation to the system of natural shaping, their formative domains will differ from one another and each will become a self-contained whole of non-transferability or *property*.

It is better to say "standing in a different relation to the same system of natural shaping," than "to varying parts of the same system." For the nature we have been given does indeed form an essential whole, and since we are not taking spatial and temporal relationships into account here, each person can only select a distinct part of this whole system as his particular formative material through the particular way in which the activity of his reason relates to the whole. It is perfectly clear, however, from what we have said in § 39 that here too it is natural shaping which is at issue in the first instance. Now, since everything which is morally organized, inasmuch as it is posited in its own right, must also be separated off in some way, a relation to something definitely varied in natural shaping as a whole must be posited in each one, as must the activity of an organization which has differed from all the others from the very beginning.

And precisely to this extent it is impossible to transfer anything which has been morally organized from one formative point to another. Neither is it possible for one to continue the activity of another. For it would no longer be the same activity, since it would be continued by means of other organs. Nor can one individual appropriate what has been formed for another; for it has been formed for another organization. Separated from its original moral point of origin each thing loses its organic meaning in proportion to its degree of particularity and recedes into the unformed mass more or less as raw material. This constitutes the moral concept of property, which is admittedly rather different from the usual legal concept; it rests on the self-contained nature of organic relationship and the indifference of every other formative point towards whatever contradicts its own drive in a definite way.[25]

---

[25] *§ 43, which follows, has been deleted in the text, and a further § 41, with gloss, crossed out in the margin and enclosed in brackets (in the text). These deletions were undertaken as early as 1816 (cf. § 55).*
41. The moral coexistence [*corrected from:* relationship] of individual beings, to the extent that they are bound up together in a single domain of commerce, is that of *right*, or the way in which appropriation and community are mutually conditional upon each other.
Appropriation is the relationship of what has been organized to the unity of the individual being, which is separated both spatially and temporally from the others. Its essence is the relationship of appropriation to community and of community to appropriation, necessarily posited in organizing activity, which rests on the fact that appropriation and community both proceed from what is identical in the plurality of individual beings. Since, in action, the individual has always constituted a unity of reason and nature, he posits himself as the result of organizing activity, i.e. as the organ of reason, and thus the formative activity of reason, acting throughout for the unity of reason in general with nature in general, i.e. for the totality of individual beings; and in this way he is in the condition of right [*Rechtszustand*]. The others strive for community, but only by acknowledging his appropriation, just as they themselves can only perfect community through appropriation, and so they enter with him into a condition of right. Where appropriation takes place without reference to a common domain of commerce, no right is present. We cannot possibly speak of right in the case of an individual who is included in the formative state, but who is completely solitary and lacks any relationship to the possibility that a number of individuals might come to join him; this is because we cannot conceive of any corresponding wrong.
Neither can the object of right be something which is organized according to the conceptual variety of individual beings, as we must describe below, because this is not the object of any moral striving for community as such. For the right of one individual necessarily presupposes the claims of others, which cannot be made in any moral way in the case of someone who has been placed right outside the domain of community. It is not moral property as such, but appropriation and what has been appropriated, which is the object of right.
To speak of right in the domain of symbolizing activity – the right of a human being to his thoughts and feelings – is a misunderstanding. No one can attempt to stop them from being produced, because there is no power that can do this, and no one would want to prevent them from being communicated either, insofar as that means simply the same [thoughts and feelings] being produced in others, something which cannot be prevented. But only to the extent that the thoughts and feelings turn into something else, i.e. to the extent that they are transferred to the domain of organizing activity.
What we have demonstrated, then, is the true moral significance of right. Right and commerce are related concepts, because and to the extent that the related nature of appropriation and community is posited in [the concept of] commerce. Community provides the basis for the claims of all against each in the domain of appropriation and by means of the same; appropriation provides the basis for the claims of each against all in the domain of community and by means of the same. Right in the individual is the acknowledgment of these claims. Wrong is the denial of the same.

43 The most confined formative domain in this sense, the smallest unity given to us, is the human body, each constituting one especial body for one especial human soul; thus life [constitutes] the most completely self-contained and non-transferable property.

The body is a formative domain in that it is an interaction of activity and result, of what was originally there and what has come into being. But strictly speaking it is only something quite simply self-contained, as it were, in the unity of all the functions which are posited in it, as life. For to the extent that one can divide one activity system from all the others, it can also be brought into greater contact with others, e.g. with the analogous activity system in another, and thus brought into community with him, although this will admittedly always remain conditional upon the unity of life. In a certain sense, then, we can even regard the individual limbs, with reference to the way they are used, as the object of commerce.

But we cannot perfectly regard even the unity of life quite simply as a self-contained formative domain, in that each one which is given in reality only arises in the moral course of things, that is, out of another, and so to some extent it is only together with the first that it forms the same unity of life. And so common possession is also posited, even in the most intensively powerful particularity.

44 From the human body to the circumference of the earth, then, as far as moral existence is concerned, everything is an interaction of singleness and variety, and property and commerce are always only partially posited as separate from each other, while non-transferability and common possession are only in relative opposition.

For since, in the tiniest instance of diversity and the largest instance of common property, both [of these things] interact, progress from the one to the other is only a decrease in particularity and an increase in common possession, and vice versa. And what constitutes a domain of particularity, a single unity, with regard to what is placed next to it, constitutes a domain of commerce for the multiplicity which that unity encompasses; so that what is particular in one respect must be something held in common in another.

45[26] As the object of the formative activity that produces uniformity and also that which produces diversity, that nature which is acted upon is the epitome of *things*.

To the extent, that is, that [nature] is given, not as something indivisible but as something that has always been manifold and divided, each part of it which is posited in its own right, in the relation we have demonstrated, is called a thing. But it is this only in the indivisible twofoldness of its possible moral value. For anything in which no property takes place at all, even though commerce with it does, or anything with which commerce does not take place even though property does, is not a thing, so that on the one hand life is not a thing,

[26] *Marginal note 1827:* NB. I have omitted this § and instead provided an introduction before § 44 that can only be decided in this way, and not so that there could be separate domains, with some things wholly for the community and others wholly for property.

and neither is the force of nature on the other; the body is one least of all, on the one hand, the elements least of all on the other.

This, however, is the indigenous concept of the thing, even in common linguistic usage, and it diverges from the dialectical and scientific concept.

46 Even though nature is split into a plurality of individual beings, the use of the term "nature" is the same in all cases, to the extent that in all of them, apart from the presence of reason, the nature to which the term is attached, the nature which is signifying and the nature which is signified are all the same.

What I mean by reason here is only this signifying activity itself, whose singleness is thus the first condition. However the reason which signifying nature is to express is exactly the same thing as the nature which stands across from it. For reason is the same thing, in a spiritual way, as nature is in a material way. This original, spiritual positing of nature in reason is what we usually call – using an expression which is readily misunderstood but which can also be correctly interpreted – innate concepts. Innate, that is, because they were pre-formed and determined in [nature] before any moral activity on the part of reason; not concepts, however, because they only become concepts in the moral activity of reason. Signifying nature, however, is the nature which has already been united with reason, containing within it the functions of consciousness. If these are diverse, then the signifying terms must also be diverse.

Thus the splitting of human nature into a plurality of individual beings takes place only when reason is active within it, to the extent that the innate concepts and the laws and procedures of consciousness are the same in everyone. It is for this reason, also, that this presupposition informs all signifying activity in a lively way, so that only by this means can it be an activity of reason.

Both these premises, however, are one [and the same]. For human nature as it is before all signifying activity, as posited originally, is only an integrating part of nature in general, so that the laws of consciousness – to the extent that they are present, so to speak, in a material way – are themselves also included in what is posited in reason in a spiritual way as innate concepts. It is impossible to claim, however, that the laws of our human consciousness constitute the essence of reason altogether, and were posited in reason, without being related in any way to the nature that belongs with it. It is rather the case that, as soon as we imagine reason belonging together with a nature which is constituted differently, we must also imagine different laws governing the consciousness which originally constituted that unification.

47 Only to the extent, however, that the signifying activity of each can be given to all the others, is it an activity which is held in common.

For to the extent that signifying activity is only among the functions of consciousness, that is, within the nature which has been united with reason, it is not something that was originally given to other individuals, like organizing activity and its products, to the extent that the whole of external nature is given to them.

If it can be given [to others], however, it can be something held in common, even given the conditions set out above. For since it proceeds from the same innate concepts and the same laws and forms of consciousness, activity, once begun, may also be continued by someone else, inasmuch as it is given, and can also be given in the same way if it is complete, standing firm in the consciousness [of another] in the same way. Thus everything in the consciousness of one individual being may also exist in that of another.

Signifying activity, to the extent that it goes back to that same nature which is alike in each one, is thus only real in individuals as a moral activity to the extent that at the same time it is something that can be communicated. However, given that both the activity and also its expression must be completed at the same time, and that as a result the activity ceases to be exclusively related to the individual being once again, the individual being – to the extent that only in this activity is it a moral being, as stated above (17) – is at one and the same time posited and superseded, maintained, that is, in a wavering [state of] existence.

48 Thus, to the extent that the same innate concepts, the same laws of consciousness, are present in a number [of individuals], there exists a common, self-contained domain of signification, in the coexistence of *thought* and *speech*.

All in all, what we call thought is an activity of which each person is conscious as something which is not especial to himself but is alike in everyone, of such a kind that each person can perform a signifying action in the same way, and each person acting in this way also produces the same signifying term, and each person in whom that term exists will also only have produced it by means of the same action. It is therefore also all the same whether the same thought is completed by the same individual or by another, and each thought determined by its content is the same in and for each one.

This is true not only of thought in the narrower sense, which lies further over towards the general and rests on consciousness, inasmuch as it is understanding; but also of imagination, which lies further over towards the especial and rests on consciousness as sense. For the equality of the tools of sense and their actions is an essential part of the equality of signifying nature.

It is obvious, however, that thought belongs to this moral activity and to no other kind. For it comes into being through the activity of reason, but only in its unification with nature, without which there can be no true thoughts; and it is not directly an organ, but each thought undoubtedly points back, however, to the system of innate concepts originally belonging to reason, and is a particular expression of it, and thus a symbol.

What we understand here by speech, finally – provisionally and in very general terms – is that becoming external which belongs to thought, as a result of which each person is able not only to hear the signifying activity of the other but also to distinguish it – because the same thing is posited in him, together with thought – so that he is in a position to absorb it into himself as regards both content and method. Without this, thought would exist as the same signifying activity in everyone, it is true, but each person would only [be aware of] his own. Speech in this general sense, however, is so essentially attached to thought that no thought is ready until it has been put into words.

Now there is a possibility, it is true, that this is a natural condition of moral existence, connecting the capacity to externalize with the capacity to absorb; in reality, however, this occurs only through the force of reason, which breaks down the barriers surrounding each person in both directions; and looked at from the point of view of both reason and nature, it is the force of the species, restoring itself by destroying the division between individuals.

49 In the broadest sense, all intelligent consciousness in the human race constitutes a single, common domain of signification.

For the whole earth is one single nature, whose life is modeled in the human reason of every individual in the system of innate concepts, and we attribute the same laws to every consciousness which we posit as human. Thus all the conditions are always present, and for this reason the moral activity of reason must also always produce communication and intelligibility.

It follows that wherever several individuals come into relation with one another, they also act on the assumption that their thinking is identical and mutually intelligible, and there is no limit to how far they can go in their absorption of each other's thought.

However, given that we do not posit what is symbolized in this way as the whole of reason, nor the whole of nature, but as something which goes beyond both, we also posit it as something self-contained and hence particular. For if we accept the idea of non-human thinking beings, we do not naturally accept the idea of intelligibility existing between them and us. And our consciousness of this fact is always essentially one [and the same] as the consciousness of how far we are intelligible to one another, and only because what is identical is at the same time posited as something that is different from other things is it something real and moral.

50 Notwithstanding the singleness of reason in everyone, the signifying of nature is something different in each, to the extent that each person's signifying nature is different, and each directs activity of a different kind towards that nature which is to be signified.

Since the totality of individual beings would not form a single species if the forms and laws of consciousness were not the same in each, diversity can only lie in the way in which its manifold functions are bound up to form a whole, i.e. in the diversity of their relationships to one another in the unity of life. Thus, to the extent that the whole of nature which is united with reason in the individual being is at work in signifying activity, and the unity of life stimulated, we may posit its diversity – and not just in the more and less of what has already been signified – the diversity that gives rise to signifying activity in one individual just as it does in another. For, morally speaking, there is only a basis in temporal and spatial relationships by chance if, given the equality of the functions and the equality of given nature, that more and less does not even itself out in each individual at every moment, so that a complete equality of all comes into being. Given the premise we have demonstrated here, equality is essentially and conceptually superseded, and diversity posited [in its place]; and only to the extent that this diversity is posited do individual beings have the right to posit that they exist in their own right in the moral domain.

It is clear, however, given this premise, that even that activity of reason which is directed towards external nature, even if that [nature] were just the same for everyone, must become something different when channeled through such a conceptually varied unity of life. For nature stands in a different relation to each different complexion of functions, and must therefore also be comprehended differently, not just to the extent that the activity is directed, strictly speaking, towards the whole of nature each time, but also to the extent that each individual towards whom it could be directed is something manifold, possessing kinship with all the functions of consciousness. This is necessary, however, in the context of the whole of nature, of which that nature which was originally posited in each human individual forms a part.

51 Only to the extent, however, that the varying signifying activity present in each person cannot be reproduced in another's consciousness is that activity non-transferable.[27]

For if it could be communicated in the same way as thought, the only difference in the consciousness of individuals would be temporal and spatial. The opposite [conclusion] is already present in our original premise, however. For anything which expresses the relationship between the whole of nature and a conceptually definite unity of life cannot be posited in another in the same way. For anything that is the same in terms of the expression must be different in terms of the content, and anything that is the same in terms of content cannot express the unity of life in the same way.

In this way, then, individuals are also divided according to the steadfastness of their being, and have a right to persist as [beings] posited in their own right; whereas if this activity, too, were communicable and transferable, their diversity would be constantly dwindling; so that even the activity of reason could not be related conceptually to these individual points and attributed to them.

52 Thus to the extent that we posit an arrangement of consciousness in each individual being which was diverse from the beginning and which constitutes the unity of his life, a particular self-contained domain of signification is also posited in each which is that of excitation and *feeling*.

All in all, what we call feeling is the expression of reason in nature, just as thought is. It is an activity of life that has come into being in nature, but only because of reason, and this is true not only of moral and religious feeling but also of bodily feeling, provided that it is posited as human, and as an entire moment of feeling. Feeling in itself is even less of an organ than thought, however, because it returns purely to itself. It is thus a definite expression of the way in which reason exists in this particular nature. For feeling, even of the very lowest kind, always expresses the effect that reason does or does not have within nature. And every feeling is always directed towards the unity of life, not towards something individual. What we emphasize in feeling, all the manifold things, everything which relates to something individual, is no longer direct feeling itself. Although it might look as if nature that is not united with reason is not in play here at all, so that feeling is either not moral at all or at least not moral on its own, but only together with something else, in fact every feeling expresses rather the effect that reason does or does not have within the nature that is united with it as a consequence of the relationship in which it

---

[27] *Marginal note, 1827:* N.B. Not altogether, presumably, for each individual [re-]constructs differently, after all.

stands to nature which has not been united [with reason]; and it is precisely this that is the excitation which is a necessary part of every feeling.

Each person, however, executes each act of feeling as something that no one else can execute in the same way, and it is through feeling that each individual expresses his right to be posited on his own terms. For there is most separateness in feeling, and to the extent that the feeling is perfect, this derives from the fact that even in the same position and circumstances no one else would feel quite the same; just as the opposite is true in perfection of thought.

53 In this sense the smallest domain of signification given to us is the consciousness enclosed in the body of each individual human being and mediated through it, so that self-consciousness is the most particular and non-transferable [aspect] of symbolizing activity.

All feeling is in fact self-consciousness. For all consciousness of another becomes thought. But [it is this] only as direct consciousness; for indirect consciousness, in which we have become an object to ourselves once again, becomes thought, and is not transferable.

One might perhaps think, however, that the highest non-transferable thing would be merely the individual moment in which one was moved in a particular way, and not the whole of human self-consciousness as a single entity, for no one is able to transfer his own feelings at a particular moment exactly to another person. This is indeed true; but just as surely as a human being is one [and the same], all the moments of feeling within him proceed from the same especial unity of life. And if we tear one single moment out of it, it can to that extent be related to an analogous moment in another's life and thus be more readily transferable. This unity of life, however, is the identity underlying everything particular in all the successive moments of feeling.[28] For this reason, however, [it is] only thought, as the common element of these feelings, and in all of them the same thought, namely the I. And only in that the particular becomes something held in common once again does it constitute something truly moral.

54 Thus, from individual self-consciousness to the collective consciousness of the human race, everything in moral being is an interaction of singleness and diversity, and thought and feeling are everywhere, and only external to each other in part; seclusion and communication are everywhere, and only relatively opposed to each other.

Precisely because of its non-transferability, there is no individual feeling where the unifying thought of the I is absent, which is just the same in everyone and is brought to completion in the same way, for personal diversity is not posited here in terms of content. In the same way, if we are conscious in all our thinking of the fact that the content and the laws of that thought are what is particularly human, this is not directly a thought, for otherwise we ought really to have been given other laws and a different content of consciousness opposed to the ones we hold in common, which is not the case; on the contrary, it is the feeling of being human, of a definite unity of life, that accompanies all certainty of all thought. If,

---

[28] *Question mark in margin.*

then, thought accompanies feeling in the innermost domain of non-transferability, while in the outermost scope of common possession feeling accompanies thought, neither is going to relinquish its hold on the other in the areas in between. For compared with these two everything can only be a diminishing of feeling-content and an increase in thought-content, or vice versa. Thus the requirement that singleness and diversity should always coexist is fulfilled for symbolizing activity in the coexistence everywhere of thought and feeling.

55 The moral coexistence of individual beings in commerce[29] is the relationship of *right*, or the way in which acquisition and community are conditional upon each other.

For acquisition and community contradict each other if each is posited in its own right. Both are necessary, however, by virtue of one and the same thing, namely the identity of organizing activity in the plurality of individuals. Each person acquires things, however, to the extent that formation can only take place on the part of reason if things are bound up with individuals; each person requires community to the extent that formative activity in the individual and in all individuals is always in relation to reason in general. At every moment each person is himself a result of organizing activity, that is, he is himself also an organ of reason, and as such comes into relation with reason in general – that is, into community with all – with what he has acquired and on the strength of it. For to the extent that he is an organ, the activity of reason should only pass through him, and in real community consciousness of coherence made as easy as possible is one of the organs of reason. We must posit acquisition and community at the same time, therefore, if acquisition is to be perfectly moral. – On the other hand, however, to the extent that reason is originally active in everyone, it does not want to be limited by what [the individual] has acquired, but strives for everything, even what has been formed by others; but only as something that has already been formed, that is, as something that has already been unified by activity, that is, something that has been acquired by them. For only in unimpeded continuation of their activity, that is, in possession, were they able to engage in formative activity. And so acquisition must be posited at the same time as community, if community is to be moral. The state of right is simply this mutual conditionality. Where one person engages in formative activity without presupposing the possibility of relationship amongst a number of people, that is, of commerce, there can be no question of right, because we cannot conceive of any corresponding wrong. What we have described above cannot possibly be the object of right either, and neither can what has been formed according to conceptual diversity, nor moral property, regarded purely as such, because it is inconceivable that another could have any claim over it, and there is an essential connection between the right of one person and the claims of others. If we were to speak of right in the domain of signifying activity, a person's right to his thoughts and feelings, this would be a misunderstanding, precisely because there cannot be any possibility of wrong with regard to the production of the same, while communication might only be prevented here and there, to the extent that thoughts and feelings could become organs. Now if the only object of right is identical

---

[29] The relationship of individuals to one another in these various relations. [*Gloss marked by* □ *in text.*]

inculcation, while wrong resides precisely in acquisition which seeks to deny community, and community which refuses to recognize acquisition, then what we have demonstrated here is the true moral significance of the state of right. Community provides the basis for the claims of all against each person, on the assumption of his acquisition and by means of that acquisition, while acquisition provides the basis for the claims of each against all in the domain of their community and by means of that community; the two things taken together constitute their relationship of right.

Thus right and commerce essentially belong together. Right can only extend as far as there are objects of commerce, and anything is only an object of commerce if it is possible to have a right to it. Thus, within the extent of right, everything is possession held in common and possessed community.

56 Right extends over the whole earth; but is not necessarily an equal relationship of each to all.

If we say that it must extend over the whole earth, we mean that one cannot imagine two people coming into real contact anywhere and acknowledging each other as such without an acknowledgment of possession arising from it and a community thereby following. Where this is absent, and a man treats another as if he simply did not possess any rights, we assume that the activity of reason has not yet developed in this relationship, because the singleness of nature in everyone and the relatedness of formative activity in everyone cannot yet have been acknowledged. If someone is treated as if he did not possess any rights, this also means, therefore,[30] that he is treated as if he were raw material in moral terms, as nature which simply has yet to be formed, nature that anyone can appropriate according to their inclination and their need.

This does not mean, however, that thereby the same relationship of right also exists between all individuals. If one does not want to take into account either the fact that the premise of singleness always involves the premise of diversity, which produces an unequal measure of transferability and commerce, and hence also of the relationship of right, then the relationship of right really only exists insofar as commerce really takes place, and this cannot take place in the same way between everyone because each person is not divided from everyone else in the same way but in different measure by space and time, so that the mobility of activities and things is not the same between everyone. We can only say that this inequality remains entirely undetermined by such things.

57 The relationship of individuals to one another in the community of articulated thought is that of *faith*, or the mutual dependence[31] of teaching and learning on the common property of language, and conversely, the dependence of the common property of language on teaching and learning.

What I mean here by faith is the conviction underlying all action in this domain that each person's word is the same as his thought and that the thought which each person connects with a word that he has received is the same as the thought from which it proceeds in any

---

[30] Therefore, *and* because (*in previous sentence*) *added in the margin, 1816.*
[31] *Corrected from:* conditionality.

other person. This is never knowledge in itself, though it can become knowledge of a kind, it is true, in individual cases, but only by a series of actions which are themselves based on that premise, and would be empty without it. It is however, a faith which no one can fend off, and because of it there exists in this domain unity of the activity of reason and the superseding of personal barriers by means of community. For since thoughts cannot be transferred directly, but only by means of utterance, transference can only take place at all inasmuch as utterance and thought are one and the same thing. It is not sufficient, in this matter, to depict it as the duty to give the truth and the right to receive the truth (cf. 55); on the contrary, the identity of the two things must be regarded as necessarily present in the activity of reason itself.

The essence of the relationship, however, rests on the fact that on the one hand, the individual develops his consciousness only by means of language and must therefore consider his thoughts to be modeled [on those of others], and the thoughts of those whose signifying terms constitute language, so to speak, as the archetype of his own; while on the other hand thoughts which the individual has generated himself are not a unification of nature and reason as long as they remain locked away in the individual consciousness, and must therefore be deposited in language before they can come into common use. Thus truth is only present in each person's thoughts insofar as it is in language, and it is only in language insofar as each person's words and thoughts are [one and] the same thing.

Teaching and learning are naturally taken here in the broadest sense, and express the very act of transferring a thought from one personal consciousness to another. – It is self-evident that this presupposes an ability to hear which is equivalent to the capacity to utter, in the faith which allowed the word to be received in the first place. The existence of the community of consciousness resides only in the fact that all thinking is both a form of teaching and a form of learning. However, just as the common possession of language is conditional upon this teaching and learning, for only as a result of constant self-renewing transmission does language continue to exist, so the opposite is true. For no one seeks to transfer another's thought, as a thought, because of his personality, in order to enter into community with an individual, but only to the extent that it constitutes an element of common consciousness.

All thought, then, is only moral to the extent that it constitutes something inscribed in language from which teaching and learning develop, and common ownership of language is only moral to the extent that individual consciousness is productive as a result.[32] Mere appropriation of thoughts which have already been deposited in language is not the activity of reason, and if we assume [the existence of] a human being whose thinking simply does not go beyond this, we consider him scarcely human. In the same way, thought that is not deposited in language is either a completed act, but in that case not a moral one, or else it is moral, but incomplete, and appears to be merely inhibited until such depositing takes place.

58 This relationship of faith is general to all people, but is not necessarily an equal relationship of all towards each, and vice versa.

It is general in the same sense as the relationship of right, in that some kind of understanding must develop on every occasion when two people come into contact. Indeed,

[32] As a result: *corrected from:* appropriates [material] from it and.

just as the most rapid spiritual progress is made by the young child, we can say that the signifying force of reason is at its strongest and faith appears to be at its most lively when there is an encounter between two people who are unable to employ their usual signifying system with each other and whose ways of thinking diverge.

The relationship is no more equal, however, than the relationship of right, and inequality is just as indeterminate from this point of view. For if we take no account of the unequal influence of particularity here either, true transference is nevertheless conditional upon a common interest in the same objects,[33] and this is just as dependent on place and time as the mobility of formative activities and of things. For even if the stimulus to communicate is greatest in the case of what is most alien, success and certainty nevertheless rest on the mass of what is identical.

59 The moral relationship of individuals to one another from within the self-contained nature of their property is that of *sociability*, or the way in which non-transferability and relatedness are conditional upon each other.

The excluding relationship of what has been particularly formed to the formative agent contradicts the unity of reason in moral activity, but is necessitated by its content. The contradiction is only superseded to the extent that the particular formative activity of each person, together with its results, is not seen as existing in its own right but as an integrating part of the whole formative activity of reason, mediated through the diversity of their natures. To posit oneself as a part of this activity, at the same time as positing the activity itself and hence one's relatedness to all the parts, forms sociability. No one regards his own particular formative activity as a moral act, except to the extent that the particular formative activity of others is posited alongside it. And here too, the fact that formative agents are placed alongside one another is merely a matter of chance if each does not use his own diversity in formative activity, closing off his own property from others. Each formative agent necessarily excludes all the others from his procedures and their results, and for this very reason posits himself as excluded in the same way from theirs. Allowing oneself to be excluded in this way, however, can only exist alongside the unity of reason insofar as we can posit at the same time, in one and the same activity, that those who exclude and those who are excluded can only perfect the organism of reason together, in the formative activity they undertake. As an organ of reason each person posits himself and the nature he has been able to unite with reason as a self-contained whole. Each person – himself reason – posits himself as a [mere] part, forming a single whole together with all the others.

This belonging together is not the same thing, however, as existing for one another in the same way as in commerce, in the relationship of right; it is conditional upon non-transferability. It does not mean merely existing alongside one another, however. For even if each person were to assume particular formative activity besides his own in general terms, in individual cases each person would still destroy the activity of the other every time they came into contact, if what has been formed in particularity did not also come to his attention as such and were not acknowledged.

---

[33] *Marginal note:* Each person wants to use the other as a mirror for the whole of nature.

All particular formative activity, then, must include the endeavor to have it acknowledged as such by others, and to acknowledge their formative sphere oneself; and in its unity this perfects the essence of sociability, which consists in the acknowledgment of alien property, in order to allow it to be opened up[34] to oneself, and the opening up[35] of one's own, in order to have it acknowledged.

Sociability and property are concepts which are related at an essential level. Where particular formative activity is not to the fore, then – leaving aside commerce – sociability is scarcely more than a mechanical keeping together, mediated by an obscure urge, a form that is admittedly unavoidable, but as yet without actual content. Where that activity is present, but without sociability, so that the sociable demands of others are met with hostile rejection, we find a selfish, morbid state where the organ has torn itself away from unity with the whole, and activity and its results no longer appear moral. Indeed, the two things are so essentially linked that if we were to invent someone engaged in formative activity in total isolation, then the more particular that activity, the more powerful we would have to assume his desire for sociable community to be, or else he would not be moral in our eyes. I mean that in his formative activity, there must also always come to the fore the thing that would allow [that activity] to be acknowledged if others were standing alongside him. For only something that can be an element in sociability constitutes property.

60 Sociability is a relationship that extends throughout humankind, but it is not necessarily an equal relationship of each to all.

It is general, for each person must presuppose – if he regards his own especial formative nature as one that has been appropriated to him, that is, if he relates it to that reason which is always one and the same as itself – that the formative activity of all the others belongs with his own, so that acknowledgment (in this case) and approval (in the former case) are one and the same action. And since the relationship of right is not an equal one either, then given the slightest diversity in the schematism of identical formative agents, it would not exist anywhere if it were not possible at least to acknowledge as differently formed those things which cannot yet be regarded as identical. Hence, where any one person comes into contact with the formative sphere of another without offering any acknowledgment, the activity of reason must be[36] either disguised or suppressed.

This does not mean, however, that sociability is shared out equally amongst everyone. Even if one does not want to look at the fact that acknowledgment, even of what is particularly formed, must be easier if it is formed according to the same schematism, and that this sameness is not necessarily always equal, variety must nevertheless be unequal, directly and to the extent that equality is not posited at the same time; that is, some people must be capable of opening up more to one another, others less. And the coexistence of acknowledgment and opening up is only real depending on the degree of contact that takes place, which cannot possibly be equal [in all cases].

61 *Revelation* is the relationship of individuals to one another in the separateness of their feeling, or the way in which the non-transferability and relatedness of feeling are conditional upon each other.

---

[34] *Corrected from:* revealed.   [35] *Corrected from:* revelation.   [36] *Corrected from:* remain.

According to our last explanation, the essence of this relationship, too, is sociability, and it could be brought under the same heading as this last, just as common language gives it exactly the same name in many cases. For we can say, just as we did there, that the diversity of individuals, in the fulfillment of their consciousness and the non-transferability of their activity, contradicts the unity of reason in the whole procedure, if the relatedness of all those various individuals were not also expressed – just as it was there – in the same action. Each one can only surrender to his own particular excitement, therefore, insofar as he presupposes at the same time that other people, apart from him and alongside him, are also in a state of excitement of a particular kind: that is, he wants them and is looking and longing for them; just as from the other point of view any way in which several people are posited as existing alongside one another, however real this is, is actually a matter of indifference from this point of view and contributes nothing to the satisfaction of this moral need, except to the extent that each person is necessarily excited in a way that is particular to him.

But looking and longing of this kind would always remain hollow if feelings could not be made known between one person and another. And here the relationship is the same as in the domain of thought. For initially feeling, too, is deep within consciousness and given its particularity, its morality is conditional upon the fact that its coming into being is also [the moment at which] it is made external, and in this utterance it is also made known to other people; and the fact that feeling can be made external in this way is likewise to be regarded as a consequence of reason striving to break through the barriers of individuality in order to be united with itself, and to supersede individual nature once more as soon as it has been posited. This is not like speaking and hearing, however, by means of whose coexistence thought itself can be transferred from one consciousness to another; and if we speak of a language of feeling this is either an incorrect expression or else the term signifies something highly mediated, which is concerned only with the utterance of one's own thoughts about feeling, and not with feeling itself. In fact gesture, taken in the broadest sense of the word, stands in the same direct and original relation to feeling as language does to thought; and just as no thought is mature and complete until it has simultaneously been made word, so no feeling is a complete and perfected act unless it has been made gesture. Our perceiving a gesture, however, does not lead to the development of the same excitation in us in the same way that the resounding of a word leads to the reproduction of the thought; on the contrary indeed, no one has a feeling because someone else's feeling has been made known to him, never mind that he ought to feel the same way himself. It is only because and inasmuch as each person knows that a certain excitation in himself is made external in a similar way that he concludes that the other person is in a similar state of excitation, whose precise nature nevertheless remains hidden from him. We are not dealing with expression and reproduction here, then, but with suggestion and intimation, not with intelligibility but with revelation.

Thus it is not something supernatural that is meant by the word here, any more than by the word "faith" earlier, but only something generally human, to which we can also trace back the supernatural meaning of these words. The direct expression of feeling allows one person's state to be made known to another, but only as something non-transferable and unreproducible, and only to the extent that the second person seeks [to understand]

and pays attention. And this making known is nevertheless the completion of his own particularity, because it is only in the various stirrings of emotion experienced by everyone else, analogous [to his own] but particular [to each individual] that nature really comes to belong to reason as a single entity.

We therefore use the expression "revelation" to signify the whole relationship, since it directly recalls, on the one hand, its similarity to what we have just described, for the sociable element is clearly apparent, but points on the other hand to the way in which it differs from that on the other side of symbolizing activity. For we can glimpse here the mysterious aspect of the relationship, the fact that we can become aware of another's feelings through the expression they are given, but without being able to absorb them into ourselves and transform them into our own.

The whole activity is, however, essentially conditional upon the fact that the elements of revelation form a whole in the community, just as thought is conditional upon language, and property upon sociability. For just as no act of feeling is complete and moral if it does not become a suggestion for anyone in search of intimation, whilst at the same time being the intimation of what others would like to suggest, so none can arise except in connection with the totality of suggestion and intimation which we must presuppose for each individual act.

62 Revelation, too, is a relationship which extends throughout humankind, but it is not necessarily an equal relationship of all to each.

It is general, by and large, for the reasons stated above. No one has any reason to regard any other person as superfluous with regard to the differentiation of reason in nature, that is, as merely duplicating some third person; thus each person is the necessary completion of every other person, a completion in search of intimation and suggestion, and each person is to every other the object of an inner desire for revelation.

However, even if we disregard that diversity which has been independently established within the singleness which we acknowledge beyond diversity – which admittedly makes suggestion and intimation more difficult – the very diversity of the nature which surrounds us and of the spheres of life in general, the source of every excitation, must produce a more and less of receptivity to mutual revelation.

63 The inequality of all community relationships for the[37] individual formative points requires a measure which will be constant for each person with regard to the others.[38]

Above all, a measure which will determine the difference. For if anyone who is ignorant of such a measure, proceeding from the assumption of singleness, establishes the narrowest of relationships where only the broadest is possible, then either he does not fulfill his activity, or else he squanders it, and in both cases the unification of reason with nature falters. – And for the same reason it must also be the same for everyone in their relationship to one

[37] The necessity and nature of measure for moral communities. *[Gloss marked by □ in text.]*
[38] *Marginal note 1827:* In 1827 I presented two different possibilities alongside each other: general diversity and a firm measuredness, the former as something not to be reproduced, the latter as something completely recognizable, and therefore postulated one alongside the other. I then left out § 65 and 66, moving straight on to § 67 and 68, and leaving out § 69 went straight on to § 70.

another, for otherwise their activities, which necessarily belong together and complete each other, will to some extent cancel each other out. It is true that this conflict will always occur as long as erroneous application of [the principle of] measure remains possible, but this only affects the individual instance and in the historical domain it will even itself out in the course of time; however, the concept of accord in activity proceeding from various points, that is, the unity of reason in the moral process, ceases to be real if that essential singleness is not incorporated in it, for without it accord will always remain something individual, occurring by chance.

64 Measure, then, must likewise proceed from something originally given, before all moral activity, and must continue to develop within the progressive unification of reason with nature.

For it is an essential component of the unification of nature with reason and can therefore only come about in the same way. If it had its basis entirely in nature, reason, whose activity is conditional upon it, would itself be suffering in the moral domain because of nature. If it arose entirely in and from moral activity, this would constitute the original entry of reason into nature, which can never occur in the moral domain.

65 If, however, the same basis of measure, given from the beginning, is posited for a number [of individuals], it will still only be exactly the same for all of them to the extent that they are at the same point of moral development.

That is, because of the second point posited in § 64. For if there is more unification of reason with nature in one individual, so that we can posit further progress or greater intension of moral being, then measure too will have developed in him to a greater extent, and will not be the same thing as it is in another, in whom we posit less that is moral. Even in the case of measure, then, there is a unity in it of what is reasonable and what is natural, which is never complete, and which we can only ever point to; and its singleness in everyone is also only really given in approximation.

66 The universality of relationships based on the identical constitution of the two kinds of activity is limited according to how strictly separated the particular constitution is; and the universality of those based on different constitutions is limited according to how far the identity of the constitution diminishes.

For each person who is engaged in formative activity according to a schematism held in common with others also uses his particularity in formation, after all, even if not to enhance it. The more such particularity diverges from that of the others, therefore, the less what has been formed can be the object of commerce. In the same way several individuals engaged in particular formative activity do so in fact on the basis of the internal and external nature which they have in common with others. Therefore, the more divergent elements appear in it, the less they will be able to recognize their particular formations as being related. The same is true of symbolizing activity. Every individual who thinks according to general laws does so at every moment on the basis of his own especial excitement, and the more this diverges from that of someone else, the less he will be able to disentangle its contribution to his thought. And a number of people excited in a particular way always derive [their excitement] from the world around them. Thus the more diverse [that world] among them, the less they will truly have an intimation of their own feeling.

67 So that each moral activity can have its measure, then, we require something twofold to have been originally given: one thing by means of which what was originally identical can nevertheless have been originally divided, and one thing by means of which what was originally separate is nevertheless originally bound together.

It is something twofold that we require since the extent of what is similar and what is diverse is mutually determined, and it cannot be rooted in the diversity of moral activity. For this cannot reinforce the particular way in which the one varies from the other, since it is itself only a gradation of more and less; neither can it enhance the singleness of nature, since it is only a difference in the activity of the same. The only possibility that remains, therefore, is that both are something originally given.

68 We do not require different measures, however, for the community relating to formative activity and the community relating to signifying activity.

For since, in its diversity from all the others, each living point is precisely one single entity, property is formed for the same diversity that is expressed in feeling, so that sociability between them can be just as great as revelation. In the same way, since the uniformity of the manner of formation rests on the singleness of natural forms, and the uniformity of thinking in its turn is dependent on the uniform pre-formation and reflection of that singleness, the relationship of right between them may be as close as the community of language.

A single measure is therefore sufficient to determine both of them, and this is particularly [true] in symbolizing activity. What has been formed according to particularity will be withdrawn from community depending on how far it relates to an excitement of which there can be no intimation, and the relationship of right cannot be other than disjointed and one-sided between people whose thought is so uniform that there can be no real permeation of each by the others.

69 The degree of development of moral activity as a whole has a greater influence on the extent of a community that relates to what is particular than it does on matters that relate to what is identical.

For what is particular, when it is offered to sociability and revelation, is to be intimated and acknowledged, but this is only possible by means of analogy. Something proceeding from a moral activity in one individual that has not yet developed in the other, however, lacks any analogy for the latter; and something proceeding from a less complete activity of reason in one individual, which in the other has already been absorbed into a higher level, cannot be for him an object of revelation posited in its own right. In commerce, however, and community of thought, this distinction arises less often, for what is imperfectly formed is to achieve more perfect form by learning from the more perfectly formed individual, and the more perfectly formed can pass into better use for the sake of the less perfect; something similar occurs in the domain of thought and language.

70 Particularity, taken as what is quite simply separate, is originally uni-fied in human nature by means of biological descent brought about by procreation; identity, taken as what is quite simply bound up, is originally divided by climatic variations between peoples, i.e. by variations in race and folk tradition. Both, then, are fixed elements of measure, which have always been given.

1. Given that new life arises through procreation as part of a life that already exists, it is evident that not only is it bound up with that life from the very beginning, and therefore only gradually becomes detached from it, but the same dependence is repeated in the life of each sibling springing from the same source, regardless of the fact that each will develop a particular life of its own. Thus as far as revelation and intimation are concerned, both parents and children, and brothers and sisters, are immediately intelligible to one another in a relationship which is specifically different from any other, since they can trace what is particular directly back to what is identical. – In the same way, with regard to commerce and the community of thought, people from different folk traditions, or who speak different languages, and to an even greater extent people of different races, find themselves separated in a way that is specifically different to any other. It is within these natural boundaries that moral relationships are determined, and everything indeterminate can be traced back to them and measured accordingly. The stamp of filial and fraternal kinship is to be found in a similarity and imitation which precedes all truly moral activity. Similarly folk tradition and, in fainter outline, racial character is a steadfast natural type which can be recognized in the form of the physique as well as in certain limitations in the capacity for language formation. Thus the first attempts of both inculcating and signifying activity to find expression rest on these elements and are conditional upon them. How the conditions of both seek to be a single entity once again [requires] a physical investigation, which can only ever be brought about by approximation, however, given that perfect cognition of the points where such bonds occur must be exclusively the province of world-wisdom. For this reason we keep to first one and then the other [form of] determination, depending on which is more clearly to the fore in any given phenomenon.

2. Both elements are admittedly always – i.e. at every point of ethical development – only relatively given. For to us procreation seems admittedly only to rest on a moral act, that is, on something that has itself become moral. On the other hand, however, we cannot really bring ourselves to imagine a first human being who did not come about through procreation and are therefore obliged to presuppose procreation as occurring in all human existence. And it maintains this character in our experience, as well, for it is indeed a moral act, but its results appear to be entirely physically conditioned, given that it is quite independent of the power of choice and will no doubt always remain so. – In the same way folk tradition, once it has emerged, creates the conditions for every individual existence in its domain; yet this too we see arising historically. For most historical peoples to be encountered in the present day only came into being out of

different elements, and developed their folk tradition only gradually. Yet this can never be brought about deliberately, either; on the contrary, the fusing of different elements into a single people can only come about where it is physically predetermined, only ever, no doubt, within the confines of the race; for a people has never yet been formed from half-breeds.

3. Connected with this is the fact that both elements are only relatively fixed. For at one moment we see only the immediate coexistence of parents and children as family and no longer recognize the same specific relatedness in the further distance; yet at another moment, that immediate coexistence appears conversely to be only a part, and the natural whole of kinship appears much greater. In the same way we sometimes find the greater natural unity in individual, definite folk traditions, sometimes more in the kinship system of several peoples, and sometimes, indeed, only the race will appear to be [the true] measure, while folk tradition appears to be more a matter of chance. Vacillation of this kind is necessary, however, because otherwise on the one hand there could be no moral development of the [concept of] measure, which consists precisely in perception of such vacillation and gradual determination of it; and on the other hand there would be no gradation between the most fixed human relationships and those that can most easily be broken off. This vacillation is limited by two opposing end-points, from which one is always thrust back without the possibility of lingering. The one is namely the endeavor to trace the whole human race back to a single family, regarding the characteristics of races and peoples as something that has come about gradually and by chance. This [point of view] seeks to establish the general uniting of humankind exclusively upon a natural element, tracing the subordinate divisions back more to what is moral. The other end-point is the endeavor to depict the diversity of the human races as characteristics that have been there from the beginning, which cannot be taken back to a common act of procreation and explained on the basis of later climatic influences. This [point of view] seeks to trace fixed divisions predominantly back to the natural element, and general unification, on the other hand, exclusively back to the moral one.

71 The positing of reason which is always the same and always like itself as an especial [aspect] of existence within a definite, measured natural whole, one, that is, which exists relatively in its own right, and which is thus both inculcating and signifying, both the center of its own sphere and linked to community: this concept is that of a *person*.

Personality and the particularity of existence are not one single thing, it is true, but they are connected in a very exact way. On the other hand, personal and numerical diversity are indeed connected in a very exact way, but there is no sense in which they are one single thing, precisely because numerical diversity can be posited without particular diversity. A particular existence is one that is qualitatively distinct from others, while a personal existence distinguishes itself from others and posits others alongside itself, and must for this very reason also be inwardly distinct. But a piece of rock that has splintered off from the rest is numerically diverse from its complement, although it is exactly the same in qualitative terms, because what is manifold about it does not relate to the same unity of space and time. We ascribe particular existence to every genus and species of animal, but we do not ascribe perfect personality to individual specimens, partly because we consider their individual particularity to be more the result of external circumstances than any internal principle, partly because their consciousness cannot entirely break through to that particular object which is the only means of distinguishing themselves from others and positing others alongside themselves. The concepts of person and personality are thus dependent solely upon the moral domain, and on the manner of being individual and many within it; for the positing of others alongside oneself is as essential to the concept as is the distinguishing of oneself. The less an individual or a people is able to distinguish itself from others, the less personally developed it is in its morality; the less it is able to posit and acknowledge others alongside itself, the less morally developed it is in its personality. There is no sense, however, in which the concept is restricted to individual human beings to such an extent that it can be applied to anything else only in a figurative sense; on the contrary, a family is a person and a people is a person in just the same way. If we were to describe these as "moral persons" in a restricted and, so to speak, improper way, then it would sound as if the individual human being were an exclusively physical person; but this is incorrect. For according to what we have said above, he too is a physical person only inasmuch as he is a moral one, and such beings are also only moral persons inasmuch as they are physical ones, that is, definitely measured natural wholes that are relatively self-contained. Indeed we can only say that the individual human being is the smallest personal whole, while, a people, in its broadest scope, is the largest, for a race does not even posit itself as a unity. The human species cannot be regarded as a person, however, because it has nothing similar which it can posit alongside itself. At the same time, to take the route of imagining reasonable beings inhabiting other celestial bodies constitutes the never-completed development of perfect personality in the human race.

Section Two

Elementary part, or, the exposition of oppositions

I Formative activity

1 Considered in very general terms

1 What is originally given is always the smallest possible quantity of the organic unification of nature with reason in terms both of extent and of intensity.

The smallest possible quantity in terms of extent, both with regard to human nature and to external nature; for the latter also always exists indirectly in an organic context; even if reason were already active, only the very least amount would have been in the power of reason from the very beginning. Similarly, in terms of intensity, both with regard to receptivity, or the activity of reason through the senses, and to independent activity, or the activity of reason through talent. For even if both were completely given, the power exercised over them by reason would be the very smallest quantity from the very beginning.

2 The total contents of the activity of reason from this given [point] onward can only be described to the extent that we may presuppose knowledge of both human nature and of external nature.

For indeed it only develops as such knowledge develops, or at the same time as signifying activity, and the one can contain no more than the other. Since our intention is only to catalogue this content in general terms here, however, we shall also proceed only on the basis of a general knowledge of this kind. It is a matter of indifference whether the expressions [used to convey] individual statements of this kind here and elsewhere are taken from a definite form of natural science, and if so, which one, or whether they are not taken from science at all but from the language of our common life. Their sense will be obvious, and every [reader] can easily transfer them into his own idiom.

3 If we take as our starting-point earliest childhood, or the very slightest degree of extension, the goal of formative activity is that the whole of human nature be brought into the service of reason, and by this means the whole of external nature also.

In this state the very smallest quantity of organic activity on behalf of reason which will still allow the possibility of human existence has already got underway, and the process of taking possession of what has been allotted to reason develops only gradually.

Activity directed towards human nature and activity directed towards external nature are relatively separate, it is true, inasmuch as reason only directly inhabits the former, but each is essentially conditional upon the other. For just as human nature in general can only be maintained in lively coexistence with external nature, so the process of becoming reasonable can only be maintained in connection with external nature.

4 If we take as our starting-point our similarity with animal existence or the very slightest degree of intensity or intension, the goal of formative activity is that everything posited in reason should find its organ in nature.

In the same way that in an animal all organic activity proceeds only from the play of the particular natural force of definite life and the natural forces in general, so too, in that state where man is closest to the animals, most [organic activity] proceeds only from this natural play and a minimal amount from the urges of reason.

Since, however, reason is only given to us in the human being, and even then only in the form of the twin activities of forming and signifying, then as far as formative activity is concerned we can only know from signifying activity what is posited in reason. It is, then, the relating of all organic activities to the reason-content which is emerging in consciousness, [a process] which is constantly developing ever further.

Since, however, perfection is nowhere given, there are also organic activities, always and everywhere, which can only achieve a lesser degree of connection with reason.

5 External inorganic nature sets fewer limits on the activity of reason than organic nature does, so that activity which is directed towards both also assumes a different character.

Inasmuch as the former is the predominant or active element, the unification of the spiritual and the material may be regarded as a steady intensification, where moral intensification, the unification of nature with reason, is merely the ultimate term. Nothing in reality is raw material pure and simple, but everything has more of a tendency to be raw material, the less life and shape it contains. It would be a contradiction, therefore, to further the connection between nature and reason by destroying life and shape where they are already present. Where no life is present, however, there is no modification that can have a degrading effect. This does not give rise to any true inequality, however. For as organic nature withholds itself more from formative activity, so it offers itself more to signifying activity, which is always directed towards it in the first instance.

6 To the extent that what is not offered at all to organic activity in and for itself can nevertheless become an organ by virtue of its relationship to signifying activity, everything else must also be able to achieve a similar indirect organic connection with reason alongside any direct one.

Celestial nature could only become an organ in this way; since we can also recognize an earthly nature, however, they must have this relationship with reason in common, which must therefore be something different from the one that is particular to earthly nature.

7 The formation by reason of all the capabilities of the senses and the talents invested in human nature is *gymnastics* in the broadest meaning of the word.

Sense and talent have already been explained. Understanding and drive,[39] considered in their organic aspect, are the starting-point here, and so on in an outward direction. Everything that can be distinguished here as a part is always conditional upon what stands in the opposite position, and no one thing can be completely separated from the other. In the same way, however, gymnastics as a whole is also conditional upon the continual development of signifying activity. For the tools of consciousness can only be formed when consciousness is materially fulfilled at the same time, namely by practice. Hence the more involuntary a life activity, the less it can become a direct organ of reason.

8 The formation of inorganic nature to be the tool of the senses and of talent is *mechanics* in the broadest meaning of the word.

That is, everything inorganic is a single entity by virtue of the unity of movement and rest, and a whole by virtue of a definite limitation placed on its shape; both are external aspects and can therefore be modified without any degrading effect. [We can define as] mechanically formed, therefore, anything that has become something new in both respects for the benefit of reason as a result of organic human influence. Mechanics cannot exist without gymnastics, however, just as the latter cannot exist without the former. For only to the extent that sense and talent have themselves been developed can external nature be formed by them for their benefit. And in the same way mechanics cannot exist without the development of signifying activity. For only what has been recognized can be formed, and only for a purpose that has been modeled in the conscious mind.

---

[39] *Corrected from:* will.

9 The formation by reason of lower organic nature in order to serve higher human nature can be summarized using the name of the dominant element, that is, *agriculture*.

In everything that belongs under this heading it is true that the individual appearances of vegetable and animal life have been destroyed; nevertheless, this takes place in a natural way, and measure and order have been imposed on this natural process, that is, it has been made reasonable. What has truly been formed, however, is the orientation of the organic forces; species are preserved and refined, nature's capacity to bring forth individual [specimens] enhanced and new varieties produced; under these conditions the destruction of individual beings does not contradict the sanctity of organic nature posited above.

Farming, just like mechanics, is connected with gymnastics, moreover, as well as with the development of signifying activity. Where the latter has been repressed to such an extent that there is not even any recognition of the relationship between the individual and the species, the fear of destruction can either extend to individual animals as well, or else human individuals cannot be excluded from destruction either. Those who eat human beings and those who do not eat animals actually share in the same moral imperfection.

10 Indirect organic use, whether of the organic or the inorganic, is the bringing together of individual entities according to similarity and diversity in order to become an organ of cognition: that is, *collection*.

Organizing activity is at its weakest here, since it merely produces spatial unity amongst what is otherwise divided, and it is most strongly conditional upon signifying activity. Now, since it is at its strongest in gymnastics and is only conditional upon symbolizing activity to the extent that it is its own production, then we have indeed determined its limits here, and there is nothing to be discovered other than what has already been stated.

11 If formative activity is not related to the existence of reason in general within nature in general, then the intensive and extensive orientations come into opposition.

In relation to the general, that is, both orientations are set to infinity, so that their coexistence and interaction are also necessarily posited; however, in relation to personality one may replace the other.[40] For one can say: the more formed things there are around me, the less formative power is needed within me, and the stronger the formative power within me, the fewer formed things I require for its sake. In that case, however, strengthened and spiritually enhanced formative power is merely something negative; the strength to remain elsewhere within the activity of reason, regardless of the lack of organs and the obstacles to be found in raw material. Yet here the activity of reason itself is something that can dwindle away almost to nothing, the mere possibility of itself; and by believing that one is promoting reasonable personality by refusing to check the intensive orientation in favor of the extensive one,[41] it imperceptibly loses its truth and its content. This is the way of thinking characteristic of the *Cynics*, which like them is rooted in a situation where

---

[40] *Corrected from:* their relationship to personality is then all that remains.
[41] I require for its sake . . . the extensive one. *Marginal addition, text crossed out and illegible.*

the general coherence of formative activity is no longer apparent, so that the individual finds himself isolated and reduces his contribution in this area to almost nothing at all, without any corresponding increase in his symbolizing activity. For since the Cynical approach ceases to hold water as soon as the task of observation comes strongly to the fore, requiring sharpened tools as well as a considerable apparatus, it must retreat ever further into distorted ethical knowledge and transcendental knowledge which is always valueless when taken on its own. The opposite way of thinking, which seeks to replace the intensive orientation with the extensive one, appears to be less moral. The formative domain which it produces is entirely negative in character; both the skills and the things which are formed by it are merely useful, and there is no attempt to posit to what end they are useful. And since this way of thinking arises only in a situation where the individual, lost in a larger context, cannot find and hold on to his own self, it leads him back ever further towards an analogy with what is animal.

12 In the same way opposition develops between the development of original tools and the inculcation of derived ones.

For in relation to the general both appear to be set in the same way *ad infinitum*, but as far as the individual personality is concerned, it seems that one may be replaced by the other. Someone who develops his skills thinks that if it is really necessary he will be able to produce something, and will not weigh himself down with things. Someone who surrounds himself with formed things thinks that he ought not to wait for activity before he can use them. The former constitutes the athletic one-sidedness of virtue in the ancient sense, the latter the effeminate, dissolute one-sidedness of wealth. Both are without value in themselves; for since it is only by chance or by magic that one can get hold of formed things without the development of skills, we find that in the latter case there is not really any confidence in what a man has, but only in what he cannot have. And since a man who does not acquire anything himself finds that everything has already been possessed, he can only extricate himself at a [given] moment by using violence or cunning, so that in this case too there is no confidence in what a man is, but only in what he ought not to be.

13 To the extent that one of these one-sided terms stems from the op-position to self-isolating desire,[42] the other from the opposition to self-isolating force, they already presuppose disaster; to the extent that each stimulates opposition, however, they produce disaster.

That is, the emergence of desire for its own sake is even more of a perversity because desire develops of its own accord from every activity, of whatever kind; and the isolating of force is also a perversity because the orientation of the individual can only be determined by need. The development of each of these one-sided notions is closely connected with the other, however.

14 Even if we split the domains demonstrated here into their smallest parts, every activity which does not exclude the other in terms of its sense and spirit is a moral one.

---

[42] *Question mark in margin.*

Definite consciousness of the relationship of each individual activity to the rest and to the whole is not in any sense necessary. Rather, this can be posited in the most varied gradations down to the vaguest of all. It is only completely and definitely lacking when an activity seeks to make its appearance at the definite expense of the others. Then, however, it severs all connection with the general task of reason and cannot be posited as a moral activity in the person [concerned]. That person is then simply an organ, and we must look for the morality of their doings elsewhere.

2 Considered under its opposing characters

a) That of singleness

15 Formative activity, which is the same in everyone to the extent that it ought to take shape in the interests of acquisition and community, requires that those who engage in similar formative activity should be located alongside one another and follow on from one another.

On the one hand these are of course natural conditions; but they could equally well be seen on the other as proceeding from moral activity. The fact that we acknowledge the singleness of the formative force in children, and that it – in a certain sense still raw material, in need of development as a result of the formative activity of others – learns of this: that is moral activity. And when we consider how formative activity, left to its own devices in a solitary state, not only falls behind but also diverges quite considerably from the type received in education, we have no alternative but to locate in that education the reason for the [endless] reproduction of the same manner of formation. In the same way, people are given alongside one another, it is true, but since each one remains together with those whose formative activity keeps pace with his own by virtue of his moral activity, regardless of the fact that each one also has an urge to venture out into the wide world, which is also implanted by moral activity, we must assume that these same individuals engaged in uniform formative activity would also have come together, [impelled by] the moral necessity of presupposing and seeking the same things.

16 Within formative activity, however, even to the extent that it is the same in everyone, steadfast variations nevertheless develop as a result of the place and circumstances in which each person is placed.

Because the human species is the most perfect, each human being is a particular individual. However, this does not prevent each person from being determined in a subordinate sense by external influences. For while practice improves individual skills in certain directions, others fall behind, as do even the first-mentioned skills in other directions and with regard to their other offshoots; this difference in *dexterities*, which is very definitely to be distinguished from what constitutes the particularity of the individual, arises from this state of affairs at times where there is a greater wealth of formative potential and subsequently remains relatively steadfast.

17 From this there arises [a situation] where each individual is inadequate in his own right, as a result of which commerce acquires the shape of *division of labor* and *exchange of products.*

As long as these differences are only slightly developed within a mass, there can be acknowledged acquisition, and acknowledged community, but no real commerce, since each person forms everything that he needs for himself. Such a development generates a double task, however. On the one hand, one-sidedness ought to be superseded, so that each person's assets can be complete; on the other hand, it ought to be retained with reference to the overall task of reason, because each person can further this most effectively with the skills which are most pronounced in himself, and least effectively the other way round. In both cases within certain limitations, of course. For a natural way of acting in a person ought not to disappear entirely, nor can we demand perfect equilibrium in an isolated phenomenon. However, the requirement that the difference should remain relates directly to the activity itself, whereas the reason why it should be superseded relates to its products. Thus both requirements are resolved in these tasks which no longer contradict each other, namely, that each person should be active for reason in general using those skills which are preeminent in himself, and that each person should supplement his assets with products generated by the preeminent skills of others. These tasks are not contradictory providing we assume that the difference of skills in other people is not the same as our own. This assumption is, however, partly given, since diversity is always originally posited in unequal measure, and partly comes into being itself in a moral way since on the one hand need generates skill, while on the other hand community will be extended to the point where its products are to be found.

18[43] Division of labor extends to all formative domains, but in an unequal way.

It is at its weakest in gymnastics; since each individual must after all exercise all his functions, for otherwise reason would not completely inhabit his nature; here, then, it is only in the higher measure of individual orientations that one individual can be supplemented by another. It is at its strongest, on the other hand, in the domain of collecting; here, inclinations of a highly individual nature appear to be [mere] amateurism and idiosyncrasy, and the whole – inasmuch as it derives from the activity of individuals – quite fragmented. Indeed, lying as it does on the boundary between organizing and symbolizing activity, we can say that there is no moral necessity posited for there to be an especial talent of this kind in each individual, for the moral property of each person is the apparatus he collects so that he himself can be recognized from it, and hence [is] a minimal contribution to the whole that arises by itself. Between these two we find mechanics and farming, with the requirement that each person practice something of both, since otherwise the connection between human nature and external nature would not be posited morally in him, and that each person be most receptive, however, to the division of labor.

---

[43] *Marginal observation 1832:* 3. Dissemination.

19[44] Where difference in dexterities has developed and division of labor has come about, there is no means of supplementing one's assets other than by exchange.

That is, when someone[45] requires a means of maintaining himself which he is unable to obtain because he is deficient in skill, he can only obtain it from other people's assets. They are not able to let anything pass out of their assets, however, without putting something back in, because otherwise these would be diminished, thus infringing the condition which alone sustains the difference in dexterities.[46]

This is clear enough in itself. The universality of the expression appears to supersede charity altogether, however, and thus by positing one moral [possibility] appears to destroy another, which always indicates error. Charity is only a necessary evil in this domain, however, because it presupposes indigence and can only in fact take place inasmuch as there is certainty, on the one hand, that whoever practices it will encounter the same in his turn if he should become indigent, thus not as the relationship of one individual to all the others; on the other hand, inasmuch as indigence must be regarded as a straitening of circumstances resulting from the division of labor, which can also only be allayed, however, by those who have been favored as a whole, and thus not as one individual to another here either. Since, then, with this single exception, the indigent individual cannot be regarded as an autonomous unity in commerce, charity too belongs in another domain, one, that is, where the autonomy of the personality is restricted.

20[47] Both of these things, division of labor and exchange, are conditional upon the community of the direct organs, which are both at once, so that what is said of each is true of both.

For things are not necessarily isolated and divided in the same way as dexterities, and so the same person cannot do everything equally well with regard to all those things that are to be formed, so that we find a community of activity directed towards the same thing, whereas it can in fact only become the property of a single person. Thus without a community of this sort, the division of labor would not achieve its purpose. Formation without appropriation, however, atrophies the personal domain just as much as giving away without recompense.

It is equally true of this community that it runs through all the formative domains; it is at its weakest in gymnastics, where it is primarily only teaching and education itself, and at its strongest in the domain of collecting, where nothing can be achieved without the unified [efforts] of several people.

Recompense can equally well be rendered in the form of products as in activities, and with regard to products, it can equally well be in the form of activities; for personal assets can be supplemented in both of these ways. What may seem rather harsher, however, is the fact that, if no one will give away activities without some recompense either, then the

---

[44] *Marginal observation 1832:* 2. Fundamental condition.
[45] *Inserted after this word in 1832:* organs for his activity.
[46] *Marginal addition 1832:* The condition of division is that no one's assets should be diminished.
[47] *Marginal observation 1832:* 1. Fundamental form.

willingness to serve is negated in the same way as charity. Nevertheless, exactly the same holds true here. No one, moreover, willingly accepts the service of others in this domain, and it is something else altogether when the performance of an activity without reference to recompense is any more than a necessary evil.

21 It is essential to any exchange that there should be agreement as to the morality of the action and agreement as to the price of what is done.

Since every activity which goes beyond personal possession is directly related to the task of reason in general, its final moment, that of being given away, can only come if there is a conviction that some part of the task of reason will really be achieved by [the process of] transference. In the same way, however, the action will never be performed if the two parties cannot reach a common decision as to the recompense [required]; for otherwise the assets of one of the two would be diminished, which goes against the original premise. One ought not to give away something one possesses for the benefit of a scoundrel at any price, and one ought not to give anything away even for the benefit of the most excellent of men if the recompense one receives is less than its value. At any rate, the action then belongs in a different domain [altogether].

22[48] Exchange is only perfect when there is trust between the two parties as well as money.

What we mean here by trust is the mutual and steadfast presupposition that one is included in the task of reason together with one's formative activity and not in the face of it, a presupposition that relieves one of the necessity of examining each individual case. Money, however, is the means of recompense accepted by the community, varying in various cases only according to quantity and measure, which replaces all specific recompense. This brings the party who is seeking and the party who is offering into direct contact, since otherwise it would only be by chance that the former could satisfy the needs of the latter, and one of them would have to undertake a second, ancillary exchange before the transaction could be realized.

The activity of reason is thus always the development of both; but neither is ever complete. Trust can never be determined and expressed with such certainty that the necessity of examination in individual cases will never arise again. And the idea of money is never so perfectly realized that it will not become something specific itself again in individual cases and in many respects, itself requiring some equalization. The fact that sooner or later the realization of the concept always comes to be fixed in metal money is something we have learned, but that cannot be explained here. Certainly the reason for this has nothing to do with the value of metals in their own right in the formative domain; for it is precisely in this sense that they themselves are goods, which always constitutes the imperfection of money. Perhaps because they have emerged from the center of the earth and so really do stand in the same relationship to all things, and because, in the interrelation of rigidity and movement, of impenetrability and light, they represent all differences. It is evident in any case that something natural lies at the root of it. At any rate it is certain that metal money and currency – as a means of equalizing the uncertainty which arises from distance – are at

---

[48] *Marginal observation 1832:* 4. Perfection.

the heart of this invention. In [the case of] other, paper money, money once again begins to require trust, thus emerging from the state of tension between them.

Where there is not yet firm trust and a definite [form of] money, all commerce is unregulated and disjointed; only where both have developed do we find a true state of contractuality. There is a gradual approximation to both by means of any number of transitions, starting from an anxious state of alienation and the most awkward of exchanges, which proceed hand in hand.

23[49] Just as both terms are essential to any action of exchange, the diversity of those actions is apparent in the relationship which binds those terms together.

That is, the more trust determines an individual to make an exchange, the less he is impelled by money, and vice versa. In all the lower forms of trade trust has the smallest part to play, because here it is a matter of the most indispensable needs; each person sells to every other without a moment's thought, and without including in his calculations the moral use [to which] the buyer [will put the goods]; we must be aware, however, that here too there is a magic circle of trust which should not be flouted. In actions of this kind, each person seeks to look after his personal assets most of all; they are the expansion of this interest in relation to the general task of reason. However, where trust is the principal motive in agreeing to do something, the money interest recedes until it is the most paltry compensation, although it ought not to disappear entirely if the action is to remain in this domain. In commerce, this is the contraction of personal interest in relation to the general interest of reason.[50]

Every domain of commerce can only be regarded as a whole if actions of both kind develop within it. And so it is only on this condition, too, that each individual is autonomous in commerce. Anyone who practices only the kind of exchange actions in which money interest predominates is base, and rather than being a self-positing formative point, is in need of moral supplementation. The same is also true in reverse, however, of anyone who wished to have no money interest in commerce; for he can no longer be regarded as an individual, and anyone who so wishes is caught in an act of presumption.

24[51] The inner essence of exchange is destroyed if the relationship between the two moments is inverted.

If, where one person is lacking in trust, the other attempts to convince him of the morality of the transaction by means of money, that constitutes bribery, and the action is immoral. If one person seeks to conceal the inadequacy of the recompense from the other with pleasant representations, that constitutes fraud, and that action is also immoral.

25[52] From each relative beginning of formative activity onward, exchange develops ever further, but gradually, and without definite boundary points.

---

[49] *Marginal observation 1832:* 5. Contraction and expansion of interest in relation to the task.
[50] *Marginal addition 1832:* Where there is no longer any reference to recompense, this does not constitute a transaction between one person and another, but simply an action performed in common.
[51] *Marginal observation 1832:* 6. Corruption.
[52] *Marginal observation 1832:* Expansion in space and time (to 3).

Because differences in dexterity are also in the process of developing, it is minimal from the very beginning, because we find more acquisition than community as long as the formative domains of individuals only rarely come into contact; it then increases until there is equilibrium between the two to such an extent that nothing is possessed that cannot also enter the process of exchange, so that there is always a crossover between one person's domain and that of the others. In the same way, on the other hand, there is more community than acquisition from the very beginning when activities are very similar, it is true, and can easily be exchanged, but few things are formed to last, and so there is a realization of the requirement – admittedly never entirely absent – that everything is only common property to the extent that the assets of each individual are posited by everyone, and vice versa.

Even the development of a state of contractuality comes into being only gradually, however, from this point, without [some kind of] leap. Trust and money introduce each other gradually as abbreviated ways of proceeding, for there are approximations even to the latter. And this relationship can only attain the highest degree of certainty and steadfastness through an increasing interest in exchange, and cannot exist except between one individual and another.[53]

26[54] Exchange decreases from each formative point outward according to distance, although also only gradually, and without definite boundary points.

The first is a matter of course, because directness and multiplicity of contact decrease, as does the singleness of the underlying representations. The last decrease also takes place gradually, however. For even if we presuppose that there is climatic diversity among people and things, it cannot appear in a definite and clearcut form even at the boundaries themselves, unless these are oceans and deserts. In that case, however, division is merely external, and once it is overcome, exchange gradually assumes the same neighborly guise and can increase until there is no distinction between an individual's relationship of exchange with his neighbor on this side of the border and his neighbor on the far side.

27[55] Thus the endeavor to perfect contractuality and the state of right does not in itself produce the state.

For on the one hand, what is most perfect can come about without giving rise to a self-contained whole which is separate from everything else; and on the other hand, we can imagine the latter without the former. It is true that no state will exist where trust and money do not exist; equally, it is not possible to find the same kind of mutuality and guarantee of trust, nor the same kind of money, throughout the earth. However, the same kind of money is not what makes the state. This is partly because the same money in the same state will always revert to being goods and will therefore stop being money, and partly because, as money, it will pass beyond the outer limits of the state.

---

53 *Marginal addition 1832:* It is for this reason that in many ancient states no jurisdiction existed in the case of delayed recompense.

54 *Marginal observation 1832:* Dilution in space (to 3).

55 *Marginal observation 1832:* Relationship to the state.

In the same way a society which guarantees trust in commerce on both sides is in no sense a state, nor is this guarantee universally one and the same thing in the state, moreover. Since in everyone's commerce with everyone else everything merges and becomes blurred, the state would always be either a whole whose outline is merely arbitrary, or else something natural, to the extent that it is delimited according to climate, but whose independent existence must always decline as soon as contact of a general nature sets in,[56] so that it was only suitable for the earliest stages of the formation process. It has been depicted as both: as an arbitrary assemblage and as an institution which everyone ought to strive to dispense with and which could only oppose such striving and secure its own foothold through the use of violence. Clearly, the basis of these misunderstandings is to be found in the one-sided emphasis of one of these factors and the total neglect of the other.

b) That of diversity

28 To the extent that, being different in each individual being, it should produce things that are non-transferable but related in kind, formative activity requires those engaged in dissimilar formative activity to be located alongside one another and to follow on from one another.

Even this, which was originally to be required as a natural condition, in fact already exists everywhere as real moral activity. In a child the particularity of the formative force is also acknowledged as it develops by training the force which forms what is identical within it, and it is not forcibly repressed, as [constituting] resistance to the prevailing norm. This is moral activity, and without it any natural tendency would be in vain, as we see wherever this freedom does not hold sway, or it would be repressed, for we see everywhere that if education is directed exclusively towards singleness, the tendency to particularity also gradually disappears. In the same way, it is true, human beings are given alongside one another as particular and diverse beings, but the fact that they restrict the orientation towards community, towards similarity, and do not become separated by directing their efforts towards perfect equality already demonstrates the activity of reason, which requires diversity as a form of completion and would therefore seek and find it – we must assume – if it did not approach of its own accord.[57]

29 Nevertheless, certain steadfast kinds of correspondence develop in formative activity, to the extent that it is different in each individual being.

The way each person varies from everyone else is necessary in the human species, but the appearance of that diversity is partly conditional upon external influences, no less than the singularity of all human beings, and partly dissimilar in itself, given that it is diversity, so that lesser diversity appears to be similarity by comparison with greater diversity, which assumes the form of dissimilarity. Such similarities in what is particular

---

[56] *Question mark in margin.*   [57] Did not approach. *Corrected from:* were not given.

are to be distinguished very definitely from those which are rooted in singleness, and in the same way, dissimilarity must be distinguished very definitely from differences in dexterity, given that these run uniformly through all the branches of activity. The two are also to be distinguished very clearly from each other, given that dissimilarities are present within the same natural compass and similarities exist which run through the most diverse natural tendencies. In this way a single type of differentiation is revealed which must be related to the essence of human nature, while on the other hand there is a plurality of masses, each of which carries this whole type within it and is an image of the whole, even if it is itself differentiated.

30 It is in this opposition of similarity and dissimilarity that the closing off and opening up of particular formative domains is rooted.

Both activity and the results of activity are closed off of their own accord because of the impossibility of transference. Our term for what is closed off in the most essential part of those results is the *house*; everything else may be regarded as its adjunct. For its reserve, its sanctity seem to be principally rooted in the fact that it epitomizes moral property. Fields and workshops are open places; even though they are the most valuable and indispensable things that he possesses, the countryman does not lock up his agricultural tools. The less particular formative activity has developed within a mass, the fewer locked dwelling-places one finds.

It is true, as we demonstrated above, that such closing off necessarily brings with it the acknowledgment of relatedness. However, if diversity were absolute or equal, such acknowledgment would remain simply the accompanying coefficient of closing off and could never emerge in its own right, nor constitute an especial activity. Given that we posit diversity as unequal, however, the closing off must also sometimes be tighter, sometimes looser, and so added to this there must also be an opening up characterized by the same variety. However, we can no more speak of right and claim here than of transference and exchange; on the contrary, opening up can only be realized in an appraisal of relatedness which coincides [on all sides]. As a result of the particular shape it assumes and the relationship it necessarily enjoys to the closed house, our term for this opening up is the hospitality of the house, the counterpart to the householder's right to privacy mentioned above. Thus we do not mean by this expression the first attempts to establish a commerce which is still some distance removed, nor a relationship to what is particular in symbolizing activity. Its overall tendency is that – always depending on the intimation of the property-owner, or as a result of goodwill on his part – another person might penetrate as far as the house's interior and be convinced of the degrees of relatedness existing between them. The less particular formative activity develops within a mass, the less hospitality is present between its members; on the contrary, even if they live alongside one another, each is mainly concerned with his own life. And because the awakening of consciousness to particularity and its opposition to singleness progress at the same rate, anyone who diverges [from the norm] is denied even the semblance of relatedness, and any attempt at penetration is treated with hostility.

31 The right to privacy and hospitality runs through all the formative domains, though unequally.

That is, the self-contained state must be smallest and hospitality greatest in the domain of the apparatus, for not only will the contribution of particularity be smallest here, the feeling of relatedness is also strongest. Again, closing off must be most rigorous in the domain of gymnastics, hospitality at its weakest; and subsequently in the domain of mechanics, because here everything is linked most closely to the innermost core of particularity, that is, to what is least comprehensible, so that only the most definite similarity can break through the barriers. In the same way, sociability in the former domain can scarcely bring about sociability in the latter. Similarly, what belongs to agriculture follows on from apparatus.

However, just as particularity is present in the same activities and their ramifications as what is identical, whatever is the result of particular formative activity can consist of elements which are identically formed, so that what is non-transferable is to be found only in the connection of the two; in the same way, elements of particularity could exist in what is identically formed. Now, to the extent that identically formed elements in what is particular could become detached from this connection and isolated, they might, if they were replaced with others of equal value, be transferred into commerce, even though a disagreeable obscuring of what is moral is demonstrated thereby. And to the extent that particular elements of what has been identically formed cannot be detached from this connection and appear only as an accessory, they cannot disrupt commerce either; for a disagreeable affectedness would be demonstrated thereby, as if it were not enough for particularity to have the constant renewal of this transient productivity in the other domain.

32 Similarity can extend as far as causing the disappearance not only of closing off but also of the consciousness of diversity; and dissimilarity can extend as far as causing the disappearance not only of opening up, but also of recognition [*Anerkennung*].

Diversity disappears here where there is community of use, which gives rise to a semblance of commerce and exchange, but is then immediately recognized as a mere semblance by the fact that it distances itself as far as possible from money. This is probably the actual, more secret meaning of the reciprocal giving of presents to one's host: they are intended to attest to the superseding of diversity [even] to the point of using things in common. A counterpart to this is joint manufacture. If one does not consider similarity to emerge to this extent in individuals, but to be universal, this would have to be the merging of two houses into one, such as we mentioned earlier.

Dissimilarity, when it appears at the same developmental stage of particularity, must remain an acknowledgment, however great it may be; yet the degree of closing off becomes greater, and a hospitable relationship can only be maintained by renewed and ever more futile attempts, which ought, however, never to be abandoned. If it is at the same time bound up with the greatest possible difference of intensity, one particularity developed to the highest degree, the other still completely repressed, then acknowledgment cannot take place. In undeveloped particularity the only moral event that can take place is the honoring of developed particularity, which can be acknowledged even where it is not understood; developed particularity, however, can only consider formative power in the first-mentioned as raw material, in terms of its particular side, but cannot begin to accept it as a closing off [into] property. When large masses which are so very different come into contact, this gives rise to a relationship of serfdom. All houses belonging to the one mass are destroyed as houses in their own right and absorbed into the others as mere components, bodies included, in order to be truly permeated by particular formative power. This relationship is only immoral if the state of right is superseded and the individual rendered incapable of acquisition, and further, if it is not directed towards the development of particularity so that the one is superseded at the same time as the other. Thus the greatest similarity and the greatest dissimilarity produce the same effect, i.e. the fusion of the houses; however, in the former [this is the expression of] equality, and in the latter, inequality. Serfdom, as a purely educative relationship, and within these limitations, considering also how it has always been a great historical tool and has often persisted purely as an inner attitude, without any external force, should decidedly not be regarded as an immoral excrescence.

33 Just as property develops out of commerce, so commerce develops in its turn out of the hospitality of property.

Since both characters are united in every real activity, property is only formed as a relative aspect of what in a different relation [constitutes] acquisition, and the more acquisition takes place, the more there can be true property, as well.

The second thing [arises] because imitation arises from hospitality, however, and here similarity is maintained and mingled, so that particularity becomes less of an obstacle to commerce because it is tinged with other secondary characteristics.

34 Hospitable relationships of every possible nuance proceed outward from each formative point, without definite points of separation.

For there is only a gradual transition from similarity to dissimilarity. However, only an abundance of relationships is fitting for the development of particularity, for surely the smaller the radius of a circle, the less development takes place in it. However, distance is not the criterion here; rather, close relationships can be established between parties who are actually distant from each other if only contact takes place, while a whole variety of relationships can be found together where there is proximity.

35 Everything also merges together imperceptibly from fusion on the one hand to serfdom on the other.

In relationships between individuals there is no definite delimitation of the various formative levels, not even by the relationship of serfdom, unless it exceeds what is intended by setting limits on the state of right. The more the semblance of this is lost, the more it becomes a purely educative relationship, which is absorbed by imperceptible transitional stages into that of tutelage.

If we now compare the educated man with his natural apprentice on the one hand, and a man who has been educated in an unfamiliar way on the other, there is a greater similarity with the former, notwithstanding the difference in educative level between the two, than with the latter, and so the basis of determination is similarly lacking, and can only be drawn from elsewhere.

II *Signifying activity*

I In general

36 What must always be presupposed before any action on the part of signifying activity is the smallest amount of unification, of reason and nature having already become one.

Since we can only comprehend one function here in terms of its opposition to the other, the latter is indicated here by the distinction between unity and unification. For formative nature is more the making ready of nature for reason, the sole means by which the latter can reside in the former; signifying activity, however, expresses more directly the existence of reason as nature and of nature as reason. Yet since there is no beginning pure and simple in moral matters, but on the contrary, everything is given as having begun, each moment of signification presupposes an earlier one, from which it follows on, so that there is no moment in human existence when reason had not already become nature and the movement of nature which formed that moment did not express the existence and essence of reason. To the extent, however, that formative and signifying nature diverge from each another, existence consisting in the exchange between the two, that very determination of existence which is absorbed into signifying activity constitutes *consciousness*. For absence of consciousness is merely the non-divergence of [the terms of] this opposition.

It is thus impossible to imagine a moment of human existence without some reasonable consciousness, even though this can be repressed to a very great extent. Indeed wherever it occurs at the earliest stage, it can only be posited as the tiniest quantity, both in terms of extent and intensity.

37 The total content of this function can only be described to the extent that we presuppose the shaping of human and external nature by reason.

For consciousness can only emerge as organs are formed, that is, at the same time as formative activity.

38 From the very beginning the aim in terms of extension is that everything posited in reason should also pass over into organic activity.

We posit the existence of something similar to consciousness in an animal, but not the expression of reason, hence only what constitutes the organic aspect of consciousness in ourselves. No definite being either, therefore, and hence no opposition between consciousness of self and consciousness of objects, but something that wavers confusedly between the two without fully developing into either. If, on the other hand, the expression of reason exists in the smallest measure of human consciousness, even where reason in the higher sense of the word appears to lie dormant, hidden away, this opposition is nevertheless present in each one, in a process of becoming, for only here are we conscious of definite being. The more dominant the analogy with the animal [kingdom] continues to be, however, the less [the terms of] the opposition diverge, and the smaller the content of reason in consciousness.

If, meanwhile, we posit a moment of definite feeling or definite perception, that is, a definite individual conscious existence, we are actually positing everything [that exists] in each individual, since we also posit in each self-posited individual a circle of relationships to everything else. However, this is not real in that same moment, but only if we presuppose infinite development, and this cannot proceed from a single act, but only once the earlier connected acts have themselves been originally taken up by a real consciousness. The real passing over of the total content of reason into organic activity is therefore only reached with the totality of all organic contact.

There is nowhere where real, complete divergence of perception and feeling in consciousness takes place, either; it is always in a process of becoming. Just as at the beginning what is confused predominates, and only the intimation of its twofold nature is true, so the opposition predominates subsequently, it is true, but confusion is also still present, even if it is repressed. We never entirely stop confusing the feeling with what is thought to be the cause of it, the existence of the object with whatever it has produced in us. If the two were ever purely separate within a single consciousness, then the totality of consciousness would have been given.

Since, however, the opposition is somehow really expressed in every human consciousness, each one is elevated in some way above mere personality; for if sense and drive are directed only towards self-preservation they can find satisfaction in the chaotic nature of animal consciousness.

The meagerness of the initial development of consciousness is clearly connected with the imperfect development of the organs. The more organs are formed and the more perfect they are, the more [frequently] contact is mediated, and so we simply cannot determine the limits of progress in terms of extent.

39 From the very beginning the aim in terms of intensity is that everything in organic movement should be permeated with the content of reason.

The content of reason is what keeps unity and multiplicity apart in consciousness, and what binds them together. Hence we assume that in animals there is only something confused that wavers between the two, and can only imagine that for human consciousness, too – if we could imagine the total absence of the activity of reason – there would remain only infinite multiplicity and indefinite unity. In human consciousness we must regard even the first utterances as an approximation to the fact that unity develops from multiplicity and multiplicity is held firm by unity. However, there is no moment of consciousness in which everything indefinite separates out completely into definite unity and definite plurality; on the contrary, there is always something confused that remains unresolved, and is not then permeated with the content of reason. Hence the whole of human consciousness is also just an alternating sequence of more or less distinct and definite moments, and posited in reason is the endeavor to elevate what is unconscious ever further towards consciousness. Since, however, the multiplicity of organic movement is infinite because of the infinite divisibility of space and time, together with the diversity of relationships at every point, the task is also an infinite one.

Elevation above purely animal interest already exists in the smallest human consciousness, however, in the closing off of a moment of this kind as something complete in itself, and resting in it; for in animals comprehension and the transition into formative activity are one and the same thing. Thus the more organic movement is permeated by the activity of reason, the more what resembles instinct recedes in humankind, and organizing activities rest upon the linking up of the definite activities of consciousness.

40 If, in all definite consciousness, plurality must be bound together by unity and unity realized in plurality, then unity in each person is also related to unity pure and simple, and plurality to plurality pure and simple.

For since in all real consciousness unity and plurality are only relative, because of the admixture of confusion in each one, they can only be kept separate by an opposing relationship of this kind. – Plurality pure and simple, where no unity is posited, is, however, simply the infinite divisibility of space and time, for in anything which is posited as fulfilling this in some way, some kind of unity is already posited. And on the other hand, a plurality which is not posited as space and time, such as is found, for example, in a sequence or body of ideas, is a plurality posited out of unity and hence not plurality pure and simple. – Unity in general, in which no plurality is posited and hence also every opposition superseded, is the unutterable unity of the most high, the purely indistinguishable absolute unity of being and knowledge.

Neither the former, divisible infinity, nor the latter, indivisible unity, are present in consciousness in their own right, but the fact that positing one necessarily entails positing the other constitutes the particular form of all human consciousness; as the content of reason becomes organic so the former supervenes, and as organic movement becomes intellectual, so the latter supervenes.

41 The transcendental and the mathematical are essential to all human consciousness; for this reason, however, it is a misconception to believe that everything that is not mathematical is [mere] appearance, or that everything that is not transcendental is [mere] appearance.

For the transcendental is simply the relationship to absolute unity demonstrated above, while the mathematical is the relationship to infinite, indefinite plurality. Both understood in the broadest sense, of course.

Doctrine of duties, final version (probably 1814/17)

Introduction

1 The doctrine of duties cannot document the totality of movement, but only the system of consciousness in which they are absorbed.

Otherwise it would be history.

2 The doctrine of duties is positioned between the other two in such a way that action in accordance with duty presupposes virtue and sets conditions on the highest good, but conversely, in the same way, it presupposes the highest good and sets conditions on virtue.

As a doctrine, however, the doctrine of duties must remain independent of the other two depictions.

3 All action in accordance with duty is thus imperfect as such, because it is positioned right in the middle between two ways of shaping virtue and the highest good.

Because, that is, the second thing that comes into being through action is something that had not previously been in existence. – Imperfection, however, must lie with the *terminus a quo* as such, and not with the *terminus ad quem.*

4 Duty is therefore rectification and production.

Either separately,[1] so that it divides along these lines, or so that each is present in the other.

5 Duty is not autonomous movement on the part of reason; on the contrary, reason is the moving [force] and nature that which is moved.

For no natural formation could come into being as the result of an autonomous movement of reason. Reason is not something we know in isolation, moreover, but only in nature.

6[2] Thus we cannot describe it solely in terms of cause, nor solely in terms of effect, but only in terms of the interaction of the two.

---

[1] *Corrected from:* divided.   [2] *Marginal note:* Passages 5 and 6 immediately after 1.

If an action is given to me solely in terms of its effect, I cannot know if it was in accordance with duty, because I do not know whether it proceeded from a movement of reason. Hence I cannot describe something which has been set in this way either.

If I am only presented with the cause, I cannot judge it either. For error might intrude, or someone might do an evil action for the sake of good.

N.B. In this way distinctions between the doctrine of duties, the doctrine of virtues and the highest good emerge of their own accord.

7 Given that every action creates a deposit in the human being himself and also in nature as a whole,[3] each one is both rectification and production.

For rectification can only take place in human nature, where every misdeed is a moral minus. Nature as a whole, however, is merely equal to zero, and in reference to nature only production occurs (except to the extent that it has already been unified, for then it is also capable of rectification).

8 Action which is to be subsumed under the concept of duty is defined as a single entity by the moment and the person.

It is only in personality that reason and nature are truly bound up together; thus it is only those things which can be traced back to a bond of this kind that constitute a single entity. It must not only proceed from a single entity, however, but must also be a single act, i.e. something willed.

9 Everything that is willed can be regarded as sharing in a single act of will.

Each individual decision belongs in a particular circle. Entry into all the circles is something coordinated and is subject to something greater. This is the will to conversion, which for that reason is infinite, and feeling demands something supernatural from it.

10 The carrying out of every decision disintegrates into a multitude of actions, which must however also be especially willed.

Action, like space and time, is infinitely divisible, but it is also indefinite, discrete division. Each part must be willed, for what is mechanical is merely imperfect, and attention must always be paid to possible breaks in continuity.

11 Between absolute unity and infinite multiplicity, unity is to be found in the purposive concept of the action.

1. The absolute single act would not be an ethical one, because reason has always already been present in nature. Moreover, the others do not stand in the same relation to it as parts to a whole, but only as something especial in relation to something general. The other decisions are not definitely contained in that single one but are only determined by something else which supervenes.

2. It is true that the small parts of individual actions must be willed, but if they are indeed parts then they are also posited in the original will, and that volition is nothing new but merely the same original volition persisting through time.

---

[3] In the human being ... as a whole. *Corrected from:* in virtue as well as in the highest good.

3. The purposive concept does not need to be actually thought, but is merely the thought that would be expressed by volition if it were thought. – Example from the composition of speech, the necessity and indefinite nature of expression and tone.

12 This unity is not to be posited as universally valid, however; on the contrary, the same thing can be regarded by one person as a single action and by others as many.

The virtuoso is able to unite more things under one [heading], because he can also comprehend straight away those determining reasons for what is subordinate which originate elsewhere.

13 In terms of natural philosophy, personality is given as something diverse; a people is a person just as much as an individual is, and the individual is also the work of other individuals.

Hence the difference in assigning to which person a given action relates, or making an assumption as to whom [a task] that has been set should relate to.

14 For this reason there must either be especial domains of duty for the individual person and the composite one, or else each concept of duty must be ordered in such a way that it can be applied to both.

To start with, the former cannot be contrived in a way that is universally valid. It is also difficult to see where we are to find the basis for determining the various concepts, since both are persons in the same way.

Without the second thing, and without putting this application into practice, it is impossible to measure out the whole of the moral domain in terms of concepts of duty. It is for this reason that even the greatest always appears to be [merely] a matter of chance.

15 We must therefore presuppose the separate existence of the acting subjects as well as divided orientation in the actions themselves.

As regards the former, we should think in terms of their existing alongside each other rather than one being subordinate to the other; but we must always bear in mind that there will be mixed assumptions as to how to assign them.

The latter is necessarily the case because a purposive concept necessarily excludes certain things in its distinction from the general will, since otherwise actions would indeed be separate, but only numerically, without any conceptual diversity.

16 With reference to persons existing alongside one another, action in accordance with duty is action that founds or appropriates community.

That is, a basis for division can only be found here to the extent that we posit identity and difference between persons. This is already presupposed in nature, however, both between individuals, by virtue of ethnic identity, and between peoples, by virtue of race etc. Those who are similar form a natural community of material, and only vary numerically. Those who are dissimilar assume relationships to material which others cannot have, and their actions relate to the others in an excluding way, as appropriation.

This distinction cannot be fixed in formulae which have universal validity, because identity and difference are relative.

17 In terms of divided orientation, action in accordance with duty[4] is also both universal and individual.

For if someone who acts is similar to another of similar nature with regard to this orientation, his action is not expressing an especial relationship and is therefore universal; the same is true of the other side.

The diverse functions of reason are not related to one another particularly here; duty is the same for the one as it is for the other.

The entire division of duty must be constructed from these two oppositions.

18 The whole of moral existence can only be expressed by means of the concept of duty insofar as every action which is in accordance with duty contains the whole idea of morality within it.

For if it does not contain it, its effect does not constitute an element of the highest good either. The imperfection mentioned above is only [located] in the *terminus a quo*, and the imperfection which is also subsequently shown in the result must not be located in the purposive concept, but must come about through the resistance of nature.

19 To the extent, however, that every action which is in accordance with duty must be constructed by means of a purposive concept, and these necessarily exclude certain things, we cannot posit the whole idea of morality as present in each one.

Only if we posit the existence of purposive concepts, however, can the totality of moral existence be expressed in a multiplicity of concepts of duty.

20 This contradiction must be resolved by the construction of the concepts of duty themselves.

It is the negative element in the so-called collision of duties, for if certain things are excluded from each concept of duty, then in fulfilling one duty we do not fulfill any of the others. We ought to have new formulae, therefore, so that we are able to decide when each duty ought to be fulfilled; otherwise, once the first proposition was established, we would be able to avoid every duty in the way of duty, and remain, once the last proposition were established, in a state of constant inactivity in order not to leave some duties unfulfilled. These especial formulae would also either have to go back to the concept of duty, however, or not. In the former case they could only be elements, so to speak, in the individual formulae of duty; in the latter, the doctrine of duties would not be independent.

21 In every action which is in accordance with duty, therefore, both must be the case in different ways.

That is, in every action [there must be] a general orientation towards the whole idea. If this is not the case, then a definite deed would not be moral. Either the orientation might be a sensory one and yet its outcome, taken objectively, be comprehended as a moral one. In that case, actions which are in contravention of duty might also proceed from the same internal basis. Or else it might be partially moral. Then, however, it will not contain the

---

[4] Action in accordance with duty. *Before this, crossed out:* The relationship of all active reason.

basis of its own measure, so that actions might proceed from it which destroy other parts of moral being.

In every [action] [there must also be] a definite excluding volition. This accords with the general volition with regard to [the act of] excluding, providing that the excluding is momentary, because everything that is moral is also indirectly furthered, after all, if one thing is perfectly posited. It accords with it with regard to its positing, if the fact of its not being posited causes the idea to be destroyed, i.e. if the result were to be a natural determining where reason is not present. The entry [upon the scene] of natural determining of this kind constitutes a demand for definite action.

General volition must be something alive in every action which is in accordance with duty: the true fundamental urge, the original movement, modified only by the demand which provides its orientation. – For this reason we should not, ethically speaking, posit general volition as a single independent act, for any act of this kind must become an especial one; as a genuine act, however, it forms the primitive component of any action.

22 General volition must vary at various moments, and the perfection of action in accordance with duty consists in internal stimulus coinciding with external demand.

For in the drive, one single part must predominate over the others, after all, in diverse subjects at diverse times, and this, given the unity of volition, produces the multiplicity of changing moral attitudes and dominant moral tendencies. There is always an imperfection when a situation arises where one is obliged to act against one's inclination or attitude. Also if one experiences imperfect stimuli without any corresponding demand.

[The key to] accord is to be divinatory in the stimulus for which the demand must [eventually] come; the basis for this lies in one's way of life (or choice of profession as far as inclination is concerned), or else in one's ability to call up the stimulus once the demand has been given.

23 Given that every action that is in accordance with duty presupposes virtue and moral being, it is part of a sequence that has already begun.

For in both the subject and the object the result of an action follows on from what is already in existence; for if moral existence is posited, it is also posited in its essential schematism so that everywhere that something ought to come into being, something exists already; the same is true of virtue.

24 Given that virtue and moral being can only have come about through action which is in accordance with duty, this is what is original.

All virtue must have arisen from the activities of reason, from individual movements. The same is true of all external natural formation, for otherwise it would be mere appearance.

25 Thus every action in accordance with duty which creates an external link is internally generative, while anything that is externally generative creates an internal link.

The only way of resolving the opposition is if each one is both things, in diverse senses.

1. Everything that gives rise to new relationships is externally generative. However, these are always predetermined (founding a state, arranging a marriage). Where there

is nothing already present, there is always hazard, and no certainty with regard to morality.

2. Since all moral relationships only exist as a result of continued action, and would otherwise founder immediately, any action which creates a link is generative all over again. Thus anything that appears merely to create a link in external terms is internally generative when one considers its effective force. If the link is not created in the same spirit as it was established, this gives rise to mechanism, and there is no longer any certainty as to the morality of the action.

I On the duty of right

1 The proposition, "Enter into a community of equals, i.e. into community with those people in whom the same kind of action on nature is posited as [you know] in yourself," is a definite moral volition which emerges from absolute volition by means of the consciousness of personality, that is, the splitting of reason into a plurality of identical subjects.

Without this it could not take place. Given this condition, it is necessary, because it is simply the acknowledgment of identity, without which absolute moral volition could not achieve any reality.

Thus it is simply one particular way of becoming that reality.

2 The volition expressed in this proposition also presupposes the opposing fact, namely that of appropriation.

For the subject can only enter into community as something that has become real, and this is only possible by means of appropriation.

In the same way, however, appropriation also presupposes community, as we shall demonstrate; thus each is conditional upon the other, i.e. both emerge uniformly from absolute volition by virtue of the same thing, that is, the character of identity.

3 Insofar as we presuppose appropriation, however, it must also be involved in action which founds community.

That is, because every action that maintains community follows on from the action that founded it, hence appropriation that was presupposed in later action must have been rooted in an earlier appropriation, all the way back to the minimum of definite moral volition.

4 We can therefore express the proposition more precisely as: "Enter into equal community, so that by doing so you appropriate in it at the same time."

This is the distinction between someone who really exists in a community and someone who is merely spatially and temporally enclosed in it. The slave, for example, does not exist in the political community but is merely enclosed by it. He would be absolutely immoral, however, if he found himself in this position as a result of freer action, producing the appearance of community without its essence.

This also provides grounds for the deduction that progress from political inequality to equality as moral consciousness develops is in accordance with duty.

5 The proposition is quite indifferent [towards the distinction between] the differing magnitude[5] of its subjects, and volition is therefore the same for the minimum as for the maximum.

As a minimum let us posit the individual, as a maximum a people. The community of peoples [*Völkergemeinschaft*] cannot be a state of right that is externally determined, because they are not all subsumed under a single unity that is itself a person, in external terms. The moral obligation is the same, however, and there is no difference in perfection. A second distinction is that one could imagine a people that has not yet come to awareness of any other; it therefore practices inhospitality towards what is alien; the maximum of such behavior is cannibalism.

6 Voluntary isolation, even in a people, is therefore moral diminution, and conflict which takes the form of positive withholding of recognition can only be moral if it is a form of punishment.

Community can be greater or smaller depending on kinship, because there is no rigid distinction between what is identical and what is different. For this reason there can be a minimum of community and a maximum, but no complete unification (even religion cannot make an order to this effect).

Aggressive war can only ever proceed from the refusal to recognize a people as a people (*la grande nation*); it can only be just to the extent that the people against whom war is waged is genuinely unworthy of community (missionary wars).

7 A people can only enter into community, however, to the extent that appropriation takes place at the same time.

1. A people that appropriates little or nothing as such (nomads) experiences little demand to become a community.
2. A people cannot enter into community if its action is not acknowledged.

8 The proposition is indifferent [towards the distinction between] the two functions of reason and is therefore equally applicable to both.[6]

[We do not find] an external state that is so very definite here either because, given that the function is an internal one, actual compulsion cannot be applied; also because precise assessment of the intention does not take place. But the moral obligation is the same.

9 Voluntary isolation of cognition is moral diminution.

The refusal to disclose thoughts[7] is contrary to duty. But this depends on the strength of one's conviction that what has been thought is real knowledge.

---

[5] Differing magnitude. *Before this, deleted:* cognitive and formative function.
[6] *Marginal addition 1827:* both for individual beings and for peoples, moreover.
[7] *Marginal addition 1827:* Absence of community of cognition between peoples only becomes immoral once the external demand and the internal urge have grown up; this is not present at the beginning, of course.

Linguistic community of peoples is in no sense a diminution in itself; on the contrary, as soon as contact takes place it is in accordance with duty.

10 Community of cognition is only to be found together with appropriation.

Community is present in language. But each person is only present in that community to the extent that he is productive, for otherwise he is merely enclosed by it, a medium of dissemination, an organ for others just like the slave.

The negative aspect of community is the overcoming of obstacles, the improvement of language, which is bad when it is not a lively production. But everyone should work on true [improvement of language].

Community of cognition between peoples always brings annihilation in its wake without lively possession of one's own [cognition]. – The attitude of the ruling power is often contradictory here depending on whether [it is exercising] a formative or a cognitive function.

11 In the formative function all form is essentially exchange.[8]

Only in this way is the entering into community which is present in each individual action also [an act of] appropriation. Each transaction must be to the advantage of both. *Do ut nec des nec facias* is of no value for community either.

The negative aspect of formative community, prevailing over the blind force of nature, is appropriation in its own right since it is a joint activity; but also in the sense that it is compensation, because one gains security.

12 To say that it is preferable not to seek to acquire anything, so that one does not need to enter into community, is the maxim of moral bankruptcy.

The limit of appropriation from the point of view of community is entirely the opposite: no longer seeking to acquire anything unless it enables one to enter into community. This is the limitation set on inequality, and the various gradations of possession develop from it.[9] Where there is great inequality one must relinquish possessions in a subordinate direction so that a more lively community can develop. Complement to 4.

13 The volition expressed in our proposition also presupposes the opposing aspect of individuality.

Because it is an essential part of human nature that individual subjects are not merely items but also individuals, a definite universal volition through which an individual identifies with others can only proceed from the absolute when what is opposed to this – the thing that enables him to distinguish himself from the others as a particular individual – is also posited as a condition or a limitation.

Universal community is based on the negative moment of personality, namely the fact that each active subject does not constitute the whole of reason; alongside this, however, there must always be the positive moment, that each person is different and in this sense a whole entity.

---

[8] *Marginal addition 1827:* In the cognitive function it is predominantly common property.

[9] *Marginal addition 1827:* Empty desire for acquisition, having no moral basis, not even in the domain of cognition.

14 We can therefore express it more precisely as follows: "Enter into universal community reserving your whole individuality."[10]

Only universal community, which does not require the sacrifice of particularity, is the right one. With reference to the state, this is the true moral concept of personal[11] freedom.

Universal community may call for the sacrificing of possessions and the activity of identical capacities into infinity, because if it is right, just as much appropriation may proceed from this. But it cannot guarantee what is individual and so it may not demand it either.

In general we can resolve this by saying that either the individual can be in and of the universal, or else the two do not come into contact with each other.

15 This definition is indifferent [towards the distinction between] the two forms and the two functions.[12]

Even if we relate it first to the analogous form, the other one is nevertheless also present, reciprocally connected to the first. – It is, however, a definition of both formative community and universal cognitive community, thus it is also directed towards both functions in both forms of what is individual.

16 Hence: "Enter into universal community without excluding individual community."

Since universal and individual are not strictly separated, individual communities can be contained within universal ones. Universal ones are then the relatively empty space, i.e. not completely filled, in which individual communities can express themselves, thus filling it up entirely, both when individual communities fall completely within a definite universal one and also when this is only partly the case. Example: the relationship between adherents of a particular religion when their nations are at war. – If they are entirely separate, however, then no conflict can take place except in time, and this does not count.

Thus there can be complete independence of individual communities alongside universal ones, and if the latter seek to restrict the former (church, family, friendship), then they are despotic [in nature]. – There is often a desire to restrict hospitality and the church as a result of political concerns; but this has its basis only in the immoral condition of civic association.

17 Enter into universal community without excluding individual appropriation.

As far as personality is concerned, the more individual someone is, the more varied are the things he enters into community with – provided, that is, that it can be comprehended as identity and is not something that struggles to resist it, which runs contrary to nature, however.

In terms of what has been externally inculcated, it might appear that the right of the universal community is curtailed by property that has been withdrawn from exchange. On the one hand, however, money, for example, is always equal to property and must first

---

[10] *Marginal addition 1827:* Universal community is never perfectly defined. Positing individuality at the same time supplements this lack of definition.

[11] *Corrected from:* political.

[12] *Marginal addition 1827:* Forms = community and stimulus, functions = cognition and formation.

be given as an equivalent; on the other hand, the individual means of each subject exists only in a particular relationship.

A state which attempts to prevent the individual development of the personality and the individual appropriation of things is a despotic one, like Sparta – even if it were entirely republican.

A language is imperfect inasmuch as it does not admit of individual treatment.

18 [13] In every universal community, then, act in such a way that it always comes closer to these rules.

That is, since each one is in a process of becoming, it would be immoral not to enter into it because none of them is perfect as it is.

What can bring about improvement is on the one hand influencing the law by establishing what is right and practical according to the constitution, and on the other hand providing the best possible exposition of the law in practice. Absolute civic volition must proceed from the most correct idea of the given community, not from the state it happens to be in at the time. [14]

19 These two determining factors determine [*sic*] the scope of universal community, from the minimum of tension – both between community and appropriation and between the universal and the individual – to the maximum.

The minimum is the horde, in which there is no acknowledgment of legal property. The maximum is the universally determined state of right within the state. Cosmopolitanism, which seeks to go beyond even this point, necessarily constitutes a reduction in community and a reduction in appropriation. The true state does not render itself dispensable, but presents itself as a maximum.

The other kind of minimum is crude coexistence determined by the same sort of instincts. [Here] the maximum is the state which is conscious of its individuality and personal freedom. Reduced, the state is merely the foundation of external commerce.

(?) In language: sign or root-language, artificial language, mannerism, in which all individuality is incorrect.

20 Enter into every universal community in such a way that you are already reconciled to it.

The natural aspect of community must already be in existence, indeed it must already be something moral, although not in the case of the active subject. Entering that community

---

[13] *Before this, in brackets:* 18. "Enter in such a way that individual community is not excluded."
   Individual communities can remain in reserve amongst those belonging to the same universal one, because it is precisely only the individual community that determines the way they will act in the universal one. If this is not the case, the individual one will be of such a kind that it does not come into contact with the universal one. Conflict can only arise if someone has no place in the universal community either. This is why we only encounter fear of friendships and religious associations in states whose composition is uncertain.
   The highest schema here is the relationship between individuals in wars between peoples who share the same religion, without offending either the one or the other.

[14] *Marginal addition 1827:* No action can be a perfect expression because of its imperfect basis.

is not merely acknowledgment of it; it is the lively consciousness that this universal community is also the proper form for all one's individual actions.

Even exceptions can only be moral to the extent that they comply with these rules. An emigrant must 1) have been expelled from the state he naturally belongs to, and 2) already have a point of contact with the state which he is entering.

The same is true of languages. We still have subsidiary mother tongues, but only in certain areas. The desire to continue transmission of a dead language is a hazardous one. However, we also need living foreign languages for purposes of commerce. For a man to take one over into his whole life would only be appropriate if he were also emigrating.

21 Reconcile yourself to community in such a way that you enter into it.

To be reconciled means to continue in action. Each time as if entering. With all one's strength, and (18) consciousness of the true idea of the state.

In the same way, all action with language must truly contribute to the formation of language.

22 In every action in universal community internal stimulus must coincide with external demand.

The volition of the community, regarded as an absolute, will also be changeable in its attitudes; in each individual, too, one inclination will emerge as the dominant one. Action is necessarily imperfect if it does not coincide with external demand; e.g. when one seeks to produce where one should protect, or when one ought to bring activities into the community, but prefers to put in things or money. Here, then, the whole of morality is dependent on harmony. It is impossible if 1) the subjects are not good citizens, or if 2) the orders of those in authority do not truly express the general need. It is only a poor substitute if 1) those in authority are given a private interest which is then expected to coincide with the general interest; 2) every possible achievement is turned into a specialized profession, so that there is always provision for people to be there who can undertake each one. For how can we be certain that those whose role is always to give the money would not like to give something else as well?

The same is true of every improvement within the community; admittedly stimulus and demand must coincide even more closely here of their own accord.

Since the same is also true of the community of the nations, we see how wrongheaded it is that the connections between them are not meant to be directed by any sort of inclination. It has always been refuted, moreover, by the existence of all living peoples.

As far as the cognitive function goes, every communication will also remain an imperfect moral action, an unsuccessful intention, if only internal stimulus is present without demand. And utterly empty if it does not set the seeds of future demand. The same is true if demand is present but with the expectation that it will be satisfied without stimulus. What is necessary here, then, above all, is the greatest possible liveliness and the greatest possible harmony.

23 All community action, which is calculated, must appear to be generated by a free urge.[15]

---

[15] *Marginal note 1827:* This is not the opposition of universal and individual.

Even if the purposive concept which arises from the definite need of the whole is something primitive, it must nevertheless stimulate free, generative fantasy, which will then increase as it is implemented; otherwise mechanism will gain the upper hand.

Everything is dead in the domain of cognition, too, if it is born out of mere calculation.

24 Everything generated by a free urge must let itself be absorbed into calculation.

Otherwise it is a service that does not affirm the whole, and one must necessarily contradict the other. Volition which has freely arisen ought not really to be implemented until its necessary place has been identified in the historical development of the whole.

In the domain of cognition everything is random that is not related to a general system.

25 The moral perfection of all universal communities – i.e. the possibility that here everyone can act in perfect morality under all circumstances – thus consists in the fact that one and the same calculating reason underlies them all, and taken together, the movements of the drive in each one form a whole.

For as a consequence of the second, no necessary movement will be absent, and as a consequence of the first, no movement which actually arises will be invalid.

II On the duty of profession

1 [16] The general proposition that one should appropriate, taken as a formula of duty, presupposes that even the most primitive expressions of this activity are already moral ones.

The first acts performed by this activity can be traced back to the animal instinct for self-preservation. If we accept this, then it holds true for all those that follow. For everything can be traced back to needs that are given later on, just as these are given originally. This is therefore the basis of every attempt to dismiss all morality as self-interest; from this point onward everything else depicts what is individual as merely additional and what is held in common as a means of appropriation.

Thus we must start from the assumption that even what comes first is already human and not to be understood simply as a product of nature, but as an activity of reason. [17]

2 We can define it more precisely in terms of the opposition of universal and individual as emerging from general volition as a result of the subject's consciousness that he forms part of the totality of reason and as such is identical to others.

For without this appropriation could only be simple and there could be no distinction between the universal and the individual. – Thus here, too, our basis is the consciousness of personality; but taken from a different aspect.

---

[16] *Marginal note 1827:* The totality of the universal process of appropriation is profession.
[17] *Marginal note 1827:* even if it is only the activity of reason in others.

3 The morality of the proposition is therefore expressed in its relation both to community as a whole and to individual appropriation.

If appropriation is willed without reference to community, then the subject is willed in absolute autonomy as a perfected end in itself,[18] but in that case not as a part of the totality of reason, so that reason is then subordinate to the natural subject and hence appropriation is immoral. If it is willed without the opposition between individual and universal, it is willed absolutely without reference to community. – On the other hand, if we posit both these things, appropriation is willed in connection with all other moral action and is hence a part of and an emanation of absolute moral volition.

Thus, even in the merely animal process of appropriation we find that both things are denied: relation to a community, which is intended to remain (for it ceases to exist as soon as the process of appropriation has reached the point of autonomy) and the incorporation of an individual into what is universal.

4 Appropriate in a way that is uniform with that of others, so that all appropriation also becomes community.

This contains the idea that all appropriation is immoral if it does not entirely take place with reference to the universal community whose schematism it bears. Thus, as far as anything that has been appropriated is concerned, nothing may be held in reserve; hence a state. A man is a bad citizen if he seeks to limit the claim on his possessions exercised by the whole.

This applies uniformly to indirect and direct appropriation. Every skill that has been inculcated belongs to the community, and every thing that has been inculcated belongs to civic commerce. Every new appropriation thus also increases the claims exercised by the whole.

5 The validity of this proposition is conditional upon the one that stands in opposition to it, demonstrated above.

For the will to appropriation would be without value if what has been appropriated were to pass into community without the community becoming a source of new appropriation. Then the subject would be merely a channel without any part of the purpose being posited within him.

6 There can only be a coincidence of the two if the general will proceeds from the individual, and the individual will from the general.

That is, the general will, which exercises a claim upon things and activities that have been formed; and the individual will, which ascribes to itself a secure state of possession.

7 The proposition is indifferent [towards the distinction between] the two functions and the power of the subjects.

Every people must be mindful of community when appropriating, and hence also mindful of a schematism which can be generally acknowledged, and must call hospitality into being. Only at the lowest level of the appropriation process is the absence of this last not positively immoral. Hospitality, that is, between one people and another.

---

[18] *Marginal note 1827:* Kantian exaggeration of this theory of the end in itself.

In the cognitive function everything that has been recognized must be deposited in language. Only where cognition still takes the form of empty, dreamy experiments is non-disclosure not positively immoral.

8 Carry out all your uniform [acts of] appropriation whilst reserving the whole of your particularity.

For a person is only an externally independent part of reason, to whom appropriation can be related, to the extent that he is also something particular. In itself, therefore, the proposition can be related equally well to individual appropriation and to community; however, the fact that the latter is also present in the proposition is a consequence more of universal community also being present on the one hand, and individual appropriation also being present on the other.

There would appear to be a greater necessity for individual appropriation to be held in check by universal appropriation, it is true, because the latter necessarily postulates universal community, whereas what has been appropriated individually cannot enter into universal community, that is, into exchange. However, 1) universal community itself postulates individual community (see above), which can only exist by means of individual appropriation, after all; 2) the two are not separate in the manner of their expression, so that in every individual act of appropriation there is also universal appropriation, and each person is all the more a part of universal community, the more he has appropriated as an individual.

9 The proposition is indifferent [towards the distinction between] the two functions and the power of the subjects.

Cognitive function. 1) A language which does not permit any particularity either in use or in combination, such as *pasilaly* [*translator's note: an artificial universal language*] would be an immoral product. 2) A language that does not lay out individual spheres for the purposes of individual communities, spheres which are relatively exclusive, would be highly imperfect.

Formative function. 1) A schematism which is so perfectly determined – both as regards the form into which things are formed and the form in which skills are practiced – that there is no room for the free play of particularity, would be positively immoral. 2) A schematism that does not allow the possibility of a cycle of art forms, or generate one itself, would be highly imperfect. With regard to the form in which capacities are exercised the Egyptian would thus appear [to represent] a minimum of morality; and with regard to the form into which things are formed, the Chinese. In the same way, as regards both, the French. Here the individual has automatically been considered more under the power of the people. For [in a people] the individual aspect is the original one, and we must simply approach the proposition in such a way that the universal appropriation which develops subsequently is not allowed to suppress the original, individual appropriation. It ought not to relinquish its national character out of politeness towards other peoples (leaving the question of imitation to one side).

10 If we take universal community and particularity as given, then as a result of their interrelation both constitute the measure for the progression of universal appropriation from a minimum to a maximum.

The minimum of community must also be the minimum of appropriation. Where the former is still merely coexistence, the formative process can only be weak as well; each person develops a meager scrap of the common form in his own way. The maximum of community (the state) is also the most versatile production: one [and the same] as the division of labor, because only then does proper community of activity take place.

The minimum of development in the opposition between universal and individual, that is, lack of consciousness of there being any such difference, is also the minimum of appropriation. When personal formative force has not yet emerged, the whole sphere of formation can only be small. The maximum of this opposition is the development of an artistic cycle in the common formative type. From this there emerges a definite distinction between formation for exchange and formation for property. Taste also enters universal production, as an accessory.

N.B. One ought also to demonstrate here that to pass this point would mean renewed diminution.

11 Enter into each process of appropriation in such a way that you are already reconciled to it.

Each genuinely new term must already have been given as a result of natural predetermination. Instances of greatest enlargement on the universal side of the formative function have their basis in natural discoveries.[19]

Since this proposition also holds true for peoples, each people must appropriate on the soil where it has been put. The migration of whole peoples is an exception, and becomes increasingly impossible the more the process within the whole is underway according to this rule. Indeed it can only be justified when a people has somehow been cast out of its natural situation. There must also be a particular climatic pull to the region it is going to. The same holds true for the emigration of individuals. In this case the pull to a definite place may depend on other affinities, those holding a similar faith, or on individual, chance relationships. To that extent, entering is also finding. The less any such determining factor is present, the more [emigration] must be preceded by expulsion. Religious or political persecution is the most obvious reason.

What is entirely arbitrary in a formative type, insofar as it is disseminated, is fashion, but only ever restricted to trivial details, established as it were to mark the limits of what can be morally determined, and partly also always forming a cycle which continually renews itself, and is therefore restricted by hidden natural conditions.[20]

Since the proposition holds true for both functions, each broadening of cognition must also already have been introduced. No true extension of scientific knowledge is ever arbitrary either. Treatment of nature leads just as surely to knowledge of nature as vice versa. And the basis for the progression of the whole process from a minimum to a maximum, regarded as an action which is in accordance with duty, lies in the way the two functions are made dependent on each other by this proposition. There is also, however, a way in

---

[19] *Marginal addition 1827:* If one does not know very much about the whole world, the difference between the part one knows and the part one does not is also very small.

[20] *Marginal note 1827:* N.B. This does not really belong here.

which nature has introduced the universal process of cognition; one such example is the natural commerce of the senses with the external world.

12 Let all reconciliation within a process of appropriation be also an entering in.

Every discovery must also enter the formative process, that is, every instance of natural predetermination that has been perceived. The perception itself is a natural emanation of general moral volition in this domain, which rests on a general presupposition with regard to nature's capacity to be formed and recognized. The way in which this takes place is determined in its turn by the following imperative.

Now, given that attention which is directed towards both the treatment of nature and the cognition of nature is channeled into individual acts, the more frequently a definite deed arising out of absolute volition is repeated, the more the whole process must develop; and the more all appropriation becomes community, [the more] consistent that development must be, whatever the starting-point.

Since the proposition also holds true for peoples, then not only is each people originally caught up in a process of appropriation on its own soil, but all individual progress must also spread to the whole people. For something that was an original act of producing for the individual subsequently becomes something to which the people must be reconciled. The proposition is also the law of internal perfection of the process. For if each reconciling is to become something new in its turn, this can only come about as the result of a more powerful turning inward. And this proposition is therefore the more intensive formula, while § 11 is the more extensive.

13 In all appropriation internal stimulus and external demand must have coincided in order for general volition in this domain to produce an individual deed.

Since the proposition is indifferent with regard to the power of the person, while actions performed at national level are the least arbitrary, we can take these as an immediate example. Internal stimulus is inclination (moods are less frequently found in peoples). External demand is need and opportunity. All progress is conditional upon these. We do not criticize a people for not having made progress in a certain area if need and opportunity were lacking, nor indeed if the inclination were lacking.

The harmony of the two cannot be an absolute equilibrium. This would be present if one were able to say: the same thing which internal stimulus has determined me to do would have come about if I had simply paid attention to external demands, and vice versa.

First of all, then, neither of the two should be entirely excluded when something is being determined. 1) The maxim that one should completely neglect external demands and simply follow an internal stimulus constitutes libertinism. It isolates reason within the subject, and however moral in itself the thing desired, an action which arises in this way will always be an egoistical one. 2) The maxim that one should always overcome an internal stimulus in order to serve external demands, because these are always derived from nature, places intelligence at the service of nature so that moral activity becomes mere receptivity. That this is correct is also demonstrated by the fact that on its own neither maxim can produce a decision. Stimulus always leaves a great multiplicity of things undetermined, and a choice between many demands could only be left up to chance.

The space between the two cannot be filled up any more closely, but the role played by each can be variously determined according to the character of each [individual]. Whether someone is right to forge ahead until he encounters a demand, given the strength of his inclination, can only be judged – with uncertainty – by someone else, after he has been successful. The person acting must not allow himself to be made uncertain even by success, supposing that he ever has been certain. Certainty can be found, however, the more he takes up one position, by also taking the other position into account. – A casuistical question: is a man right to give up the profession on which he has embarked in order to support his dependants more easily?

The conflict between stimulus and need in a community naturally creates a division of transactions; and this is a means of compensation as natural and necessary as a person's definite way of life. (It proceeds from discovery of the difference in stimuli, however, i.e. from what is individual, that is, the urge to love.[21])

14 Any definite decision can only emerge in a moral way from the general will to appropriate when calculating intelligence (reason) coincides with the intelligence of free formation (fantasy).[22]

Action arises [either] more in the form of the purposive concept or more in the form of desire; but the two must both be present. The purposive concept, which is a construct, cannot produce a deed unless it becomes an urge, a strong emotion. Desire cannot be translated into action so swiftly that [there is no room for] reflection to intervene and transform it into a purposive concept.[23]

Construction cannot produce a decision on its own. On the one hand, as far as external formation is concerned, one can confront each task with its opposite, e.g. that of increasing vegetable provision with that of reducing consumption. On the other hand, as far as internal formation is concerned, intensive and extensive enlargement ought to be constructed at the same time, even in relation to the same need, e.g. improving memory or acquiring the ability to construct, learning or putting into practice, etc.

Fantasy cannot produce a decision on its own either. There is simply too much that it is obliged to leave indeterminate. E.g. it can only determine the type of profession, not the exact branch.

A decision arising purely from construction, then, would always be precipitate, while one arising purely from fantasy would be arbitrary, as a result of which reason would no longer be in connection with the other subjects acting; thus appropriation would not be predicated on community.

---

[21] *Marginal addition 1827:* On the influence of community on appropriation. It is an imperfect state if profession is determined from the outside; neither by family nor state. – The community must have [power of] confirmation, however.

[22] *Marginal addition 1827:* The particular volition which emerges from general volition is characterized by free formation. Calculation is the process in which one engages with external demand.

[23] *Schleiermacher erroneously substitutes the word* desire *here.*

In between the two there is plenty of scope for each to contribute in differing proportion. In each individual one element, the one which constitutes his moral character, will predominate, but within this there will nevertheless be fluctuations in approximation. In this respect all duties are analogous to the duty of conscience.

The highest ideal is harmony between calculation and fantasy; included in this is harmony between individual and general consciousness.

Closing remarks. Since this is the domain of perfect duty, i.e. what is usually treated as the only strict domain of duty, it begs the question as to whether our treatment [of the topic] has covered everything. 1) The way in which all moral volition belonging under this heading is derived entirely from general volition is clearly apparent; so that, if people always act in this way, complete morality must be achieved in this domain. 2) It is surely also readily apparent that any immoral elements which might come to the surface in an individual could not be put into practice if our formulae were consulted. Any traces of laziness or selfishness immediately come into conflict with the general propositions; just as anything capricious and illegitimate conflicts with our more closely worded definitions. It is clear, therefore, that according to our formulae what is immoral could not build on what is moral. 3) Do those same formulae determine, however, how what is moral might build on some immoral element and develop further on this basis, and not how something immoral might produce a different outcome? This would definitely have been made clear throughout if the fact that all moral action must also be rectifying had been carried through to its conclusion at every point. As far as a) immoral elements in the individual are concerned, there is a clear basis for the duty of compensation in our formulae, because otherwise the harmony between appropriation and community is disturbed. One of the most important tendencies of a certain state of civic [development], moreover, is that of punitive justice, and it becomes an individual's duty to participate in the process of punishment even if this is detrimental to himself or another. If this state is still imperfect enough to admit of instances of self-defense, then the only defense can be that of intention (although the outcome of that intention can vary enormously). The violent individual is to be regarded as a natural obstacle, something which is to be overcome but which is also, as moral material, to be unified [with reason]. b) If, however, the representation of civic society itself turns against morality, then the combination of both functions imposes a duty to make this apparent in any way possible. Then, however, to resist; but only ever a minimum [of resistance], taking as a benchmark the fact that every element of the social form that is still available and undamaged is not only to be spared but also used, so that one is always building on moral elements that are already present.

The individual aspect

Preliminary remarks. Since this is frequently considered to defy strict treatment according to the concept of duty, it would appear necessary to begin by examining the supporting arguments for its not being coordinated with the universal. The first of these is deeply skeptical towards what is individual and sees it as a moral non-entity, simply the result of external influences; that is, as something which could not be produced by moral action. At its head is the proposition that all human beings are born equal. The second [view] concedes that the individual has some moral content, but states that this does not need to be brought out specially – cannot be, indeed – but comes into being of its own accord. In favor of this view, it is true, is the fact that what is individual cannot be absorbed into concepts, so that construction is only ever directed towards what is universal. However, nothing moral can proceed from construction on its own; on the contrary, desire is equally necessary, and this is what is particular from the very beginning; and even what is universal could not have been constructed without relating it to what is individual. Indeed, even the apparent imperfection attributed to what is individual is something that we have also found in the fundamental construction of what is universal, namely the free play between stimulus and demand, construction and freedom, which goes back, after all, to what is particular in character. Everything depends, therefore, on whether the consciousness within human nature – which we have made the basis of our argument – that reason enters actively into the process of individualization and becomes human reason by virtue of that fact, is also made part of the basis of the argument. If not, then marriage and religion must be excluded from any moral treatment, which on the other hand is also admittedly done by those who seek to disparage what is ethical, so that then finally all that remains for the concept of duty are continuing actions.

We will stay with the first point of view and will turn first to what is most closely related to the last subject treated, namely individual appropriation.[24]

---

[24] [*The location of this footnote is not clear from the original text.*] *Marginal addition 1827:* For the individual aspect, community is based on appropriation, so that this must come first. The fundamental fact is the entry of intelligence into the process of individualization.

As far as the nations are concerned, no one can claim that they were born equal.

Here – since particularity is never completely comprehended in objective consciousness – the entering in is simply feeling, as individual self-consciousness, passing over into the will.

Question as to whether the domain of profession and the appropriation of art could be one and the same.

Different peoples do not relinquish their type when engaged in the same [sort of] appropriation. And so they then enter in all over again.

This autonomy of command is the basis of the non-transferability of the body and, for peoples, the non-transferability of the fatherland.

III On the duty of conscience

The basis of this designation will become clear once we have surveyed the whole.

1 The proposition that one should be caught up in individual appropriation proceeds from general moral volition, conditional upon personality, inasmuch as particularity is the genuinely human aspect of personality.

Just as appropriation in general [is based] on the fact that the individual person should be autonomous, his own starting-point, so individual appropriation [is based] on the fact that he ought to be entirely this; for otherwise he would be without any organ for his particularity.

2 This proposition is indifferent [towards the distinction between] peoples and individuals and between cognitive and formative activity.[25]

The formative action of a people is something universal as far as the individuals who make it up are concerned; as far as the people, taken as a single entity and coordinated with other peoples, is concerned, it is something individual. This appropriation is more readily present in it than community with other peoples. If it did not have its basis in a moral command, then from the moment when it formed such communities the people would have to throw off its own particular schematism and derive everything from one held in common. The fact that this is not acceptable is the root of all individual appropriation.

The same is true of cognition. A people would have subsequently to relinquish its own particular concept formation and language in order to turn its community into a universal one.[26]

Now, if individual appropriation must subsist within peoples, and an individual community is also to proceed from it which is different from the universal community, the same must also be true of individuals. For them, national schematism is what is universal. They may not venture outside this in their external natural formation because the acknowledgment of folk traditions is based on it; what is individual must remain within it. Personal formation remains within the limits of what is consonant with the people of its own accord, because no one can shed their national character; thus what is individual appears here to come to the fore.

The same holds true for the cognitive function. No one can venture outside language, and what is individual must remain within it as a combination; in feeling, however, which

---

[25] *Marginal addition 1827:* If what is individual must be allowed, then it must also be commanded. Since, however, what is individual cannot be established in consciousness and we must assume it to be an internal impulse, the command can only be negative as far as imitation is concerned, or affectation with regard to what is not determined by the universal. Intermediate entities between the people and the individual are bad when they are constituted by imitation. Disintegration is bad if it is determined by what is arbitrary.

Linguistic appropriation of a people is only possible when the two communities are very unequal, or where new objects are concerned; in any case it will always be individualized.

[26] *Marginal addition 1832:* Community of language must be inaugurated each time by one [individual] together with other individuals. – On foreign meter in German [poetry]. Everything depends on the purity of one's disposition, i.e. the life of a language in the individual.

signifies absolute personality, what is individual comes to the fore and what is universal – common feeling – is present of its own accord.

3 Appropriate in such a way that you are reconciled as you begin and begin as you are reconciled.

All free action, then, builds on what is given and so does not emerge as something arbitrary; but every time something builds on something else [this takes place] with full consciousness of will and, indeed, as something distinct from the universal. It is precisely in this way that consciousness of particularity is brought about.[27]

Hence also the tracing back of particularity to the paternal, and the positing of one's own individuality as the germ of others'.

4 Appropriate in your own particular way, so that appropriation also becomes community.[28]

Non-transferability, keeping itself to itself, might otherwise swallow up the whole of universal appropriation.

Everyone ought to desire to be what he can for everyone.

[*Interpolated 1832:* The quantity of difference in hospitality can be explained on the basis of the formula concerning impulse and demand.

Diversity of style.

On obscurity in surrender on the side of the cognitive function.

Moral basis in the desire to communicate when one is uncertain of success.

Limits. False; true.]

5 Appropriate in an individual manner whilst reserving what is universal.

Constitutes non-transferable property by means of commerce itself; but also vice versa. Unlimited claim of the domain of right.

IV   On the duty of love[29]

1 The proposition that one should establish ties of individual community proceeds from the general one [concerning community], if we presuppose the capacity for revelation.

---

[27] *Marginal notes 1832:* Original involuntariness. Migration of souls as moral fiction. Here demand is doubtless only the assets of both functions. Stimulus is the quantity of the determination itself.

[28] *Marginal addition 1832:* Communications [do] not [take place] on their own, but are for purposes of mutuality. But community is not only individual but also universal. It also enters the commerce of things and experiences.

[29] *Marginal additions 1832:*
Here the stimulus is to be found in the impression, the demand in natural affinity.
In misalliances the demand is absent. Demand is the common domain. Hence the limited nature of connections with alien tribes. Mistrust of stimulus.
Enter into individual community with the whole of your universal orientation.
Marriage must be within the state; also friendship. The church is within the state but as something that transcends its boundaries. Even the community of members of a church is affected by the relationship between states, however.

2 The two functions cannot be separated but must supplement each other. Even communication on the part of a writer remains an imperfect revelation without knowledge of [the writer's] life.

3 The development of the community is dependent on its capacity to comprehend. Each person must simply desire all degrees [of comprehension].

4 Individualization of the species [*translator's note: or possibly* of gender] – of the national constitution – of speculation – of feeling.

5 All community must be appropriation. Not merely enjoyment.

6 All individual community must also posit the universal. Marriage produces the essence of the household. Speculation on real science. Religion and art.

> Individual community with universal appropriation.
> No hospitality without possession.
> Let the foundation of community be [in] finding.
> The predetermination which is only acknowledged; there is nothing that can be done arbitrarily.

Index

Note: This index incorporates the earlier index found in Friedrich Schleiermacher, *Werke. Auswahl in Vier Bänden*, edited by Otto Braun and Johannes Bauer (Leipzig: Felix Meiner, 1910–13; reprint ed. Aalen: Scientia, 1967), II, 677–703.

limit
  of cognition, 18
  of community, 228
  of ethical existence, 179
  of inculcating activity, 177
  of the organizing function, 17
lives, becoming one, 62
love, 68, 103, 109 ff.
  duty of, 128, 241 f.
  sexual, 109

magnificence, 97
male, 62
man, 65 f.
manifestation, 148, 152, 159
marriage, 61, 63 ff., 69, 81, 111, 241
  as possession of persons, 61
  forms of, 63
  indissolubility of, 62
mass, 55, 159
  of families, 69
materialism, 11
mathematical, the, 42, 81, 220
matter, 109
maximum, 9, 10, 15, 41 f., 128, 180, 227, 234
  and minimum, 9, 13, 15, 41 f., 128, 180, 227, 234
measure, 61, 141, 198 ff.
  for moral communities, 198
  for the progression of appropriation, 234 f.
mechanical, the, 149
mechanics, 27, 205, 209
Mechanism, 97, 110, 226, 232
memory, 51, 129, 148
method, 137
  critical, 140, 166
  technical, 161, 166
mind, presence of, 118
moment, 26, 38, 124, 191
  closing of a, 219
  of steadfastness, 122
monarchy, great and small, 72
  universal, 72
money, 32 ff., 35 f., 48, 74, 211, 213, 231
  metal, 211
  paper, 212
moods, 20, 56, 118
morality, 16, 58, 68
  of individual property, 37
morals, doctrine of, 150, 151 ff.
  applied, 161

movement, 5, 53
  epitome of all, 164
  ethical process as, 123
  of the drive, 232
  organic, 219
  to depiction, 58
  totality of, 13
multiplicity, 219
  of concepts of duty, 224
  of goods, 174
  of virtues and duties, 163
mysticism, 55

nation, 76, 95
nationality, 61, 68, 87 ff.
nature, 82, 109, 133, 147, 168 f., 187, 198
  connection with, 133
  domination of, 6
  earthly, 179 f.
  human, 159, 179 f.
  knowledge of, 150, 156
  reason becoming, 155
  reason in, 9 f.
  shaping, 184
  signifying, 187
necessity, 94, 124
  objective, 126, 131
need, 236
nobility, 67

obedience, 69, 110
Objectivity, 62
objects, 19
  natural, 18 f.
  to be communicated, 96
old age, 38, 67
oneness, of reason and nature, 155
one-sidedness, 207
  extinguishing of, in marriage, 63
opinion, 137
  public, 78, 81
opposition, 142, 157
  between cognition and depiction, 127
  between formation of community and appropriation, 127
  between freedom and necessity, 160
  between individual sphere and common good, 34
  between science and life, 43
  in particular forms of knowledge, 5
  knowledge consists in, 142

Cambridge texts in the history of philosophy

Titles published in the series thus far

Aristotle *Nicomachean Ethics* (edited by Roger Crisp)

Arnauld and Nicole *Logic or the Art of Thinking* (edited by Jill Vance Buroker)

Bacon *The New Organon* (edited by Lisa Jardine and Michael Silverthorne)

Boyle *A Free Enquiry into the Vulgarly Received Notion of Nature* (edited by Edward B. Davis and Michael Hunter)

Bruno *Cause, Principle and Unity* and *Essays on Magic* (edited by Richard Blackwell and Robert de Lucca with an introduction by Alfonso Ingegno)

Cavendish *Observations upon Experimental Philosophy* (edited by Eileen O'Neill)

Cicero *On Moral Ends* (edited by Julia Annas, translated by Raphael Woolf)

Clarke *A Demonstration of the Being and Attributes of God and Other Writings* (edited by Ezio Vailati)

Condillac *Essay on the Origin of Human Knowledge* (edited by Hans Aarsleff)

Conway *The Principles of the Most Ancient and Modern Philosophy* (edited by Allison P. Coudert and Taylor Corse)

Cudworth *A Treatise Concerning Eternal and Immutable Morality* with *A Treatise of Freewill* (edited by Sarah Hutton)

Descartes *Meditations on First Philosophy*, with selections from the *Objections and Replies* (edited by John Cottingham)

Descartes *The World and Other Writings* (edited by Stephen Gaukroger)

Fichte *Foundations of Natural Right* (edited by Frederick Neuhouser, translated by Michael Baur)

Hobbes and Bramhall on Liberty and Necessity (edited by Vere Chappell)

Humboldt *On Language* (edited by Michael Losonsky, translated by Peter Heath)

Kant *Critique of Practical Reason* (edited by Mary Gregor with an introduction by Andrews Reath)

Kant *Groundwork of the Metaphysics of Morals* (edited by Mary Gregor with an introduction by Christine M. Korsgaard)

Kant *The Metaphysics of Morals* (edited by Mary Gregor with an introduction by Roger Sullivan)

Kant *Prolegomena to any Future Metaphysics* (edited by Gary Hatfield)

Kant *Religion within the Boundaries of Mere Reason and Other Writings* (edited by Allen Wood and George di Giovanni with an introduction by Robert Merrihew Adams)

La Mettrie *Machine Man and Other Writings* (edited by Ann Thomson)

Leibniz *New Essays on Human Understanding* (edited by Peter Remnant and Jonathan Bennett)

Malebranche *Dialogues on Metaphysics and on Religion* (edited by Nicholas Jolley and David Scott)

Malebranche *The Search after Truth* (edited by Thomas M. Lennon and Paul J. Olscamp)

Melanchthon *Orations on Philosophy and Education* (edited by Sachiko Kusukawa, translated by Christine Salazar)

Mendelssohn *Philosophical Writings* (edited by Daniel O. Dahlstrom)

Nietzsche *Beyond Good and Evil* (edited by Rolf-Peter Horstmann and Judith Norman)

Nietzsche *The Birth of Tragedy and Other Writings* (edited by Raymond Geuss and Ronald Speirs)

Nietzsche *Daybreak* (edited by Maudemarie Clark and Brian Leiter, translated by R. J. Hollingdale)

Nietzsche *The Gay Science* (edited by Bernard Williams, translated by Josefine Nauckhoff)

Nietzsche *Human, All Too Human* (translated by R. J. Hollingdale with an introduction by Richard Schacht)

Nietzsche *Untimely Meditations* (edited by Daniel Breazeale, translated by R. J. Hollingdale)

Schleiermacher *Hermeneutics and Criticism* (edited by Andrew Bowie)

Schleiermacher *Lectures on Philosophical Ethics* (edited by Robert B. Louden, translated by Louise Adey Huish)

Schleiermacher *On Religion: Speeches to its Cultured Despisers* (edited by Richard Crouter)

Schopenhauer *Prize Essay on the Freedom of the Will* (edited by Günter Zöller)

Sextus Empiricus *Outlines of Scepticism* (edited by Julia Annas and Jonathan Barnes)

Shaftesbury *Characteristics of Men, Manners, Opinions, Times* (edited by Lawrence Klein)

Adam Smith *The Theory of Moral Sentiments* (edited by Knud Haakonssen)

Voltaire *Treatise on Tolerance and Other Writings* (edited by Simon Harvey)